Blessed Louis, the Most Glorious of Kings

Notre Dame Texts in Medieval Culture

Blessed Louis

The Most Glorious of Kings

Texts Relating to the Cult
of Saint Louis of France

M. Cecilia Gaposchkin

Translations with Phyllis B. Katz

University of Notre Dame Press

Notre Dame, Indiana

Copyright © 2012 by University of Notre Dame
Notre Dame, Indiana 46556
www.undpress.nd.edu
All Rights Reserved

Manufactured in the United States of America

Library of Congress Cataloging-in-Publication Data

Blessed Louis, the most glorious of kings : texts relating to the cult
of Saint Louis of France / [edited by] M. Cecilia Gaposchkin ;
translations with Phyllis B. Katz.
      p.   cm. — (Notre Dame texts in medieval culture)
   Texts in Latin with English translation; introductory material
and study in English.
   Includes bibliographical references.
   ISBN-13: 978-0-268-02984-5 (pbk. : alk. paper)
   ISBN-10: 0-268-02984-9 (pbk. : alk. paper)
   E-ISBN: 978-0-268-08070-9
   1. Louis IX, King of France, 1214–1270—Cult—Sources.   2. Church
and state—France—History—To 1500—Sources.   3. France—Kings
and rulers—Religious aspects—Sources.   4. France—Church history—
987–1515—Sources.   I. Gaposchkin, M. Cecilia (Marianne Cecilia), 1970–
   DC91.A2B54   2012
   944'.023092—dc23

                                                        2012019012

∞ *The paper in this book meets the guidelines for permanence and*
durability of the Committee on Production Guidelines for Book Longevity
of the Council on Library Resources.

CONTENTS

Preface and Acknowledgments

Louis IX, king of France between 1226 and 1270 and twice crusader, was canonized in 1297. He was the last king canonized during the medieval period, and was both one of the most important saints and the most important kings of the later Middle Ages. This volume presents the first editions and English translations of two little-known but early and important vitae of Saint Louis, as well as the most commonly used liturgical texts composed for Louis' feast day and two unedited sermons in honor of Louis by the Parisian preacher Jacob of Lausanne (d. 1322). The aim is to present to a diverse readership the Louis as he was known and experienced in the Middle Ages, as a saint celebrated by the faithful for his virtue and his deeds.

This volume grew out of textual discoveries I made while working on the cult of Saint Louis for an earlier book, which itself grew out of my doctoral research. Thus, the work here would not have been possible without the help I received during my graduate training and in my first years out of graduate school, starting foremost with that of my doctoral advisor, Geoffrey Koziol. Many other generous scholars, mentors, archivists, librarians, colleagues, and teachers have helped me along the way. I thank them all. For this project, I must single out a few in particular.

Without question, the most important is Phyllis B. Katz, who endeavored to come on board and translate the Latin texts with me. This was a task of unanticipated difficulty, which I would have never undertaken without her. In addition to her generous gifts of time, immense knowledge, and great patience, I thank her for many hours of collaborative intellectual rigor and pleasure shared in translation and discussion. Further, I thank her for bringing her poet's talents and instincts

to the liturgical office, the interpretive poetic translations of which are hers alone. I have learned a great deal from her in the process, not only about translation but also about reading and interpreting Latin texts.

To Elizabeth A. R. Brown I owe a large debt of intellectual generosity and common interest, as well as a host of archival discoveries, critical challenges, and insights.

Sean Field has helped me at every stage, from sitting down with manuscript copies in order to resolve difficult passages, to reading every word of my text, often multiple times. I am fortunate to have him as a colleague, one who shares my overall questions and research interests, and even more fortunate to have him as such a good friend.

John Zaleski has edited and revised the text, and has checked and disputed translations. His eye is remarkable, and his instinct for the language of medieval texts is extraordinary. I have been uncommonly fortunate to have had a student who has taught me so much.

Patrick Nold took precious time at the Vatican library to consult Vat. Reg. Lat 534 for me, to examine the manuscript itself, and to check my transcription, which had been completed from a microfilm copy.

Eric Rice read the materials that deal directly with the liturgy and the music and has been extremely helpful in clarifying my confusions and correcting mistakes. Stan Metheny, though we have never met, has been of great and frequent help with numerous issues involving liturgy.

William Chester Jordan, throughout my work on Louis, has been an invaluably generous and accessible authority. Many small issues have been helped by his vast knowledge, and he has answered innumerable queries.

Larry Field, at a late date, read through the entire text of the Latin, correcting a number of errors and suggesting no few improvements.

I also owe a special debt of gratitude to Charles Briggs, who generously reviewed translations for me in their final stages and caught and corrected a number of mistakes.

For all of their suggestions I am deeply grateful. Of course, it goes without saying that all errors here and throughout the text are mine alone. I simply hope that they are not so numerous as to render these texts unhelpful to those whom they might interest.

Thanks also to Leslie Butler, Robert Bonner, Jane Carroll, Margaret Darrow, Allen Hockley, Richard Kremer, Jennifer Lind, Christopher MacEvitt, Edward Miller, William North, Monika Otter, Daryl Press, Kevin Reinhart, Walter Simons, Andrea Tarnowski, and Thomas Madden for their friendship, help, and engagement.

As always, words do not exist to properly acknowledge my debt to, and gratefulness for, my family—my mother and father, my brothers, my in-laws, and in particular, my husband Paul and my son Michael.

ABBREVIATIONS

AH   *Analecta hymnica medii aevi.* Edited by Guido Maria
            Dreves and Clemens Blume. 55 vols. Leipzig: Fue's Ver-
            lag (R. Reisland), 1886–1922. Reprint, New York: John-
            son Reprint Corp., 1961.

BHL   *Bibliotheca hagiographica latina antiquae et mediae ae-
            tatis.* Brussels: s.n. 1898; and Henri Fros, ed., *Bibliotheca
            hagiographica Latina antiquae et mediae aetatis: Novum
            Supplementum* (Brussels: Imprimerie Cultura, 1986).
            Online at http://bhlms.fltr.ucl.ac.be/

BL   *Beatus Ludovicus* (text edited herein)

BLQRF   *Beatus Ludovicus quondam rex Francorum.* "Beati lu-
            dovici vita e veteri lectionario extracta." In RHF vol. 23,
            160–67.
                     The text can also be found in P. Albanus Heysse,
            "Antiquissimum officium liturgicum S. Ludovici regis,"
            Archivum Franciscanum Historicum 10 (1917): 559–75;
            and Marcy Epstein, "*Ludovicus Decus Regnantium*: Per-
            spectives on the Rhymed Office," *Speculum* 53 (1978):
            283–334. (The text is also presented herein.)

BNF   Bibliothèque Nationale de France, Paris

CCSL   Corpus Christianorum: Series latina. Turnhout: Brepols,
            1953–.

GB   Geoffrey of Beaulieu. "*Vita et sancta conversatio piae
            memoriae Ludovici quondam regis Francorum.*" In RHF
            vol. 20, 1–27.

GR   *Gloriosissimi regis* (text edited herein)

HLF   *Histoire littéraire de la France.* 41 vols. Paris: Imprimerie
             Nationale, 1832–1974.

LDR   *Ludovicus decus regnantium* (text presented herein)

PL   Patrologia cursus completus: Series latina. Edited by
             J.-P. Migne. 221 vols. Paris, 1844–1891.

RHF   *Recueil des historiens des Gaules et de la France.* Edited
             by Martin Bouquet. 24 vols. Paris, 1738. Reprint, Farn-
             borough: Gregg Press, 1967.

WC   William of Chartres. "De vita et actibus inclytae recor-
             dationis regis Francorum." In RHF vol. 20, 27–44.

WSP *mir*   Fay, Percival B., ed. *Guillaume de Saint-Pathus: Les
             miracles de saint Louis.* Paris: Champion, 1932.

WSP *sermo* H.-François Delaborde. "Une oeuvre nouvelle de Guil-
             laume de Saint-Pathus." *Bibliothèque de l'École des Chartes*
             63 (1902): 261–88.

WSP *vie*   Guillaume of Saint-Pathus. *Vie de Saint Louis.* Edited
             by H. François Delaborde. Collection de textes pour ser-
             vir à l'étude et à l'enseignement de l'histoire 27. Paris:
             A. Picard, 1899.

YSD   Yves of St.-Denis. "Gesta sancti Ludovici Noni, Franco-
             rum regis auctore monacho sancti Dionysii anonymo."
             In RHF vol. 20, 45–57.

Manuscript Sigla

Gloriosissimi regis

A: Vatican Reg Lat 534, 242v–246r (base manuscript)

B: Vienna ÖNB 12807 (9394), 141r–146r (base manuscript for fifteenth-century expansion)

C: Vienna ÖNB 12706 (9367a), 225r–232v

D: Brussels Bibliothèque Royale 197, 25r–29v
    (NB: I have opted for four sequential letters here to represent sequential production.)

Beatus Ludovicus

O: Orleans BM 348, 1r–18r

Sermons of Jacob of Lausaune

Rex sapiens

P_1: Paris BNF Lat 14799, 191rb–193r (base for *Rex sapiens*)

P_2: Paris BNF Lat 14966, Pt II, 25r–26r

V: Vatican Lat 1259, 162va–164rb

Videte regem Salomonem

P_3: Paris BNF Lat 15962, 25v–28r (base for the first part of *Videte regem* and for *Videte regem$_1$* in second part of sermon)

V_1: Vatican Lat 1259, 164r–167v (base for *Videte regem$_2$* in second part of sermon)

V_2: Vatican Lat 1250, 102r–104r (*Videte regem$_1$*)

W: Avignon 601, 460r–462v (*Videte regem$_2$*)

INTRODUCTION

Louis IX of France (b. 1214, r. 1226, d. 1270) was canonized in 1297, twenty-seven years after his death in Tunisia while on crusade. Louis was undoubtedly one of the most significant kings of his era, the only king canonized in the thirteenth century and the last saint-king of the Middle Ages. He represents the crystallization of the medieval idea of the saint-king, which went back to the beginnings of Christian rule, and also the paradox of how the later Middle Ages made a strong king into a saint at a time when sanctity was chiefly defined through poverty, humility, and renunciation.

The move to have him canonized was begun shortly after his death. In 1282–1283, formal proceedings were held at the Benedictine Monastery of St.-Denis, where Louis had been buried and where miracles had occurred, and two vitae were written in the process of advocating Louis' sainthood, by two court Dominicans, Geoffrey of Beaulieu, O.P., and William of Chartres, O.P. Today, we know Saint Louis best through Jean of Joinville's *Vie nostre saint roy Looÿs,* written by 1308. Joinville's vivid and compelling narrative, readily available in multiple translations and routinely assigned in the classroom, has primarily shaped the modern understanding of the saint king and his sanctity. But this reliance on Joinville misrepresents the Saint Louis of the later Middle Ages, since Joinville's text was virtually unknown beyond the royal court before it was first printed in the sixteenth century.[1]

For what medieval people knew of Louis, for how the medieval devout made sense of his sanctity and interacted with him as a saint and intercessor, we are better served by more traditional hagiographic and liturgical texts of the type presented here. The aim of this volume is to make available to modern readers Saint Louis as he was known to

1. Boureau, "Les Enseignements absolutistes de Saint Louis."

the Middle Ages, by presenting some of the texts that were involved in the construction of Louis' saintly persona and in the formation and propagation of his cult.

The composition of a number of lives and liturgies honoring Louis is witness to the flush of enthusiasm following his canonization. In addition to Joinville's account, these included the works of the Franciscan William of Saint-Pathus, based on the records of the canonization proceedings and finished by 1303; two works by historians at St.-Denis (William of Nangis and Yves of St.-Denis); and a short vita that the Dominican, Bernard Gui, included as part of his enormous *Speculum sanctorale* (a series of saints' lives that followed the Dominican calendar). With the exception of Gui's text, which remains unedited, these have long been available to historians, in part because they were published in volume 20 of the *Recueil des historiens des Gaules et de la France* (1840). Serious students of Louis' life and cult have routinely consulted these texts, but they are still available only in Latin.

This phase of early memorialization also included the composition of two other vitae: *Gloriosissimi regis* and *Beatus Ludovicus,* which are published here for the first time.[2] *Gloriosissimi regis* and *Beatus Ludovicus* are ideal witnesses to the development of the cult of Louis and his construction as a saint in the period immediately following his canonization. They represent an important stage in both the textual and the hagiographical development of, in Jacques LeGoff's words, the "production of royal memory."[3] They demonstrate the image of Louis that emerged from the canonization proceedings—an image made to conform to the shifting patterns and expectations of sanctity in the later Middle Ages, a sanctity predicated, above all, on the ideals of renunciation and active charity that characterize the century of Saint Francis. These two vitae also offer several new details about Louis, and they help clarify the process by which his cult was propagated in the

2. The two vitae were known to the compilers of the *Bibliotheca hagiographica latina* (BHL nos. 5047, 5042, and 5043b).

3. LeGoff, *Saint Louis* (Paris: Fayard, 1996). English edition, *Saint Louis,* trans. Gareth Evan Gollrad (University of Notre Dame Press, 2009)."The production of royal memory" was the name LeGoff gave to the second of the three "parts" of his extensive biography. Citations of page numbers throughout are from the English edition.

Middle Ages. Above all, they enrich the early hagiographic record and demonstrate the fervent creative activity in the years following Louis' canonization. In addition to these two vitae, this volume includes an interpretive translation of the most widely disseminated of the liturgical offices (*Ludovicus decus regnantium*) and the proper mass for Louis, as they were celebrated at the royal court on Louis' feast day (August 25),[4] as well as two sermons by the Parisian Dominican preacher Jacob of Lausanne, which were written to be preached in Paris following the liturgical celebration.

LOUIS IX TO SAINT LOUIS

Louis IX ruled the kingdom of France from 1226, when he was crowned at the age of twelve, to 1270, when he died on the shores of North Africa on his second crusade.[5] He had the good fortune to be king during generally peaceful and prosperous years in France, and he presided over a growing consolidation and strengthening of the French monarchy and the articulation of an increasingly focused royal ideology.[6] Administratively, Louis instituted mechanisms and procedures of centralization, many of these born from his desire to rule well, to effect justice throughout the kingdom, and to standardize royal administration. This included the establishment of Parlement, the institutionalization of royal justice, and the creation of the office of the *enquêteurs*, agents of the crown who were meant to seek out and correct royal abuses. Louis also sought to raise funds for a number of projects very

4. Paris Mazarine 413, 228v–230v (Missal from the Capella regis; includes a third prosa); Mazarine 406, 229v–300r (Capella regis, shortened); BNF Lat 911, 29r–35r (fourteenth century, Ste.-Chapelle or Capella regis); BNF Lat 8890, 59r–61v (sixteenth century, Ste.-Chapelle; with some changes to the prosa).

5. For the best recent treatments of Louis' reign, consult Jordan, *Louis IX and the Challenge of the Crusade*; LeGoff, *Saint Louis*; Richard, *Saint Louis*; Strayer, "The Crusades of Louis IX." A good overview is Hallam, *Capetian France, 987–1328*. The classic works are Tillemont, *Vie de Saint Louis* (1847–1851); de Wailly, *Histoire de Saint Louis* (1868).

6. Weiss, *Art and Crusade*; Jordan, *Visualizing Kingship*; Stahl, *Picturing Kingship*; Cohen, "An Indulgence for the Visitor."

close to his heart, such as the building of the Ste.-Chapelle in Paris, his endowments of religious institutions throughout France, and in particular, his crusades. He went on crusade twice. The first time followed a sickbed vow of 1244; he raised an important army and spent four years in planning and preparation before sailing in 1248, but the crusade was an utter disaster, and ended in 1250 with him and his army in captivity in Egypt. After his ransomed release, he went to the Levant for four years, where he became the de facto ruler of the ailing Kingdom of Jerusalem, before returning home in 1254 to take back the reins of French rule. These years were later memorialized by his friend, Jean of Joinville, in his account of Louis' life and sanctity. Louis' second crusade was equally disastrous. Louis fell ill and died outside the walls of Tunis, and the army soon packed up and returned home. Those returning to Paris brought with them the bones of the dead king, which were subsequently buried, along with Louis' forebears, at the Benedictine Abbey of St.-Denis, north of Paris. Miracles had begun to occur on the trip home from North Africa, and these multiplied in Paris, at the court, and particularly at St.-Denis.[7]

Miracles were the sign of sanctity—of a special relationship to God and the ability to intercede on behalf of men—and it was clear that a popular sentiment existed that Louis was a saint. Even during his lifetime, Louis had been widely considered pious and just. That said, by 1250 the making of a saint was not a simple matter, and even popularly venerated saints often did not achieve official recognition by the papacy. Successful canonizations required concerted effort and the backing of a well-funded constituency.[8] In Louis' case, in addition to the support of Pope Gregory X, who instituted proceedings in 1272, both his son Philip III (1270–1285) and his grandson Philip IV ("the Fair,"

7. On the miracles of Saint Louis, see Chennaf and Redon, "Les miracles de Saint Louis"; LeGoff, "Saint de l'Eglise et saint du peuple"; Farmer, "Down and Out and Female in Thirteenth-Century Paris"; Farmer, *Surviving Poverty in Medieval Paris*; Skoda, "Representations of Disability in the Thirteenth-Century *Miracles de Saint Louis*"; Gaposchkin, "Place, Status, and Experience in the Miracles of Saint Louis."

8. The single best treatment of the canonization process remains Vauchez, *Sainthood in the Later Middle Ages*. Still very useful is Kemp, *Canonization and Authority.*

1285–1314) were deeply committed to the process, both out of sincere devotion, but also, not surprisingly, because of the promise of the prestige that a king-saint would bring to the French monarchy. In 1297, France was the only major monarchical power that could not boast a saint in its royal history.[9] England had Edward the Confessor. Germany had Henry II and Charlemagne. But the kingdom that claimed that it had the most Christian kings had not, until then, been able to claim a saint among them.

Louis' canonization followed the basic format for saint-making in the second half of the thirteenth century. Immediately after Louis' death, the pope-elect, Gregory X, asked Geoffrey of Beaulieu, one of Louis' Dominican confessors, to write a vita in anticipation of the inquest into Louis' sanctity, and also asked Simon de Brie to quietly begin inquiries regarding Louis' canonization.[10] Another Dominican cleric in Louis' court, William of Chartres, composed a second vita, probably in the second half of the 1270s. In March 1282 the formal inquest was begun. Held at St.-Denis, where Louis was buried, it lasted through May 1283. The inquest brought together witnesses to the events of his life and to his character, and, more important, to the miracles he had effected after his death.[11] Among those who testified were Louis' son Philip III, now king; Charles of Anjou, his brother and by then King of Sicily; and his friend Jean de Joinville, seneschal of Champagne. A report was sent to Rome, but the canonization was delayed for another sixteen years, until Boniface VIII included it in a package of concessions that he was giving to Louis IX's grandson, Philip the Fair of France. At Orvieto, on August 11, 1297, Boniface VIII solemnly canonized Louis IX of France as a confessor saint and instructed churches throughout Christendom to add his feast day—August 25—to their liturgical calendar.[12]

9. Klaniczay, *Holy Rulers and Blessed Princesses*; Folz, *Les saints rois du Moyen Age en occident.*

10. Ripoll, *Bullarium Ordinis FF,* vol. 1, no. 1, 503; Potthast, ed., *Regesta Pontificum Romanorum,* vol. 2, no. 20511, 1652. This is summarized in Carolus-Barré, *Le procès de canonisation.* And see Gaposchkin, *Making of Saint Louis,* 33, 36–37.

11. Carolus-Barré, *Le procès de canonisation.*

12. Gaposchkin, *Making of Saint Louis,* 48–66; RHF vol. 23, 154–60.

Sourcing Sanctity: How the Devout Interacted with Their Saints

The most direct mode of interaction with a saint was to visit the saint's shrine, often in the hope and anticipation of a miracle. Testimonies of miracles were necessary for official recognition of a saint by papal canonization, which in turn led to the composition of intersecting texts, music, and images that were designed to celebrate, commemorate, and praise the virtue of the saint and to hold the saint up as a model for imitation and devotion. Hagiography, liturgy, devotional images, and sermons constituted some of the principal ways in which devotees interacted with a saint. They are important for historians because they define how contemporaries understood the saint, why they admired the saint, and the qualities of character and virtue that they valued enough to prize as saintly. Indeed, it is almost axiomatic that the saints that a society chooses reflect essential values and also define and valorize core virtues and social ideals.[13] The texts and images that explicitly celebrated the saint for these values constitute the sources that together shape his (or her) cult, and they allow us, as historians, to reconstruct the importance and meaning of that cult for men and women of the Middle Ages.

Saints usually had one or more vitae written for them. *Vita* (plural, *vitae*) means simply "the life," but the medieval vita was itself a genre that followed essential rules of composition and was specifically designed to showcase the virtues and characteristics of a saint.[14] Vitae were often structured according to different saintly virtues (such as chastity, humility, charity), and they generally treated a saint's birth, upbringing, life and major accomplishments, and good death. Sometimes a list of miracles—the proof of sanctity—was part of a vita, and at other times it constituted a separate work. Vitae were often guided by, but not bound by, chronology. Vitae could be written prior to canonization as part of the dossier that was compiled in order to make the case for a saint's admission into the catalogue of saints, and often new vitae were written once canonization had been secured. In Louis' case,

13. Weinstein and Bell, *Saints and Society.*
14. Heffernan, *Sacred Biography.*

as we saw, two important texts were written prior to 1297, but the canonization then spurred a host of new literary productions.

Once a saint was officially recognized by the church, he or she would then be inserted into the ecclesiastical and liturgical calendar. Typically, as in Louis' case, the feast day was the anniversary of the date of his death—called the *dies natalis* (birth day), since it was the day a saint was reborn into heaven. For Louis, this was August 25. Sometimes other feasts were added to the ecclesiastical calendar. In 1306, when Louis' grandson Philip the Fair had the relics of Louis' head brought from the Abbey of St.-Denis to the Ste.-Chapelle, the palace chapel, a new annual feast was established to commemorate this Translation (that is, the event of the transfer of relics), falling in May on the Tuesday after Ascension.[15] The way in which and extent to which a saint was honored could differ geographically and even among different kinds of monastic or ecclesiastical orders. In Louis' case, the elaborate celebration of his feast day was limited for the most part to French churches, especially in the Paris area. A Cistercian house might use a different set of liturgical rites than a Franciscan house or a secular church. Ecclesiastical institutions thus would often have special texts written for the mass (the Eucharistic celebration) and the office (the daily prayer cycle) that honored a particular saint.

The mass and the office constituted the core ritual and liturgical work of medieval clergy and was one of the principal ways in which the cult of a saint was defined. The liturgical office, called the *Opus Dei* (the work of God), was the longer and fuller text of the two, since it comprised chant for the eight liturgical hours of the day (Vespers, Compline, Matins, Lauds, Prime, Terce, Sext, and None). Liturgical offices were of unparalleled importance in the construction and validation of a saint. We tend to read the hagiographical accounts of saints in part because they offer the kind of historical, biographical element that so often interests historians; but it was more often through liturgy and sermons that medieval men and women most directly and actively interacted with the saint. The long night-time service of Matins, in which celebrants would awake at midnight to sing the office, included both sung texts (antiphons, responsories) and also lections—"lessons" or

---

15. Brown, "Philippe le Bel and the Remains of Saint Louis."

"readings" that were intoned following particular chants. These were hagiographical in nature and often consisted of a vita that was specially written for the office or drawn from an existing vita. In the case of *Ludovicus decus regnantium*, the liturgical office offered here, the lections were comprised of a hagiographical text that was itself an edited version of the vita *Beatus Ludovicus*, and that began with the same words, *Beatus Ludovicus quondam rex Francorum*. Indeed, these texts and liturgies were often highly interdependent.

The liturgy, however, was performed and celebrated by elite clergy in Latin. The translation and the further development of the identity and virtues of the saint for the faithful as a whole was the work of the sermons that were preached by the clergy to the laity on the saint's feast day. Although mostly preserved in Latin, these sermons would have been preached in public in the vernacular. Often inspired by the hagiographical and liturgical record, they could also be vehicles for preaching other themes.[16] Two fourteenth-century sermons are offered here as representative of the way in which the cult of Louis was transmitted by preachers to the non-elite, nonliterate faithful.

THE HAGIOGRAPHIC AND LITURGICAL TRADITION FOR SAINT LOUIS OF FRANCE

The cult of Saint Louis embraced all these different kinds of texts. The hagiographic tradition proper for Louis IX had begun in 1272, with Gregory X's request to Geoffrey of Beaulieu, Louis' Dominican confessor. Geoffrey had known Louis for over twenty years, and he had accompanied Louis on both of the king's crusades. His vita, entitled the *Vita et sancta conversatio pie memorie Ludovici quondam regis Francorum* (The life and saintly manner of Louis, of pious memory, the former king of the French), is divided into fifty-two chapters, organized for the most part according to Louis' virtues, but also treating events such as the Crusade of 1250 and the Crusade of 1270.[17] Geoffrey's text

16. Useful treatments of late medieval sermons can be found in Bériou, *L'avènement des maîtres de la Parole*; Kienzle, ed., *The Sermon*; D'Avray, *Preaching of the Friars*.

17. RHF vol. 20, 3–27. See discussion in LeGoff, *Saint Louis*, 256–58.

was highly influential, being quoted or paraphrased in all subsequent hagiographical accounts.[18]

William of Chartres' text, in contrast, was less directly influential.[19] William, another Dominican cleric in the royal court and a colleague of Geoffrey, was also present with Louis during his captivity in 1250 and at his death in 1270.[20] William wrote his vita—the *De vita et actibus incliti recordationis*[21] (The life and actions of Saint Louis of noble memory)— because, as he explained in his prologue, Geoffrey of Beaulieu left out important materials bearing on Louis' rule, his captivity in Egypt, and his death.[22] It is generally assumed that William died before 1282, because otherwise he would surely have appeared as a witness at St.-Denis for the canonization inquest. The text is a terribly interesting one, but it did not have the impact on later writings that Geoffrey of Beaulieu's did, and it is not even clear whether a copy of the text was included in the canonization dossier sent to Rome at the end of the inquiry.

A number of important texts about Louis were written at St.-Denis, which at the time was also the most important center of historical writing in France.[23] William of Nangis wrote his *Gesta sancte memorie Ludovici* around 1285–1295, before the official canonization.[24] Another short vita in twelve chapters, which is credited in the *Recueil des historiens des Gaules et de la France* to an anonymous monk at St.-Denis, was probably written about 1317 by Yves of St.-Denis as part of his sweeping treatment of the role of Saint Denis in the history of France.[25]

18. Carolus-Barré, who reconstructed the events of the canonization (see n. 28 below), called Geoffrey's vita the first act in the process.

19. Kaeppeli and Panella, *Scriptores Ordinis Praedicatorum Medii Aevi,* vol. 2, 95–96; RHF vol. 20, 27–41.

20. On William, see Carolus-Barré, "Guillaume de Chartres clerc du roi." The vita survives in only one manuscript from the fourteenth century.

21. RHF vol. 20, 27–44. The full title as found in BNF Lat 13778, 41v, is *De vita et actibus incliti recordationis regis francorum ludovici et de miraculis que ad ejus sanctitatis declarationem contigerunt.*

22. RHF vol. 20, 28.

23. Spiegel, *Chronicle Tradition of Saint-Denis.* On the cult of Louis as it developed at St.-Denis, see the important works by Elizabeth A. R. Brown, "The Chapels and Cult of Saint Louis at Saint-Denis" and "Burying and Unburying the Kings of France."

24. Spiegel, *Chronicle Tradition of Saint-Denis,* 101–2; RHF vol. 20, 310–465.

25. RHF vol. 20, 45–57.

Both of these were written within the Dionysian context of royalizing historiography for which the abbey was famous, and William of Nangis's text was later incorporated into the *Grandes chronique de France,* a kind of national history of the French monarchy.[26] Last, an otherwise unknown monk, Gilon of Reims, wrote a (lost) life of Louis, of which we know only because William of Nangis tells us that he consulted both this account and Geoffrey of Beaulieu's vita in composing his own.[27] Given how much William of Nangis relied on Geoffrey's text, we can assume that much of Gilon's work is preserved in William's *Gesta sancte memorie Ludovici.*

Because Louis was buried at St.-Denis, the abbey was chosen for the formal inquest into his life and miracles. The canonization itself produced two immediate literary products, both now lost.[28] The first consisted of the records of the canonization proceedings themselves, that is, the collection of documents and testimonies assembled at St.-Denis in 1282–1283. Two copies, at least, of the records from those proceedings existed in 1300. One copy was sent to the papal court, and Boniface VIII consulted it when he canonized Louis in 1297. We do not know what ultimately became of this copy, although we do know, from Boniface, that the records were so voluminous that they were more than could be transported by a single ass.[29] Another copy was housed at the Franciscan convent in Paris and was probably lost in a fire of 1580 that devastated the convent library.[30] The second text coming out of the can-

---

26. Spiegel, *Chronicle Tradition of Saint-Denis.* On the role of St. Denis in memorializing Louis, see LeGoff, *Saint Louis,* 266–80; Brown, "The Chapels and Cult of Saint Louis at Saint-Denis"; Gaposchkin, *Making of Saint Louis,* 137–51.

27. Molinier and Polain, *Les sources de l'histoire de France,* 116, no. 2541.

28. A fragment of Charles of Anjou's testimony survived in a compilation of materials dealing with holy war, and some of the miracle testimony survived as well. See Riant, "Déposition de Charles d'Anjou pour la canonisation de saint Louis"; Carolus-Barré, "Consultation du cardinal Pietro Colonna sur le IIe miracle de saint Louis." For the process of the canonization and the eventual outcome of the documentation, see Carolus-Barré, *Le procès de canonisation* and "Les enquêtes pour la canonisation de Saint Louis."

29. RHF vol. 23, 151–52. "Et ita per tot et totiens examinatum est, rubricatum et discussum negocium, quod de hoc plus factum est de scriptura quam unus asinus posset portare."

30. Beaumont-Maillet, *Le Grand couvent des Cordeliers de Paris,* 199–205, 255–57.

onization proceedings was a summary account of the canonization proceedings and of Louis' life—what William of Saint-Pathus would later refer to as the *vita curia approbata*—which, he explained, was sent down to and "approved" by the curia,[31] and which Boniface VIII (or his aide) probably used in composing his canonization bull and the two sermons preached for the event.[32]

We know most of this from a third text, the *vie* written by William of Saint-Pathus.[33] William of Saint-Pathus was the Franciscan confessor of Louis' wife, Marguerite of Provence, after her husband's death. William himself never knew Louis, but after Marguerite's own death in 1295 William also became the confessor to Louis' and Marguerite's daughter Blanche, who lived in lay residence at the Franciscan convent of St.-Marcel (Lourcines). Blanche requested that William compose a life of Louis, which he wrote in 1302–1303, drawing on materials derived from the canonization proceedings of 1282–1283. He seems to have had before him the actual recorded testimony of the witnesses, since he repeatedly refers to their specific testimony. He also had access to the *vita curia approbata,* the existence of which we know only by his reference to it. In his prologue he explains that his aim was to reproduce what he found in the canonization documents, and he tells his readers that one can check the actual record in the copy housed at the Franciscan convent, where he was in residence.[34] He also explains that he ordered the material according to theme, rather than by chronology, which was a method he had taken from Bonaventure's *Legenda maior* of Saint Francis.[35] William drew on Geoffrey of Beaulieu's vita, either because this last had been incorporated into the canonization record or into the *vita curia approbata,* or because he was able to consult an independent copy. But, curiously, very little of William of Chartres' text seems to have made it into William's redaction at this stage. William of Saint-Pathus' text, like Geoffrey's (and like Bonaventure's Life of

31. Delaborde, "Une oeuvre nouvelle de Guillaume de Saint-Pathus," 270, 278.
32. RHF vol. 20, 310.
33. RHF vol. 20, 58–121. On this process, see Vauchez, *Sainthood in the Later Middle Ages,* 33–103.
34. Guillaume of Saint-Pathus, *Vie de Saint Louis,* 3–4; RHF vol. 20, 60. The account is written in the first person.
35. Gaposchkin, *Making of Saint Louis,* 157.

Saint Francis), was organized according to Louis' different virtues, cull-
ing together precious anecdotes that had been offered at the proceedings. William also summarized a list of sixty-five miracles purported at
Louis' tomb, miracles that had largely accrued since Geoffrey and Wil -
liam of Chartres had written their vitae, sixty-three of which were subsequently approved by the papacy.[36] William may have written in Latin
in 1302–1303, but all that survives is a French text (either a translation
or simply the vernacular original) that was copied sometime in the first
third of the fourteenth century.[37] We also have, however, a Latin sermon that William of Saint-Pathus wrote in Louis' honor, which reproduces much of the material included in his *Vie monseigneur saint
Louis*,[38] though it is substantively shorter and ordered differently.[39]

The canonization, as discussed, itself spurred the composition of
a number of new hagiographical accounts, as well as a series of liturgical offices for Louis' feast day. It is rare for a hagiographical account to
be unrelated to earlier hagiographies or liturgical texts, and these texts
were often intertwined.[40] But for the most part, the texts that came
out of the canonization process were the basis for a series of new accounts that included Yves of St.-Denis' *Vita et passio sancti Dionysii*,[41]

36. RHF vol. 20, 121–89; Fay, ed., *Guillaume de Saint-Pathus.*

37. The text survives in three manuscripts: BNF Fr. 4976, Fr. 5722, and Fr.
5716. On these manuscripts, see Guillaume of Saint-Pathus, *Vie de Saint Louis,*
xv–xx. On the issue of French versus Latin, see P. Paris, "Le Confesseur de la Reine
Marguerite, auteur de la Vie et des Miracles de saint Louis." There was some de-
bate after Delaborde published his 1899 edition about whether William himself
was the translator or someone else. See Levillain, "La Vie de Saint Louis par Guillaume de Saint-Pathus."

38. In his preface, William referred to his text as "La vie monseigneur saint
Loys, jadis roi de France." See Delaborde, *Vie de Saint Louis,* 1.

39. Delaborde, "Une oeuvre nouvelle de Guillaume de Saint-Pathus."

40. The sole example of an outlier is a vita that exists in a compendium of
saints'-lives owned by the Benedictine monastery St.-Germain-des-Près. See RHF
vol. 23, 167–76. The manuscript is BNF Lat 11754. This last text bears the influence
of letters written in 1275 by French prelates to the curia, asking for Louis' canonization. Gaposchkin, *Making of Saint Louis,* 30–33. I extend my thanks to Elizabeth
A. R. Brown, who was able to identify this manuscript as belonging to St.-Germain.

41. On Yves of St.-Denis, the text is printed in RHF, vol. 20, 45–57, under the
title *Gesta sancti Ludovici noni, francorum Regis, auctore monacho sancti dionysii
anonymo,* and in Duchesne, *Historiae Francorum scriptores coaetanei . . . ,* vol. 5,

Bernard Gui's still unedited life of Louis in his *Speculum sanctorale*,[42] and the two vitae offered here. These two vitae, *Beatus Ludovicus* and *Gloriosissimi regis*, were thus part of the creative dynamic of saintly production in which the history of Louis as a saint (as opposed to Louis as a king) was constructed.

For *Gloriosissimi regis*, authorship and context are vexed. We have two early versions of it—one, ca. 1300, which represents its complete early form (Vatican Reg Lat 534), and a highly edited version of that early text (Mazarine 1718).[43] The most complete copy (Vatican Reg Lat 534) appears to have been made in Toulouse around 1310.[44] In both cases, the texts are found as additions to manuscript copies of Jacob of Voraigne's *Legenda Aurea*, which suggests Dominican authorship.[45] *Gloriosissimi regis* draws heavily on Geoffrey of Beaulieu and seemingly on the canonization proceedings as well. At GR 4.1, the author refers to having heard the story of Louis' embarkation at Aigues Mortes directly from Philip III (d. 1285) which, if we accept this, means that the author was probably a member of the court in the 1280s. The text has many echoes of, and overlaps with, William of Saint-Pathus' text (including the opening line), which William states was drawn directly from the canonization testimony, indicating that *Gloriosissimi regis* dates to *after* 1283; but since the early version of it does not mention

---

395–406, under the title "Gesta alia S. lvdovici noni francorvm regis avthore monacho sancti dionysii anonimo." Spiegel, *Chronicle Tradition,* 112–15, did not realize that this vita was part of Yves of St.-Denis' larger work. I am indebted for my understanding of these issues to Elizabeth A. R. Brown.

42. BNF Lat 5046, 152r–155r. Kaeppeli and Panella, *Scriptores Ordinis Praedicatorum Medii Aevi,* vol. 1, 210, no. 612. The entry on Louis appears in Part IV of Gui's *Speculum sanctorale,* the volume dedicated to "confessors and virgins." A small portion of this text was printed under the title "Brevis Chronica de progressu temporis sancti ludovici, auctore Bernado Guidonis" in RHF vol. 23, 176–77. Bernard drew on Boniface's canonization bull for Saint Louis, as well as either the *vita approbata* or *Beatus Ludovicus*. On Bernard, see Lamarrigue, *Bernard Gui.* On Bernard Gui's *Speculum sanctorale,* see Dubreil-Arcin, *Vies des saints, legends de soi.*

43. I thank Elizabeth A. R. Brown for sharing this text with me.

44. Cherubini, "Un manoscritto occitanio della *Legenda aurea,*" 123.

45. Vatican Reg Lat 534; Mazarine 1718 (originally belonging to the College of Navarre).

the canonization, there is no proof that it was not written before 1297. That said, it seems more likely that it was written on the heels of the canonization. Someone who had known Philip III in the 1280s could very well still be alive. The text—or rather, the first few chapters of the text—was immediately exploited for liturgical lections. It is first found in a royal breviary as lections accompanying an early version of *Ludovicus decus regnantium* (before the confection of BLQRF), which further argues for a compositional context close to the royal court.[46] And it was soon consistently paired with the Franciscan office, *Francorum rex magnificus* (which echoed or drew on a number of its themes), which may in turn argue for a Franciscan origin. Since the earliest example of the Franciscan office is found in a manuscript that can also be identified with a member of the royal court,[47] it is possible that the author was one of the many Franciscans known at court in the final decades of the thirteenth century. Whether Franciscan or Dominican in original authorship (or some other possibility entirely), it enjoyed the afterlife of a second recension. It was expanded in the middle of the fifteenth century with the addition of material from BLQRF and some other materials originally emanating from the court at a convent of canons-regular in the Lowlands called Rooklooster (Rouge Cloître), and was afterward adopted by the famous hagiographer Johanne Giel - lemans in his collection of Brabantine "Hagiology."[48]

Beatus Ludovicus was also an early composition, compiled around 1300 and then tightened up shortly thereafter for liturgical use with *Ludovicus decus regnantium* (as BLQRF). The author of *Beatus Ludo - vicus* was surely a Dominican, and he may well have also been attached to the court. He was able to consult the Dominican William of Chartres' otherwise little-disseminated vita in composing material on the saintly quality of Louis' governance (see BL 9). He included biographical details known only from that vita, and he redacted the seventeen miracles that William had included as part of his vita.[49] And he tellingly intro-

46. Washington, DC, Library of Congress MS 15.
47. BNF Lat 1288; Allirot, *Filles de roy de France*, 119–20.
48. Hazebrouck-Souche, *Spiritualité, sainteté et patriotisme.*
49. Chapter 9 includes materials not echoed in William of Saint-Pathus, *Gloriosissimi regis*, or Boniface VIII's text, and derived from William of Chartres.

duced into the tradition a detail about how Blanche entrusted Louis'
upbringing and education to Dominican teachers. (Shortly thereafter,
someone added the words "et minorum" to the text so that Louis' education was said to be entrusted to Dominicans *and* Franciscans, a detail that was transmitted into most versions of the text but always elided
by Dominicans.)[50]

Compare, for example, *Beatus Ludovicus,* "Consuetudines vero iniquas quantumcumque iniquos quantumcumque longevas, faciebat quantum poterat aboleri,"
with William of Chartres, "Consuetudines si quidam iniquas et pravas quantumcumque longaevas, ut commode poterant, aboleri, et exactiones indebitas amoveri
jubebat" (RHF vol. 20, 33). This chapter of *Beatus Ludovicus* relates to materials
that are not closely echoed in its sister-texts, but that do seem to have roots in a section of William's vita that deals with Louis' acts of rulership as king, his outlawing
of duels, his hatred of Jews and management of usury, and his exercise of justice
against magnates. The discussion of Louis' abstinences speaks of how he desisted
"on the advice of his doctors" ("consilium medicorum," BL 3.2; WC, p. 35), a detail
and phrase from William of Chartres that appears nowhere else. The author of *Beatus Ludovicus* follows William's miracle account very closely. William's *De vita et
actibus* survives today in only one medieval copy, now BNF Lat 13778 (old 1610), a
manuscript that also includes Geoffrey of Beaulieu's vita, which once belonged to
the Dominicans of Evreux. My thanks to Sean Field for help on this point.

   50. The idea of Louis' instruction by *either* Dominicans *or* Franciscans was
not in the original canonization documents. *Gloriosissimi regis* states only that
Blanche raised him religiously (*religiose nutrivit*), a characterization that began with
Geoffrey of Beaulieu. It says nothing of Louis' teachers, per se. William of Saint-
Pathus, in a chapter entitled "De sa sainte norreture en enfance" (on the saintly instruction of his youth), states only that Blanche was upright in words and deed and
that she loved religious people. In 1297, Boniface reported only that when Louis
turned fourteen, Blanche made sure that he had "proper teachers, who imbued him
with the knowledge of letters and formed him in good mores" (RHF vol. 23, 156).
The (Dominican) author of *Beatus Ludovicus* inserted the detail about Dominicans.
"Mater eius domina Blancha regina quondam castelle filia uno suo ac domino sic
orbata beatum Ludovicum adhuc puerum diligentissime enutrivit, et bonis et religiosis viris precipue fratribus ordinis predicatorum in sanctitate ac sciencia scripturarum tradidit imbuendum." However, when *Beatus Ludovicus* was edited into
BLQRF at the royal court, the redactor added the term "et minorum" (Quem ipsa
tenerrime diligens sub cura specialis magistri et consilio religiosorum maxime ordinis fratrum predicatorum et minorum in scientia litterarum tradidit imbuendum).
The phrase is awkward, since "ordinis" is in the singular, while the inclusion of both
Franciscans and Dominicans would seem to require "ordinum." Copies of the text
found in volumes associated with the Ste.-Chapelle or the royal court, and indeed

The single manuscript example of *Beatus Ludovicus* distorts its importance for the development of the hagiographical image of Louis, because it is *this* text that formed the basis of the liturgical vita that constitutes the single most frequently copied and disseminated of *all* hagiographical texts on Louis in the Middle Ages. This liturgical vita, BLQRF, lifted its opening phrase, "Beatus Ludovicus quondam rex francorum," from its source. Sometime after 1297—during which time the royal court of Philip the Fair was busy promoting the cult of Louis at the Ste.-Chapelle, adding new feasts to the calendar, and promoting indulgences for those who visited Louis' relics there—this text was redacted to accompany the court's fancy new liturgical office, *Ludovicus decus regnantium,* and was included alongside it in a shrine book that may well have been made for the Ste.-Chapelle or the royal court (BNF Lat 911).[51]

---

all copies made in non-Dominican contexts, including the rites of Paris, Tours, Evreux, and so forth, include the reference to the Franciscans, which was derived from the royal version found in 911—crediting both Dominicans and Franciscans with his education: BNF Lat 13238, 290v (Ste.-Chapelle); BNF Lat 1023 (Capella regis), 561r; BNF Lat 10485, 430r (Paris); BNF Lat 1026, 252v (Paris); BNF Lat 1028, 334v (Paris); Arsenal 582, 583r (Paris); St. Genevieve 2626, 331r (Rouen); BNF NAL 388, 311r (Evreux); BNF Lat 10491, 115r (Roman rite); BNF Lat 1032, 96v (Tours). In some versions they were both edited out: BNF Lat 1029 (Auxerre). On the other hand, the tradition as it was transmitted in a Dominican context always included only the Dominicans. In all Dominican versions of the text—including the copies in British Library Add. 23935 (St.-Jacques), Mazarine 374, 309r (St.-Jacques), Arsenal 603, 313v (Poissy), and also the simplified and shorter lections at the General Council meeting of 1306—the lections speak only of Dominican instruction (MOHP vol. 4, 21–23. The phrase appears on 21: ". . . tenerrime diligens, sub specialis cura magistri et consilio religiosorum, maxime ordinis fratrum predicatorum, moribus et sciencie literarum tradidit imbuendum").

51. BLQRF is an edited and simplified version of *Beatus Ludovicus.* The number of chapters was edited from twelve to nine, since *Ludovicus decus regnantium,* a secular office with nine responsories, required only nine readings. As with the incipit for the vita as a whole (which begins with the words *Beatus Ludovicus quondam rex francorum*), the incipits for many of the individual chapters were retained (chs. 1, 4, 5, 6, 7, 9/8, 10/9), and the two versions follow the same basic line of narrative. BLQRF's redactor cut out well over 60 percent of the original text and tightened up the language and presentation. He also added, here and there, some explanation, including, for instance, typological comparison that brought the lections into line with the liturgical office. When *Ludovicus decus* was initially confected,

It was edited down by more than half and cleaned up, and some new rhetorical elements (such as the addition of Old Testament comparisons) were added, but the biographical content and the first seven miracles in the text were essentially derived from *Beatus Ludovicus*. However, the miracle account, which constituted the readings for the octave, was updated, including a number of miracles that had occurred after 1297 in Evreux, Poissy, and near Beauvais, bringing the text, as it were, "up-to-date."[52] Some version of BLQRF appears in dozens if not hundreds of fourteenth- and fifteenth-century breviaries, and it can be accessed in several modern editions.[53] Its influence on the memorialization of Louis in a wider sense is also testified by its influence on sermons written in Louis' honor.[54] Ultimately, the text found its way into manuscripts as a traditional hagiographical life, including in expanded versions of Jacob of Voragine's *Legenda Aurea* (since the original, written ca. 1260, did not include a vita for Louis).[55] When William Caxton printed an English translation of the *Legenda Aurea* (*The Golden Legend*) in the late fifteenth century, it included a translated version of BLQRF.[56]

---

lections were taken from the early sections of our other vita, *Gloriosissimi regis*. The earliest versions of BLQRF of which I am aware are BNF Lat 911, the liturgical compendium devoted to Saint Louis, and BNF Lat 1028, an early fourteenth-century breviary of Paris usage, in which the feast is a later addition to the back of the manuscript after 1297/1298. BNF Lat 1028, fols. 328–341, is less complete, including neither the octave items nor the items for the little hours. Both paired the liturgical office, *Ludovicus decus regnantium,* with the liturgical vita (BLQRF).

52. The redactor of BLQRF included the first seven miracles from the miracle account in BL (itself taken from WC); since *Beatus Ludovicus* relied on William of Chartres' miracles, all from that account had occurred in 1270 or 1271. BLQRF's redactor also included a number of miracles that had occurred after Louis' canonization, which can also be found in greater detail in the additions made to *Gloriosissimi regis,* 14.8–14.15.

53. See the list of abbreviations at the front of this volume.

54. An example of the influence of BLQRF on preaching is Jacob of Lausanne's sermon *Rex sapiens,* included in this volume. The best example of such influence is a Franciscan sermon found in BNF Lat 3303, which is structured around BLQRF.

55. Jacob of Voragine, *Legenda Aurea,* 915–18. This is the only modern edition of the Golden Legend of which I know that includes the text for Louis. The text is a slightly altered version of BLQRF. On the *Legenda aurea,* see Reames, *The Legenda Aurea.*

56. See Jacob of Voragine, *The Golden Legend.*

The hagiographic texts reproduced here cannot be separated from the context of liturgical composition. At roughly the same time that *Gloriosissimi regis* and *Beatus Ludovicus* were being composed, as noted above, a number of liturgical offices and proper masses were written for the feast day of Saint Louis. The Dominicans, Franciscans, and Cistercians each quickly produced an office: *Nunc laudare, Francorum rex magnificus,* and *Lauda celestis,* respectively.[57] At the royal court, Philip the Fair probably hired a famous liturgist, Pierre de la Croix, to compose a fancy liturgical office, *Ludovicus decus regnantium,* which was a reworking of the Dominican office *Nunc laudare*; this office may have been the one that was used at St.-Denis for the inaugural translation in 1298. Meanwhile, at St.-Denis and St.-Germain-des-Près (another Benedictine monastery, directly across the Seine from the royal palace), a revamped version of the Cistercian *Lauda celestis* was incorporated into the liturgy, which itself adopted liturgical items from *Ludovicus decus regnantium*. And then, in 1306, when Philip translated the relic of Louis' head to the Ste.-Chapelle in order to augment the royal chapel as the center for the cult of kingship, Philip had a new office, *Exultemus omnes,* composed for the translation feast.

The sermons of Jacob of Lausanne presented here must also be understood as part of the same complex dynamic of writings, memory, and devotion that characterized the production of the hagiographic and liturgical texts. Preachers offered sermons on a variety of topics pertaining to the Christian faith, and often preached a sermon on a particular saint following the daily mass on his or her feast day. About fifty such sermons in Louis' honor survive.[58] As with Jacob of Lausanne's sermons, authors of such saint's day sermons would often consult a hagiographic account of some kind to garner necessary biographical and devotional details for use in the sermon. In Jacob's case, these were the liturgical readings (BLQRF) for the *Ludovicus decus* office just discussed. Preachers might also use books of Exempla to find set-piece stories or other received information to fill out or spice up the sermon.[59] But authors of sermons were often interested in using the saint to de-

---

57. Gaposchkin, "*Ludovicus Decus Regnantium*"; "Philip the Fair"; "The Monastic Office," 143–74; *Making of Saint Louis,* 86–92.

58. Gaposchkin, *Making of Saint Louis,* 284–89.

59. Berlioz and Polo de Beaulieu, *Les Exempla médiévaux.*

velop themes that were not necessarily inherent in the hagiographi-cal record; the saint's life served as a jumping-off point, as it were, for other ideas or arguments altogether, in which case the sermons repre-sent the deployment of a saint toward different pastoral goals. Many sermons survive only in single copies, but in other cases sermons were copied into model sermon collections, which other preachers could use as a basis for their own preaching.[60] In this case, too, the two ser-mons included in this volume represent the dissemination of the story of Louis' life and sanctity into the larger cultural arena from which that life also took its meaning.

This brief history of hagiographical production of Louis is not complete without some discussion of the best-known account of Louis' saintly life: that of Jean of Joinville. Joinville probably (though the point is arguable)[61] had begun writing down his own memories of the crusade of 1250 long before Louis' canonization, perhaps in the 1270s or 1280s. After Philip the Fair's queen, Jeanne de Navarre (d. 1305), asked him to write a life of Louis, he retooled his account into the form that we now have it, completing it by 1308.[62] Joinville's text, although critical to mod-ern estimations of Louis, did not have much (if any) influence on the tradition in the fourteenth century, although it was itself in parts de-pendent upon that tradition.[63] Joinville incorporated materials derived ultimately from Geoffrey of Beaulieu's account, which he obtained from a French translation that had made its way into a copy of the *Grandes chronique de France*.[64] And because he had testified at St.-Denis, certain

60. D'Avray, *Preaching of the Friars*; Kienzle, ed., *The Sermon*.

61. The issue of dating is vexed. For the view that Joinville wrote the entire text between 1303 and 1308, see Monfrin, "Introduction," in *Vie de Saint Louis*, 69–79. For the view that the text was composed over a much longer period of time, in at least two sections, see the recent treatment by Smith, *Crusading in the Age of Join -ville*, 48–76. Smith is defending a position initially taken by G. Paris, "La composi-tion du livre." I am of this view as well; *Making of Saint Louis*, 182–85.

62. The standard edition and translation is now Jean de Joinville, *Vie de Saint Louis*, ed. Monfrin. There are many English translations, the most recent of which is now also the best: Joinville and Villehardouin, *Chronicles of the Crusades*, trans. Smith, 137–336.

63. Boureau, "Les Enseignements absolutistes de Saint Louis"; Viollet, "Les Enseignements," 1–56.

64. Viollet, "Les Enseignements"; Delaborde, *Jean de Joinville*; Maureen Slattery, *Myth, Man and Sovereign Saint*; Boutet, "La méthode historique de Joinville," 93–108.

of his own memories of the king found their way into the canonization record. But his written memoirs, as we know them, largely stand apart from the otherwise interconnected hagiographical tradition. In a sense, Joinville's text is the most distinct and most unrepresentative example of what people thought of Louis, and of the ideas and anecdotes that were preached about Louis, around 1300. Thus, although we recognize in the hagiographical and liturgical representations of Louis the man we know from Joinville, his Louis appears less as the man who fulfilled the pious mold of saintly expectation than as the individual and deeply charismatic personality so vividly represented in Joinville's extraordinary vernacular prose. It is in *this* sense that Joinville's portrait is so remarkable. But it is also fundamentally unrepresentative of the *medieval* understanding of why Louis was remarkable.

THE SANCTITY OF SAINT LOUIS IX OF FRANCE IN 1300

For this—for the *medieval* understanding of Louis—the vitae, liturgical texts, and sermons included in this volume offer a better picture of how the Middle Ages reconciled Louis' kingship and crusade with his sanctity. They belong to a family of texts that were designed to show how Louis conformed to the patterns and expectations of holiness in the period. And thus, these texts should be understood, and the image of Saint Louis presented in them must be understood, within the context of the developing history of sanctity and sainthood at the end of the Middle Ages. Sanctity, as André Vauchez has outlined, was increasingly open to laypeople and predicated on personal renunciation (the idea of "asceticism and sainthood") and active charity (the idea of "saints of charity and labor").[65] The sociology of sanctity in general had been deeply affected by the spiritual and religious movement that gave

---

65. Vauchez, *Sainthood in the Later Middle Ages,* 190–99. For scholarly treatments of the sanctification and memory of Saint Louis, see Folz, *Les saints rois du Moyen Age en Occident*; Beaune, *The Birth of an Ideology,* 90–125, 327–30; LeGoff, *Saint Louis* (Part II); Klaniczay, *Holy Rulers and Blessed Princesses*; Gaposchkin, *Making of Saint Louis*; Rathmann-Lutz, *"Images" Ludwigs des Heiligen*; Allirot, *Filles de roy de France.*

rise to the mendicant orders early in the thirteenth century; its effect on royal sanctity was to depress the production of saint kings after 1200 but to reward an increasing number of queens and princesses with sainthood. The best interpretation of this phenomenon is that during the rise of new monarchies, the requirements of successful kingship had become essentially inimical to the ideals of renunciation and asceticism that now animated sanctity.[66] By 1297, no king had been canonized for over one hundred and thirty years.[67] This is one reason why Louis is so interesting, since his three most salient characteristics—his kingship, his unsuccessful crusading activity, and his sanctity—seem to be somehow in tension with one another, in the context of a historical period in which concepts of monarchy, crusading, and sainthood were all in flux.

Both vitae offered here, *Gloriosissimi regis* and *Beatus Ludovicus,* integrate a chronological narrative that begins with Louis' parentage, birth, and upbringing and ends with his death, and both share a chapter structure that highlights individual virtues or qualities of his sanctity. As a whole, these texts are primarily interested in manifestations of active Christian piety, charity, humility, and devotion in ways that conform to the principal themes of late medieval sanctity and define the emergence of lay sanctity.[68] Most of their chapters are organized around basic virtues of Christian devotion. In this regard, the chapter titles are indicative of the authors' aims. Both authors included chapters on how Louis was raised (GR 1, BL 1), how he raised his children (GR 3 and 4, BL 2), on his bodily sufferings ("how he punished his body," GR 5, BL 3), on his humility (GR 6, BL 4), on his alms-giving (GR 7, BL 6), and on his devotion to relics (GR 8, BL 7). *Gloriosissimi regis* alone includes a chapter on his chastity and his undertaking of a

66. Klaniczay, *Holy Rulers and Blessed Princesses.*

67. Charlemagne was canonized in 1166 by an anti-pope, Paschal II, as part of Frederick Barbarosa's political agenda. Although his cult was celebrated in parts of Germany, his sanctity never rang true in the way that, for instance, the sanctity of Edward the Confessor or Henry II did. Edward the Confessor was canonized in 1161, and Henry II was canonized in 1146.

68. The best discussions of Louis in the context of the history of sanctity include Vauchez, *Sainthood in the Later Middle Ages*; Klaniczay, *Holy Rulers and Blessed Princesses*; LeGoff, "La sainteté de Saint Louis"; LeGoff, *Saint Louis.* My own treatment of the subject is found in *The Making of Saint Louis.*

chaste marriage (GR 2), thus highlighting monastic and ascetical qualities that *Beatus Ludovicus* ignored. *Gloriosissimi regis* also includes a
chapter on his love of the cross, dealing not with the crusade but rather
with his devotion to the form of the cross itself.

Louis' two crusades are the subject matter of three chapters in each
vita. *Gloriosissimi regis* consolidates the discussion of both his crusades and his death on his second crusade in the last three chapters
(GR 10–12). The title of the tenth chapter, "On his first assumption of
the cross and his liberation from prison and the danger of the sea," indicates the interpretive approach to Louis' crusading as a mark of his
devotion, the testing of his faith, and his miraculous protection by
God. For both authors, his second crusade served primarily as the stage
set for his good death, although the author of *Beatus Ludovicus* was
more invested in the topic and devoted more of the text to it. In both
vitae, the treatment of the crusades follows the pattern set out first by
Geoffrey of Beaulieu and repeated by William of Saint-Pathus, interpreting the events of 1250 and 1270 as manifestations of Christian
suffering and a desire to work in Christ's name, and looking for ways of
explaining the catastrophic events of both crusades.

One place where the two vitae diverge in their interpretation of
Louis' sainthood is the issue of his rulership. In an age where sanctity
was heavily invested in ideals of poverty and renunciation, the exercise
of power inherent in royal authority was potentially problematic.[69] This
is one reason why both vitae (indeed, all the vitae) emphasize Louis'
humility (dressing in a simple manner, personally ministering to the
poor, feeding lepers), a humility all the more marked by the exalted
royal status to which it was compared. But beyond this, two different
approaches to Louis' kingship could be taken—to avoid the subject of
his kingship and rule as an element of his sanctity altogether, or to emphasize the justice of his reign as a quality of his saintly character. In
general, the pre-canonization materials were less occupied with Louis'
rulership, favoring the image of royal mercy and piety over the image
of royal magnificence, but the record did include discussions of his
good justice, his appointment of good advisors, his establishment of

69. A paradox masterfully treated by Klaniczay, *Holy Rulers and Blessed
Princesses*.

the *enquêteurs*, and his comportment in Parlement. To be more spe -
cific, Geoffrey of Beaulieu was restrained on the issue of Louis' rulership, while William of Chartres was less so, and the evidence of the
canonization proceedings relayed by William of Saint-Pathus suggests
that many witnesses were impressed by the quality of Louis' exercise
of his authority over justice. *Beatus Ludovicus* thus took up materials
from William of Chartres—the second approach—and the author included a rich chapter on Louis' kingship, entitled "Concerning his dedicated preservation of justice and peace" (ch. 9). He showed Louis rendering justice equally to everyone, making certain that the agents of the
crown upheld true justice, not allowing the duel, not selling royal offices,
taking legislative measures against the Jews and usury, and punishing
magnates. The image of Louis sitting outside his palace twice weekly in
order to hear the cases of the poor, which became very popular in later
years, originates in this text.[70]

The other approach was simply to downplay Louis' royalty—to
minimize the extent to which the elements of his sanctity were located
in his royal identity and even to avoid depicting Louis as a king. *Gloriosissimi regis* includes no material on Louis' rule and kingship, and in
fact, is striking for its studied avoidance of any depiction of Louis as a
king.[71] The only two references to Louis' kingship in *Gloriosissimi regis*
are instances where Louis expresses the desire to *renounce* his kingship. The first appears in the second chapter, which recounts Louis' desire to abdicate the throne to his son and to enter a religious house (a
story known from Geoffrey of Beaulieu), and the second appears in the
fourth chapter, in his speech exhorting his sons to be willing to give
up family and kingdom for the church. A complementary theme was
that of Louis' desire to enter the religious life. So absent was kingship
that the fifteenth-century scribe at Rooklooster who expanded the
text imported the entire eighth chapter/lection from the liturgical vita
(BLQRF), itself derived from *Beatus Ludovicus*, which treated these
themes, and which he entitled "On his prudence in his rule and concerning the equity of his justice in all his judgments."[72]

---

70. See BL 9.2. Cf: Joinville, *Vie de Saint Louis,* §59.
71. GB, chs. 6, 20, 35; WSP *vie,* ch. 17.
72. "De prudentia eius in regimine: et de iusticie equitate in omni suo iudicio."

This divergence between *Gloriosissimi regis* and *Beatus Ludovicus* over the issue of Louis' rulership in fact points to the issue that hagiographers faced around the year 1300 when dealing with Louis. That is, the most distinctive element of his biography—his kingship—was potentially the most problematic for his sainthood, since sanctity, as already mentioned above, was increasingly predicated on renunciation and humility. The author of *Gloriosissimi regis* solved this problem by emphasizing Louis' desire to renounce the throne, by speaking to themes of humility, asceticism, and devotion, and by side-stepping the issue of his royal authority. In *Beatus Ludovicus,* the discussion of aspects of Louis' kingship in one sense echoes more traditional themes of the "just king," but in a way that was modeled on the themes of active charity and true justice that animated the social and charitable aspects of thirteenth-century sanctity. The trials of his two crusades—captivity on the first and death on the second—also played into the traditional trope of the "suffering leader," reconciled with the notion of passion and compassionate suffering with and for Christ.[73] The formulations of sainthood in *Gloriosissimi regis* and *Beatus Ludovicus* thus reflect the ways in which Louis' hagiographers understood his saintly virtue, the priorities of the new sanctity of the thirteenth century, and also the general tenor of the spiritual and religious ideals that influenced Louis himself.

A Few Notes on Transcriptions, Sources, Translations, and Practices

In preparing each text for this volume, I have chosen a base manuscript. I have generally followed the orthography of the base manuscript, although I have expanded common abbreviations, standardized *u* and *v, i* and *j,* and some (but not all) *c* and *t* to modern usage, and imposed punctuation.[74] Except for Orleans BM 348, which is a unique witness to

73. Vauchez, *Sainthood in the Later Middle Ages,* 158–67. Klaniczay, *Holy Rulers and Blessed Princesses,* 243–45, 295–96; Gaposchkin, "Role of the Crusades," 195–209.

74. I have sought to follow principles of "critical transcription," on which, see Maier, *Crusade Propaganda and Ideology,* 71–73; D'Avray, *Death and the Prince,* 8–10.

its text (*Beatus Ludovicus*), I have collated the base manuscript against one or more available manuscripts, and on occasion have adopted readings from one of these when they offer a superior or clearer reading. Changes in word order or orthography in the comparison manuscripts have not usually been noted unless they affect meaning, although omissions and additions are noted.

The transcription of chapters 1–12 of *Gloriosissimi regis* is that of the shorter, early life in twelve chapters, which is known to me in only one manuscript: Vatican Reg Lat 534, 242v–246r (siglum A). It is thus used as the base manuscript, and I have generally followed its orthography. The notes furnish the expansions made at Rooklooster in the fifteenth century, and I have included the additional chapters compiled there, as found in B, C, and D, that comprise chapters 14 (on miracles) and 15 (the translation) of the expanded text, although some of this was suppressed in D. Some additional materials (as in the extended prologue found in C) have been placed in the notes. In this way, a reader has access to both the text of ca. 1300 and the text of the mid-fifteenth century.

The transcription of *Beatus Ludovicus* reproduces the text found in Orleans BM 348, fols. 1–18, as the only known version of the text. Where the text is clearly faulty and the grammar unworkable, I have sparingly emended it, based on comparison with either Geoffrey of Beaulieu's text or manuscript versions of the liturgical vita BLQRF (which depends on it), and so indicated in the notes.

The texts for the mass and liturgical office, *Ludovicus decus regnantium,* including the office and octave lections, *Beatus Ludovicus quondam rex Francorum* (BLQRF), have been edited and printed by Heysse (1917). Epstein (1978) edited the office (including the music, but not including the octave readings). Both based their editions on BNF Lat 911.[75] An older edition of the chant texts based on a greater number of manuscript sources can be found in the *Analecta Hymnica.*[76] The Latin text of the office presented here is based on two manuscripts, BNF

---

75. Epstein, "*Ludovicus Decus Regnantium*: Perspectives on the Rhymed Office"; Heysse, "Antiquissimum officium liturgicum S. Ludovici regis."

76. Dreves and Blume, eds., *Analecta hymnica,* vol. 13, pp. 185–88 for the office, vol. 11, pp. 177–78 for hymns. The edition in the *Analecta Hymnica* is drawn from a variety of manuscripts.

Lat 911 and Washington, DC, Library of Congress MS 15[77] (although the octave items are not found in the latter). The lections (BLQRF) have been previously printed, both by Heysse and Epstein and also, divorced from the office chant, in the *Receuil des historiens des Gaules et de la France,* in a version drawn from BNF Lat 10872.[78] My references to BLQRF are taken from the *Receuil,* although a reader might prefer to consult the more modern editions found in Heysse or Epstein.

In both *Beatus Ludovicus* and *Gloriosissimi regis,* I have noted where material was derived from Geoffrey of Beaulieu's vita (GB), and I have noted parallel passages in each other, as well as in William of Saint Pathus' French vita (WSP *vie*) and his Latin sermon (WSP *sermo*). Occasionally, when it is of interest, I have noted parallels with other authors, such as Yves of St.-Denis, writing ca. 1317 (YSD), William of Chartres (WC), or Joinville. I have not indicated parallels between *Beatus Ludovicus* and the liturgical lections, BLQRF, since the latter was derived directly from the former.

In quoting and referencing scripture, I have followed the numbering of the Latin Vulgate. We have generally used the Douay-Rheims Bible for English translations of scripture, although sometimes we have silently altered this version to better address context and meaning. Biblical language and phrases in both the Latin texts and the translations are identified with italics.

In translating, we have generally tried to split the difference between a literal translation that reflects and respects the original language and vocabulary, and the language that we, as English speakers, would have naturally used if expressing the idea in our own idiom. If some of the translations seem awkward, it is usually because we have not wanted to stray too far from the Latin. Some passages remain oblique to us and will surely invite disputed interpretation.

77. The text used here is found in Gaposchkin, *Making of Saint Louis,* 153–83.
78. RHF vol. 23, 160–67.

1 ~

GLORIOSISSIMI REGIS

Vienna ÖNB cod. ser. n. 12807 [siglum B], 143r. Courtesy
Österreichische Nationalbibliothek.

Gloriosissimi regis represents one of the early attempts to model the portrait of Saint Louis that emerged from the canonization proceedings into a structured hagiographical and para-liturgical narrative. It echoed many of the themes found in William of Saint-Pathus' *Vie,* and may have been based on mutual sources. It prizes themes of humility, piety, renunciation, and charity. The text exists in two versions. The earlier, in twelve chapters, was probably compiled around 1300 (BHL no. 5047). A second, longer version (BHL no. 5042) was redacted in the second half of the fifteenth century at Rooklooster (Rouge Cloître), a convent of canons regular in the Lowlands, outside Brussels.

The early version of *Gloriosissimi regis* was composed by someone who had known Philip III (d. 1285) and seems to have been part of the early efforts by the court to promote Louis' sanctity. Lections were drawn from it for an early (if not the earliest) copy of the liturgical office for Louis, *Ludovicus decus regnantium,* in a royal breviary perhaps made for one of Louis' own sons.[1] This pairing was never again repeated and was probably a provisional usage, when the tradition was still in flux. However, the Franciscans quickly adopted *Gloriosissimi regis* as the readings (lections) for their office, *Francorum rex,* and it is through their liturgical manuscripts that the early parts of this tradition were chiefly disseminated.[2]

The text was then substantially expanded in the fifteenth century at Rooklooster. Founded in 1374 in the Zoniën (Soignes) woods as a hermitage for regular canons, Rooklooster was a leader in the *devotio moderna* movement and became a great center of learning, mysticism, and hagiography in both Latin and Middle-Dutch in the late fourteenth and fifteenth centuries. It boasted one of the premier medieval monastic libraries and owned dozens of works of hagiography, sermons, and

---

1. Washington, DC, Library of Congress MS 15, 553v–560r. Rebecca Baltzer has suggested that the breviary was made for Robert of Clermont. See Baltzer, "A Royal French Breviary from the Reign of Saint Louis."

2. Cambridge Dd V5, 294v–299v; London British Library Harley 2864, 368v–370v; New York Pierpont Morgan M 149, 465v–470v; New York Pierpont Morgan M 75, 484v–487v; BNF Lat 1288, 491v–494v; Padua, University of Padua 734, 375r–377r.

histories.[3] All three manuscripts that preserve the longer version were written there.[4]

The expansion was done by taking the existing text in twelve chapters and incorporating into it text from BLQRF (itself derived from *Beatus Ludovicus*), along with an original set of lections that was written, in or after 1306, for the Office of the Translation of Louis' head to the Ste.-Chapelle (*Exultemus omnes*), and a miracle account. The latter included miracles that had occurred after 1297, which seem to have been tracked at the royal court. The result was a text of fifteen chapters, which included the insertion into the narrative (as the new chapter 9) of the eighth lection of BLQRF, which treated the otherwise missing theme of Louis' good rule, and two added chapters at the end (chapters 14 and 15, here), which dealt with post-canonization events. The fourteenth chapter comprised simply the octave readings from BLQRF that narrated some of Saint Louis' miracles. The fifteenth chapter, drawing from the lessons from the Translation of the Head that had been composed at court, dealt with Louis' canonization and Philip the Fair's role in the sanctification of his grandfather and the translation of the head relic to the Ste.-Chapelle. It includes the astounding royalizing formulation that "where the head of the entire kingdom of France is [that is, the royal palace], there the head of that one who so gloriously ruled over and benefited France . . . shall be forever worshipped" (see GR 15.11).

We can identify the very manuscript in which this expansion occurred: Vienna ÖNB 12807 (9394), 141r–146r (before 1465) (siglum B), a collection of "Vitae Fratrum Predicatorum."[5] No name can be attached

---

3. *Corpus Catalogorum Belgii,* ed. Derolez, vol. 4, 178–209. Rooklooster's catalogues do not include its liturgical holdings, from which some of the additions to the earlier life may have derived (p. 179).

4. For Vienna ÖNB 12807 (9394), see "Catalogus codicum hagiographicorum qui vindobonae," 257. For Vienna ÖNB 12706 (9397a), see "De codicibus hagiographicis Iohannis Gielemans," 9–11. For Brussels, Bibliothèque Royale 197, see *Catalogus Codicum Hagiographicorum Bibliothecae Regiae Bruxellensis,* vol. 1, 97–99.

5. "Catalogus codicum hagiographicorum qui vindobonae," 257. The catalogue of contents runs from 257 to 261. The manuscript was listed in the fragmentary catalogue of 1503 and the Bench catalogue of works before 1522. See *Corpus Catalogorum Belgii,* vol. 4, 191 (no. 77), 197 (no. 87).

to this manuscript. A contemporary table of contents lists the vitae of forty different saints, of which Louis' is the twelfth. All of the substantive additions that appear in the two later manuscripts (sigla C and D) are found in B, up through 144r (chapter 12/13), and were systematically added interlinearly or in the lower, upper, and side margins of the page in the same hand responsible for the body of the text. The scribe's process of work is evident; he copied out *Gloriosissimi regis* as we know it from a copy of the text known from A, and then went back and added into the margins and sometimes interlineally the materials that he took, first, from *Beatus Ludovicus* and then from the translation lections, that were not already part of the text. Between folios 142 and 143 he added a smaller folio in order to include a section on Louis' rule (BLQRF lection 8), and then had to change the subsequent chapter numbering to accommodate the inclusion of a new eighth chapter. His version of BLQRF included the miracle stories that were part of the octave readings in more complete versions of the office.[6] The last chapter, chapter 14, drew from the original lections written in 1306 for the Office of the Translation of Louis' head.[7]

This text, as augmented in B, was subsequently copied into C: Vienna ÖNB 12706 (9367a), by Johannes G(h)ielemans (d. 1487), one of Rooklooster's well-known canons and a prominent hagiographer, who has left us over twenty volumes of his writings.[8] Sometime between 1476 and 1484, Gielemans compiled in two volumes a collection that he entitled the *Hagiologium Brabantinorum,* which consisted of various hagiographical texts honoring Brabantine lineage.[9] His interest in Brabantine history is indicated by another collection he compiled, called

---

6. RHF vol. 23, 165–67. The octave appears in BNF Lat 911 and a number of other manuscript versions of the office.

7. This text is known from an early transcription found in BNF Lat 14511, 180r–v. The first portion of this text consists of the lections as they are generally found in breviary versions of the Translation office. Note that much of the language in this text is close to that of Boniface's bull of canonization.

8. "De codicibus hagiographicis Iohannis Gielemans," 8; Maes, *Sur les traces des chanoines reguliers de Rouge-Cloître,* 103.

9. For a catalogue of contents, see "De codicibus hagiographicis Iohannis Gielemans," 42–61. *Gloriosissimi regis* is no. 70 in vol. 1. On Gielemans's manuscripts and his larger historical and hagiographical project, see Hazebrouck-Souche, *Spiritualité, sainteté et patriotisme.*

the *Historiologium Brabantinorum*.[10] Gielemans sought to establish the virtuous lineage of the line of Brabant and in particular its descent from Charlemagne, and the entire *Hagiologium* is predicated on Gieleman's interest in connecting local saints and figures to Charlemagne.[11] The *Hagiologium Brabantinorum* included the "vita of the most glorious and saintly Charles, named 'the Great,' duke of Brabant, king of France, and emperor of Rome, after whom is called the Carolingian lineage"[12] (no. 47), along with vitae of Clovis and Clothild (no. 13), Dagobert (no. 14), and a number of saints identified as "de stirpe Karolidarum" (nos. 27, 28, 29, 30, 31, 34). To the life of Louis, which is otherwise directly dependent upon, and probably copied from, B, Gielemans added a unique prologue, in which he linked Louis and Charlemagne in a Brabantine lineage (see GR, n. 2 of the Latin, n. 1 of the translation).

The version of the vita found in D, Brussels 197, also belonging to Rooklooster, was further modified. A note on fol. 237 indicates that the volume was copied by a regular canon named Johannis Back (Jean Bac, d. 1472) and finished in 1465.[13] The text of *Gloriosissimi regis* was based on the version established in Vienna ÖNB 12807, but was somewhat shortened by the omission of certain passages and some minor reordering of text. In all cases, the additions and then subsequent omissions are indicated in the notes to the text.

The basic text proffered here in translation is the earlier text in twelve chapters. The transcription of this version reproduces the text as found in Vatican Reg Lat 534, 242v–246r (siglum A), since it is the only full version I know that includes the early life, and is thus used as the base manuscript. Included also, as an appendix consisting of chapters 14 and 15, are the substantive additions made in the fifteenth century. The notes furnish the other expansions made at Rooklooster. In this way, a reader has access to both the text of ca. 1300 and to the text of the mid-fifteenth century.

10. See "De codicibus hagiographicis Iohannis Gielemans," 11, 80–88.

11. See Gielemans's prologue to the *Hagiologium Brabantinorum*, printed at "De codicibus hagiographicis Iohannis Gielemans," 11.

12. "De codicibus hagiographicis Iohannis Gielemans," 48, no. 47. "Vita gloriosi ac sancti Karoli cognomento Magni, ducis Brabantinorum, regis Francorum et imperatoris Romanorum, a quo denominatur stirps Karolidarum."

13. *Catalogus Codicum Hagiographicorum Bibliothecae Regiae Bruxellensis*, vol. 1, 99, no. 7; Maes, *Sur les traces des chanoines*, 36.

GLORIOSISSIMI REGIS

[1.0] Incipit vita beati Ludovici confessoris quondam regis francorum.[1]

Quam sancte educatus fuerit et vixerit. Primum capitulum.[2]

[1.1] Gloriosissimi regis Ludovici vite ordinem percurrentes, et si non omnia de multis tamen gesta eius aliqua que certa fide comperimus[3] ad laudem divini nomini et edificationi[4] fidelium enarramus. [1.2] Pater eius Ludovicus, qui et ipse francorum rex christianissimus, zelo fidei accensus contra hereticos in albientium[5] partibus, fidei christiane adversantibus,[6] auctoritate ecclesie crucem assumpsit. Et viriliter peregrinatione aggressa ac potenter, superbia illorum suppressa,[7] dum inde rediret, feliciter in via migravit ad dominum. [1.3] Mater eius Blancha[8] regina venerabilis, que viro defuncto filium annorum

---

1. regis francorum] francorum regis incliti B
2. C *includes a unique prologue*: Incipit prologus in vitam beati Ludovici francorum regis incliti, de stirpe karolidarum propagati.
Ad hoc gesta sanctorum proponuntur fidelibus in ecclesia, ut ex eis in hoc mundo caligioso illuminentur et ad imitationem incitentur. Hinc est quod ad modum stellarum que locantur in firmamento celi et illuminant noctem, sancti virtuosis actibus illuminant omnem hominem venientem in hunc mundum, docentes nos quid agere et quo pergere debeamus. Sequamur itaque eos per viam qua precesserunt, quia ducent nos ad civitatem supernam quam ipsi feliciter intrare meruerunt. Insuper cum sponsam camicis surgamus civitatem ecclesie circueamus, et per vicos ac plateas quam diligit anima nostra queramus, quia secundum beatum Gregorium, sancti spiritus organum precipuum sunt nonnulli vite secularis, qui aliquid imitandum habeant de actione virtutis. Quorum unum libet hic ad medium deducere, quem virtuosissimum fuisse ac deo plurimum placuisse, miracula crebra testantur; beatum Ludovicum videlicet regem francorum et prolem brabantiorum, cuius vita virtutibus plena refulsit, sicuti sequentia evidenter declarabunt. Explicit prologus. Incipit vita eiusdem; et primo, de ipse orgine. Capitulum primum C
3. comperimus] compe C
4. nomini et edificationi] nominis et edificationem BCD
5. albientium] albigensium BCD
6. adversantibus] adversantes BCD
7. suppressa] depressa C
8. Blancha] regis castelle filia *add.* B *[margin]* CD

THE MOST GLORIOUS KING

[1.0] Here begins the life of blessed Louis the confessor, the late king of the French.

Chapter 1. How he was educated and lived in holiness.[1]

[1.1] In recounting the course of the life of the most glorious king Louis, we reveal those things of which we are certain so as to praise the divine name and edify the faithful, although we have not described all of his many deeds.[2] [1.2] His father, Louis [VIII], most Christian king of the Franks, burned with the zeal of faith against the Albigensian heretics opposing the Christian faith. He took up the cross with the authority of the church, and having courageously undertaken a pilgrimage, he overcame the arrogance [of the heretics] with great force. On his way home, he departed joyfully to the Lord.[3] [1.3] [Louis']

---

1. Unique prologue, found in C only: Here begins the prologue to the life of blessed Louis, illustrious king of the French, descendant in the lineage of the Carolingians.

The deeds of the saints are recounted to the faithful in the church so that from them [the deeds] they [the faithful] may be enlightened in this dark world and encouraged toward imitation. They are given here because, in the manner of the stars which are located in the firmament of heavens and illuminate the night, so the saints, through their virtuous acts, illuminate every man who comes into this world, teaching us what we ought to do and how we ought to go forth. And so, let us follow them through the life which they have led, because they lead us to the city above, which they themselves joyfully deserved to enter. Moreover let us rise up with the bride [in the white shirt] and let us encompass the city of the church, and let us seek throughout the villages and streets [the church] which our soul loves, because, according to Blessed Gregory, the many saints are the special instrument of the Holy Spirit for the secular life, who must be imitated in their action of virtue. Many miracles testify to that one among these whom it is appropriate to bring to the fore, that one who is extraordinarily virtuous and very pleasing to God, that is, of course, blessed Louis, king of the French and descendant in the Brabantine line, whose life shone full with virtue, just as the following will clearly declare. Here ends the prologue. Here begins his life, and the first chapter, on his birth. Chapter 1.

2. Cf. the opening line, "Gloriosissimi regis Ludovici," with WSP *vie* 1 (p. 12): "Li tres glorieux saint Loys, jadis rois de France."

3. Cf. GB 3 (p. 4); WSP *vie* 1 (pp. 12–13); BL 1.1.

duodecim[9] regnare incipientem religiose nutrivit et[10] feminee cogitationi ac[11] sexui masculinum inferens animum, strenue, industrie, potenter, et[12] iuste administravit[13] iura regni et contra plurimos adversarios qui tunc apparebant, sollerti providencia[14] defensavit.[15] [1.4] Huius laudes[16] devotus[17] filius sepe recolens et quandoque referens: "dicebat" inquit "de me quem super omnes mortales creaturas diligebat quod si infirmarer ad mortem et sanari non possem nisi tale quid faciendo quo peccarem mortaliter; prius permitteret me mori[18] quam vellet me illud faciendo meum dampnabiliter offendere creatorem." [1.5] Quod videlicet verbum pie matris adeo religiosi filii animam penetravit; quod quinquagenita sex[19] annis quoad vixit,[20] ab omni culpa quam confessor suus mortalem iudicaret teste viro iusto et perito qui per viginti[21] annos confessionem eius audivit semetipsum divina favente[22] gratia custodivit.

9. duodecim] xii B
10. et] ac BCD; et et A
11. ac] et BCD
12. et] ac C
13. administravit] amministravit BCD
14. providencia] et tutela *add.* B *[margin]* CD
15. defensavit] Filium ac tenerrime diligens sub cura magistri specialis de consilio religiosorum, maxime ordinis predicatorum et minorum, in moribus et in [*om.* C] scientia bonorum tradidit inbuendum. At [D: Ac] ipse velut alter salomon puer ingeniosus, et *add.* D: bonam [C: *bona*] sortitus animam; supra coetaneos suos profecit laudabiliter in utrisque, cuius profectum plurimum congaudebat pia mater. B *[margin]* CD. This passage is derived from BLQRF 1.
16. laudes] *om.* D
17. devotus] *om. et add.:* quoque devote matris D
18. mori] temporaliter *add.* B *[margin]* D
19. quinquagenita sex] lvi B
20. quoad vixit] quo advixit BCD
21. viginti] unigeniti A; xx B
22. favente] faciente A

mother, the revered queen Blanche, after her husband died, piously raised her twelve-year-old son as he began his reign. Bringing to bear a masculine spirit, joined to the intellect and sex of a woman, she attended to the rights of the kingdom with vigor, industry, power, and justice, and she also defended them with deft foresight against the many adversaries who appeared at that time.[4] [1.4] Her devoted son, who remembered and described her with praise, related that "she said of me, whom she loved more than any other mortal creatures, that if I were sick unto death and could not get well except by committing mortal sin, she would rather let me die than that I, by [sinning] so, should offend my Creator to the point of damnation."[5] [1.5] The pious mother's saying so penetrated the soul of her religious son that he lived by it for fifty-six years. According to the testimony of his confessor, a just and learned man who heard his confession for twenty years, [Louis] guarded himself by divine grace against all sins that his confessor considered mortal.[6]

4. Cf. GB 4 (p. 4): "quam struenue, quam industrie, quam juste, quam potenter dicta mater administraverit . . . femine cogitationi ac sexui masculinum animum; WSP *vie* 1 (p. 13); BL 1.

5. Cf. GB 4 (pp. 4–5); WSP *vie* 1 (p. 13); BL 1.3.

6. Cf. GB 5 (p. 5); WSP *vie* 15 (pp. 123–24); WSP *sermo* 8 (p. 279); BL 1.4.

[2.0] Quam caste matrimonium susceperit et servaverit est.[23] Capitulum secundum.[24]

[2.1] Iuvenis itaque omnium[25] oculis gratiosus et amabilis factus providente matre et[26] regni sapientibus[27] uxorem[28] duxit primogenitam comitis provincie, dominam scilicet Margaritam. [2.2] Cum qua nuptialis thalami ingressus secreta, magni[29] angeli[30] edoctus consilio ac Thobie informatus exemplo[31] priusquam ad eam accederet, tribus noctibus orationi se dedit, et ipsam facere similiter docuit, prout ipsa postmodum enarravit.[32] De eiusdem itaque domine regine consensu vir sanctus per totum adventum, et per totam[33] quadragesimam, nichilominus quelibet[34] ebdomada similiter[35] in vigiliis et[36] diebus magnorum festorum, insuper et in sollempnitatibus quibus communicare solitus et[37] pluribus diebus ante communionem et pluribus diebus post, a carnali opere[38] continebat. [2.3] Castitatis quoque zelator per plures annos antequam deo redderet spiritum ad culmem omnimode perfectionis aspirans, corde devoto firmiter proposuit quod adulto filio primogenito uxoris[39] habito consensu religionem intraret. Sed cum dictum propositum nacta oportunitate secreto regine aperuisset, astringens eam quod hoc alicui nullatenus revelaret, ipsa probabiles rationes[40] assignans ad contrarium minime consensit, deo forsitan

23. Chapter titles and divisions are omitted in D. The chapters are designated by a paragraph marking in red.
24. secundum] ii B
25. omnium] omni A
26. et] ac C
27. regni sapientibus] proceribus ne tam nobile regnum regali successione careret BCD; proceribus *interlin* B. Note that this is derived from BLQRF.
28. uxorem] *om.* D
29. C: 225v
30. angeli] raphaelis *add.* BCD
31. Cf. Tobit 6–18, 8:4–5.
32. prout ipsa postmodum enarravit] *om.* D
33. totam] omnem BCD
34. quelibet] certis diebus qualibet *add.* BCD
35. similiter] et *add.* BCD
36. et] in *add.* D
37. et] ad *add.* A
38. opere] se *add.* C
39. D: 25v
40. rationes] ratione A

[2.0] Chapter 2. How he undertook and maintained a chaste marriage.

[2.1] And so the youth [Louis], made pleasing and beloved in every-one's eyes by a prudent mother and the wise men of the kingdom, mar-ried the lady Margaret, the eldest daughter of the Count of Provence.[7] [2.2] Having entered the privacy of the marriage chamber with her, fol-lowing the advice of the great angel [Raphael],[8] and inspired by the ex-ample of Tobias, [Louis] gave himself over to prayer for three nights be-fore he went to her, and as she later recounted, he had her do the same. With the consent of this same lady queen, the saintly man refrained from carnal acts during all of Advent, during all of Lent, and also in other weeks on the eves and days of the great feasts, and especially on solemn days when he was wont to take communion, and for many days before and after communion.[9] [2.3] This zealot of chastity, aspir-ing by all means to the apex of perfection for many years before he rendered his spirit up to God, with a devout heart steadfastly deter-mined that when his firstborn son attained his majority and his wife had given her consent, he would enter a religious order. But when the opportunity presented itself and he secretly revealed this intention to the queen, obliging her to tell no one under any circumstances, she, pointing out credible arguments to the contrary, was of hardly the same mind, [arguing] that perhaps God foresaw something better for

---

7. Cf. WSP *vie* 16 (p. 129); WSP *sermo* 21 (p. 285).
8. For Raphael and Tobit, see Tobit 6–18, esp. 8.4–5.
9. Cf. GB 11 (p. 6); WSP *vie* 16 (p. 129); WSP *sermo* 21 (p. 285). Note that "domine regine consensu" appears in WSP *sermo* but not WSP *vie*. Cf. GB 11 (p. 6).

aliquid melius providente, videlicet utiliorem[41] ipsum fore in statu pristino ad regnum in pace servandum et ad tocius ecclesie negotia pro-
movenda. [2.4] Desideria[42] tamen eius omnia ex alto[43] prospectans
suaviterque disponens haut[44] divina defuit sapientia que vota[45] eius
complens, eidem inspiravit secundo crucem assumere. Et sic etiam si
coniunx non consensisset que remansit, thorum licite declinans vidu-
alis saltem continentie premia non amisit,[46] nam taliter ab uxore sep-
aratus defunctus est.[47]

[3.0] Quam religiose prolem[48] nutrierit et instruxerit. Tercium capitulum.[49]

[3.1] Susceptam igitur prolem de tam sancto coniugio curavit summopere vir sanctus religiose educare et ad amorem dei contemptum mundi
ac[50] cognitionem sui salutaribus[51] monitis et exemplis informare.[52]
[3.2] Volebat siquidem quod pueri sui iam adulte etati proprinqui cotidie non solum missam sed et matutinas diurnasque horas canonicas
cum cantu audirent, et quod ad audiendum sermones secum adessent,
quod que singuli litteras addiscerent, et horas beate virginis dicerent
etiam quod semper cum ipso[53] ad completorium quod post cenam
suam cotidie sollempniter et in fine antiphonam[54] de domina nostra
devote faciebat cantari, pariter convenirent. Dictoque completorio, ad
cameram cum pueris revertebatur et aqua benedicta a sacerdote circa

41. utiliorem] ultiorem A
42. Desideria] desiderio A
43. ex alto] exalto A
44. haut] hanc A
45. vota] devota A
46. amisit] admisit A
47. Desidera tamen . . . defunctus est] *not known from other sources*
48. prolem] filios suos B
49. B: Quam religiose filios suos nutrierit et instruxerit. Cap iii C: Quam religiose filios suos nutrierit et instruexerit. Capitulum tercium. D: *title omitted.*
50. ac] et C
51. A: 243r
52. informare] Et quando sibi secreto vacare poterat eos personaliter visitans
de eorum profectu diligenter requisivit, et velut alter Thobias dabat eisdem monita
salutis, docens eos super omnia timere deum, et ab omni peccato iugiter abstinere.
add. B *[margin]* CD; cf. BLQRF 2.
53. cum ipso] ipso B; cum eo C; *om.* D
54. et in fine antiphonam] cum anthiphona D

him—that is, that Louis would be more useful as king[10] for preserving the peace of the kingdom and advancing the work of the entire church.[11] [2.4] Nonetheless, divine wisdom, beholding all things from on high and sweetly setting them in order, in no way neglected his desires, and inspired him to take up the cross a second time, thus fulfilling his vows. And so, even if his wife, who stayed behind, did not give her consent, he, as if now widowed, turned away, as lawfully permitted, from the marriage bed. And in this way he, at least, did not forgo the reward of continence since he died thus separated from his wife.[12]

[3.0] Chapter 3. How he raised and instructed his offspring religiously.

[3.1] This saintly man took particular care to educate religiously the offspring born from so sacred a marriage, and to instill [in them] the love of God, contempt for the world, and self-knowledge through salutary admonitions and examples.[13] [3.2] He therefore wanted his sons, as they approached adulthood, daily to hear not only the mass but also matins and the singing of the daily canonical hours, and he wanted them to hear sermons with him, and desired that each one should learn [to read] texts, and that they should recite the hours of the Blessed Virgin. He also wanted them to join him every evening after dinner at Compline, at the end of which he had the antiphon of our Lady devoutly sung. When Compline was over, after a priest had sprinkled holy water around the bed and throughout the room,

10. The Latin has here "pristino statu" = original state, or given status. We have found this rendering far clearer.

11. Cf. GB 12 (p. 7); WSP *vie* 16 (pp. 129–30).

12. This passage seems to reflect the view that equated entering a monastery with going on crusade, and similarly, equated the monastic vow with the crusade vow, or the life of the monk with the life of the crusader. See Constable, *Crusaders and Crusading,* 110.

13. Cf. BL 2.2.

lectum et per cameram aspersa, quia illa hora eruditioni[55] liberorum[56] familarius vacare poterat, solitus erat[57] bona verba et edificatoria eis dicere,[58] omnibus residentibus circa ipsum. [3.3] Serta de rosis seu[59] capellos quosque nolebat quod dicti liberi sui umquam sexta feria deportarent propter coronam tali die impositam capiti redemptoris. [3.4] Ordinavit etiam et in suo testamento scribi voluit quod duo filii qui sibi nati sunt ultra mare, unus apud fratres minores alius apud fratres predicatores Parisius mansionibus pro eis[60] ibidem sumptibus regiis decenter preparatis educarentur, et illic sacris institutis et litteris instruerentur, desiderans ut domino inspirante loco et tempore religiones intrarent, quas precipue vir sanctus amabat. [3.5] Dicebat enim quod si de[61] corpore suo duas posset facere portiones, unam daret uni religioni reliquam alteri.[62] [3.6] Filiam quoque[63] primogenitam que postea fuit regina Navarre vir sanctus tam in se quam in liberis suis cupiens perfectionis appicem attingere, cum[64] adhuc erat ultra mare per litteras speciales quas manu propria inscripserat[65] ad mundi contemptum[66] religionis amorem et ingressum induxit quantum potuit[67] et devote. [3.7] Haut dubium quod pius eius affectus non caret premio et corona quamvis Illo *cuius providencia in sui dispositione non fallitur*[68] aliter ordinante sancta eius voluntas optatum effectum non fuerit consecuta.

55. B: 141v
56. liberorum] filiorum C
57. erat] dare *add.* B *[margin]* CD
58. dicere] *om.* BCD
59. seu] vel C
60. eis] eis pro eis *add.* B *[manuscript repeats phrase twice]*
61. C: 226r
62. Dicebat enim quod . . . reliquam alteri] *om.* D
63. quoque] suam *add.* C
64. in se quam in liberis . . . attingere cum] *om.* D
65. inscripserat] scripserat BD
66. contemptum]et *add.* B
67. potuit] sollicite *add.* C
68. A common liturgical formulation quoted frequently by medieval authors: "Deus cuius prouidencia[m] in sui dispositione non fallitur, te supplicis exoramus ut noxia cuncta submoueas, et omnia nobis profutura concedas." It is found in the Gelasian sacramentary (eighth century) and made its way into the later Roman Ordines. See PL vol. 74, col. 1190; Moeller ed., *Corpus Orationum*, vol. 2, 154–55, no. 1188; CCSL vol. 160A.

he would return to his bedchamber with his sons because at that hour he was free to instruct his children in private, and he would speak good and uplifting words to them as they all sat down around him.[14] [3.3] He did not want his children to wear garlands of roses or hats of any sort on Fridays because that was the day the Crown [of Thorns] was placed on the head of the Redeemer.[15] [3.4] Further, he arranged and wanted written in his testament that his two sons who were born overseas should be educated, one with the Friars Minor, the other with the Friars Preacher, at houses set up for [the orders] in Paris at royal expense. He ordered that they be instructed there in sacred teachings and texts, desiring that—God choosing when and where—they should enter the religious life which this saintly man especially loved.[16] [3.5] He said that, if he were able to split his body in two, he would give one part to one religious order and the remaining part to the other.[17] [3.6] The saintly man, desiring for his firstborn daughter (who was later Queen of Navarre) as much as [he desired] for his sons—that is, that she reach the height of perfection—encouraged her from overseas with special letters that he wrote himself to have contempt for the world and to devoutly love and take up religion as much as she was able.[18] [3.7] There is no doubt that his pious disposition earned him the reward and the crown [of glory]. If the One, *whose providence is not lacking in His plan*, had arranged it otherwise, [Louis'] saintly will would not have achieved its desired effect.

14. Cf. GB 13 (p. 7); BL 2.2.
15. Cf. GB 13 (p. 7); BL 2.3.
16. Cf. GB 14 (pp. 7–8).
17. Cf. GB 12 (p. 7).
18. Cf. GB 14 (p. 8).

[4.0] Quartum capitulum.[69] Quam perfectione primogenitum specialiter verbo et facto erudierit.[70]

[4.1] Pretermittendum nequaquam arbitror[71] quod eius primogenito domino philippo rege francorum christianissimo referente, ipse libenter audivi. [4.2] "Dum" inquit "ad aquas[72] mortuas naves ascensuri dominum genitorem nostrum ego et fratres mei et Iohannes et Petrus deduxissemus ad suam alias pro nobis paratas postmodum intraturi ipse in navem sursum levatus nos in barga[73] qua veneramus aspiciens[74] deorsum, audite ait 'filii audite patrem vestrum.' [4.3] "Et nos pariter instruens, ad me tamen sermonem dirigens, 'placet' inquit 'quod mecum hucusque veneris, priusquam equorum nos spatiis et fluctibus comittamus. Interdum enim accidit quod in diversis lignis licet eodem momento ingredientes maria se nunquam de cetero sunt visuri.'[75] [4.4] "'Considera'[76] ait 'fili quod ego iam grandevus alias pro Christo transfretavi, et quod mater tua regina in diebus suis processerit. Regnum nostrum favente deo sic possedimus pacifice quod non fuit qui ganniret diviciis, honoribus, delitiis que[77] temporalibus prout libuit et licuit perfruentes. Te quoque et[78] fratres tuos ac[79] sorores prolem genuimus generosam. Vide igitur quod pro fide Christique[80] eius ecclesia nec mee parco senectuti, nec matris tue desolate misereor delicias honores relinquo, ac expono pro Christo divitias te quoque qui regnaturus es et fratres tuos ac sororem primogenitam mecum duco etiam quartum adduxissem filium si pubertaris annos plenius actigisset.[81] Que idcirco

69. capitulum] cap. iii. B
70. erudierit] erudivit C. Quartum capitulum . . . erudierit] *om.* D
71. neququam arbitror] non est C
72. aquas] naves B
73. barga] bergan C
74. aspiciens] *corr. from* aspiens A; aspiciens BC
75. Pretermittendum nequaquam eruidierit arbitror. . . . decetero sunt visuri] Denique testamentum quibus pauloante quod migraret ad dominum ordinavit. Manu propria scripsit et fuit domino philippo filio suo primogenito tradit eisque dixit D. Note that this passage appears at the end of the chapter in A and B.
76. D: 26r
77. delitiis que] deliciisque D
78. et] ac C
79. ac] et C
80. christique] christi et BCD
81. delicias honores relinquo . . . annos plenius actigisset] *om.* D

[4.0] Chapter 4. With what perfection he specially taught his firstborn son by word and deed.

[4.1] I think we should not omit what I gladly heard myself from his firstborn, Lord Philip, most Christian king of the Franks. [4.2] He said: "While at Aigues Mortes, I and my brothers John and Peter, just before we were to board our ships, had led our lord father to his [ship]. As we were about to get aboard the other [ships] that had been readied for us, [Louis], high above us and looking down on us below in the barge on which we had come, said 'Listen, sons, listen to your father.'[19] [4.3] And instructing us all equally but directing his sermon to me, he said, 'it pleases me that you have come this far with me, before we commit ourselves to the expanse and waves of the seas. It sometimes happens that [persons] on different boats, although they enter the sea at the same moment, never see one another again.[20] [4.4] 'Consider,' he said, 'sons, that I, now aged, have crossed other seas before for Christ, and that your mother the queen is far advanced in years. We have possessed our kingdom in peace through God's favor, which is not something to complain about, enjoying temporal riches, honors, and pleasures as was good and right. We bore noble offspring, both you and your brothers and sisters. See that for faith in Christ and his church I neither spare my old age, nor do I take pity on your forsaken mother. I relinquish delights [and] honors, and, for Christ, I offer my wealth, and I lead you, who are about to reign, and your brothers, and your firstborn sister, with me, and I would have even led my fourth son, if he were of age. And therefore I wish that you listen and

19. Cf. BL 10.5.
20. Cf. BL 10.6 (where the story is in the third person).

audire te volui et animadvertere in te ipso ut post obitum meum cum[82] ad regnum perveneris, pro ecclesia dei et eius fide sustinenda ac defendenda[83] nulli rei parcas nec tibi nec tuis seu regno vel uxori aut liberis tibi enim[84] et fratribus tuis do exemplum ut et vos similiter faciatis.'"[85] [4.5] O beatus discipulus perfectum imitatus[86] magistrum, qui quod verbo docuit opere adimplevit. [4.6] Denique testamentum quod paulo antequam migraret ad dominum velud[87] obitus sui prescius manu[88] propria[89] scripsit et in fine eidem primogenito tradidit, testamentum quidem non de rebus temporalibus, sed de fide et moribus. Quod quia nunc[90] properamus ad alia—ad informationem omnium Christianorum et maxime principum[91]—in fine presentis opusculi adiuvante domino subscribemus.[92]

[5.0] Qualiter corpus suum per asperitates disciplinarum ciliciorum castigaverit.[93] Quintum capitulum.[94]

[5.1] Omni[95] septimana semel ad minus sexta scilicet feria vir iustus de consuetudine habebat devote et humiliter confiteri, et quasi in

82.　cum] regnaveris *add.* D
83.　defendenda] defensanda C
84.　enim] etiam BD
85.　faciatis] opus fuerit similiter *add.* B *[margin]* CD; Testamentum quidem vobis relinquo non de rebus temporalibus, sed de fide et moribus. *add.* D
86.　imitatus] imitatum A
87.　B: 243v; velud] *om.* D
88.　manu] sua *add.* C
89.　propria] sua *add.* BC
90.　quia nunc] quia A
91.　Principum] principium A
92.　O beatus discipulis . . . adiuvante domino subscribemus] *om.* D
93.　Qualiter . . . castigaverit. Qualiter corpus suum perasperitates disciplinavit Cap. v B; qualiter corpus suum persaperitates disclinaverit. Capitulum quantum. C; *title om.* D
94.　capitulum] Et quia sciebat quod in divitiis pietas in delitiis castitas, et in honoribus humilitas periclitari solet [D: solent]; ideo [D: idcirco] sobrietati humilitati, et misericordie animum dedit. Ab insidiis mundi. carnis. et dyaboli. [C: 226v] sollicite custodiens se, et exemplo apostoli corpus suum castigans, et in servitutem redigens castigatione [C: vexatione] multiplici; suo spiritui servire cogebat, vigiliis orationisbus laboribus et aliis secretis abstientiis ac disciplines iugiter se affligens. *add.* B *[margin]* CD. Note that this is derived from BLQRF 3.
95.　Omni] siquidem *add.* B *[interl.]* CD

consider well in your own minds, so that after my death, when you attain the kingdom, you spare nothing for the preservation and defense of the church of God and the faith—neither yourself, nor what belongs to you—not your kingdom, not your wife, not even your children. I give this example to you and your brothers so that you will all do the same.'"[21] [4.5] O, blessed disciple, imitating the perfect teacher, who taught with words what he fulfilled with works. [4.6] And in the end, shortly before he journeyed to the Lord, foreseeing his own death, he bequeathed his testament, which he wrote with his own hand to that selfsame eldest son, a testament which was not about temporal things but about faith and morals. But, because now we are moving on to other things, for the instruction of all Christians and especially of princes, we will transcribe it, with God's help, at the end of the present little work.[22]

[5.0] Chapter 5. How he punished his body through the harshness of discipline [and] hair shirts.

[5.1] This just man was in the habit of devoutly and humbly confessing at least once each week on Friday, and he arranged for a secret and

21. Cf. BL 10.7.
22. This is a reference to the so-called *Enseignements* (The Teachings), instructions on Christian rule that Louis wrote for the future Philip III near the end of his life. Geoffrey of Beaulieu included a version of the *Enseignements* as chapter 15 of his vita (where they are called *salutaria documenta*). For the critical edition, see O'Connell, *The Teachings of Saint Louis*. Note that the promised transcription did not make it into A, nor is it found in the later recension.

quolibet suo manerio locum ad hoc secretum et aptum providebat. Nam semper post confessionem[96] per manum confessoris disciplinam recipiebat de quinque cathenulis[97] ferreis simul[98] iunctis capitibus earum in fundo parvule pixidis eburenee decenter infixis,[99] que virgule ad ictus disciplinares de pyxide[100] exeuntes dependebant, et peracta disciplina ut[101] reconderentur pulchre multum in eamdem iterum plicabantur. Hanc[102] pixidem in bursa secum portabat ad zonam. Si quando[103] delicatissime cuti eius confessor compatiens remissius feriebat, quod fortius percuteret, ipse per signum aliquod innuebat. Et hanc disciplinam pro nullo umquam festo recipere omittebat.[104] [5.2] In adventu Domini et quadragesima, etiam in quatuor vigiliis virginis gloriose, clam ad carnem cilicio utebatur. Tandem confessor eius manifeste cognoscens quid[105] caro eius tenerrima[106] asperitate cilicii nimium gravaretur, cum instancia obtinuit quod vir sanctus uti cilicio pretermisit. In[107] recompensationem tamen huius asperitatis voluit rex pius quod idem confessor in[108] illis diebus quibus ante portabat cilicium[109] quadraginta solidos parisiensis[110] secreto pauperibus erogaret.[111] Nec hoc conten - tus non numquam in quadragesima fascia[112] quadam de cilicio[113] se cingebat. [5.3] Ieiunabat omni tempore eisdem diebus sextis videlicet

96. et quasi in quolibet . . . aptum providebat nam] *om.* D
97. cathenulis] catenulus D
98. similis] simul D
99. infixis] infixit A
100. de pixide] *om.* D
101. B: 142r
102. Hanc] autem *add.* BCD
103. quando] eius *add.* BC
104. Si quando delicatissime . . . festo recipere omittebat] *om.* D
105. quid] quod BCD
106. tenerrima] tenrima A
107. In] cuius tamen *add.* D
108. in] *om.* B; tamen huius asperitatis . . . quod idem confessor in] *om.* D
109. cilicium] *in marg.* B; pro qualibet die C
110. parisiensis] parisiensium C
111. erogaret] voluit erogari D
112. fascia] fascias A
113. cilicio] in quadregisima *add.* C

suitable place for this at whichever manor house he was staying. After confession he always received from his confessor's hand a discipline from five little iron chains, which were all joined together and fixed properly on the base of a little ivory box. These [chains] hung down, attached to the box by a little rod, and were removed from the box for the rod's disciplinary blows. The discipline done, they were folded up beautifully to be hidden away in that little box. He carried this little box in a purse with him on his belt. If ever his confessor, pitying him, struck his skin too lightly, he would signal that [the confessor] should strike him more forcefully, and he never failed to receive this discipline on account of a feast day.[23] [5.2] During Advent and Lent, and even on the four vigils of the glorious Virgin, he would secretly wear a hair shirt on his flesh. After some time, his confessor realized that his very tender flesh was being overly burdened by the harshness of the hair shirt, and insisted that the saintly man stop wearing the hair shirt. However, in exchange for these asperities, the pious king wished that on the days on which he had previously worn the hair shirt, his confessor now secretly distribute forty Parisian *solidos* to the poor. Not content with this, he sometimes wrapped himself with a strip of hair shirt during Lent.[24] [5.3] Throughout the entire year he fasted on Fridays,

23. Cf. GB 16 (p. 10); WSP *vie* 14 (pp. 122–23); WSP *sermo* 25 (p. 287).
24. Cf. GB 17 (p. 10); BL 3.1; WSP *vie* 14 (p. 122); WSP *sermo* 25 (p. 287).

feriis[114] quarta quoque feria semper a carnibus et sanguine[115] abstinebat. Simili modo abstinuit aliquandiu[116] die lune, donec discretorum
virorum usus consilio secunde ferie dimisit ieiunium[117] propter corpus
suum debile quod ita[118] crebras abstinencias non poterat sustinere.[119]
Panem et aquam tantummodo in vigiliis festorum beate virginis similiter in[120] parasceve et aliquibus aliis sollempnibus[121] ieiuniis per annum
in cibo sumebat, sextis quoque feriis in quadragesima et adventu[122] a
piscibus et fructibus abstinebat, nisi quod interdum propter debilitatem corporis accipere saltem de uno genere piscium et fructuum
suadenti confessori acquiescebat.

[6.0] De eius humilitate quanta semper[123] fuerit. Sextum capitulum.[124]

[6.1] Omnium virtutum decor humilitas in eo gratiose se dedit velut
gemmula[125] *carbunculi in ornamento auri*[126] [Sir. 32.7] qui quanto magnus extitit,[127] tanto se humilem in omnibus exhibuit.[128] [6.2] Quolibet
namque sabbato consueverat flexis genibus in loco secretissimo[129] pauperum pedes abluere et[130] post ablutionem tergere, ac humiliter osculari. Similiter aquam devote fundebat eorum manibus abluendis et
postmodum cuilibet cum manus osculo certam denariorum summam porrigebat. [6.3] Frequenter quoque centum viginti pauperibus

---

114. eisdem diebus sextis videlicet feriis] feriis sextis D
115. et sanguine] *om.* D
116. aliquandiu] in *add.* C
117. ieiunium] seu abstinenciam *add.* BC
118. ita] tam C
119. Simil modo abstinuit . . . non poterat sustinere] *om.* D
120. in] *om.* D
121. solempnitatibus] sine *add.* C
122. adventu] domini *add.* C
123. semper] *om.* C
124. B: *chapter title illeg.* D: *title omitted*
125. gemmula] gemma BCD
126. Sir. 32.7
127. extitit] velud alter David *add.* B *[margin]* CD; cf. BLQRF 4.
128. exhibuit]et coram deo in oculis suis semper vilior apparuit *add* B *[mar-gin]* CD; cf. BLQRF 4.
129. secretissimo] quorumdum *add.* B *[margin]* CD
130. D: 26v

of course, and he abstained from meat and blood on Wednesdays. In the same vein, for some time, he abstained on Mondays, until, because his weak body was unable to sustain such frequent abstinences and acting on the advice of wise men, he abandoned Monday's fast. He ate only bread and water on the vigils of the feasts of the blessed Virgin, and on Good Friday and on any other solemn days of fasting throughout the year. Further, on Fridays during Lent and Advent he abstained from fish and fruit, except for times when, because of bodily weakness, he would acquiesce to his confessor, who persuaded him to take at least one kind of fish and fruit.[25]

[6.0] Chapter 6. On his humility and how great it always was.

[6.1] Humility, the glory of all virtues, bestowed itself graciously on him *like a ruby in a setting of gold.*[26] And by the same degree that the gem shines out, to this same degree did Louis show himself to be humble in all things.[27] [6.2] Sometimes on Saturday on bended knee in a very secret place he would wash the feet of some of the poor, and after washing them, would dry and humbly kiss them. Then he devoutly poured water on their hands to wash them, and then kissed their hands and gave them some money.[28] [6.3] Frequently, too, he would personally

25. Cf. GB 18 (pp. 10–11); BL 3.2; WSP *vie* 14 (p. 121); WSP *sermo* 26 (p. 287).
26. Sir. 32.7.
27. Cf. WSP *vie* 12 (p. 102): "Humilité qui est biauté de toutes vertuz, s'assist gracieusement au benoiet roy saint Loys, ausi comme la pierre precieuse de l'escharboucle . . ."); BL 4.1.
28. Cf. GB 9 (p. 6); WSP *vie* 12 (p. 104); WSP *sermo* 18 (p. 283); BL 4.1.

qui cotidie in domo[131] eius habundanter[132] reficiebantur ipsemet serviebat et in vigiliis festorum sollempnium ac[133] quibusdam certis die -
bus per annum ducentis pauperibus discumbentibus manu propria
priusquam ipse comederet fercula ministrabat. [6.4] Semper in prandio et cena prope se tres senes de pauperioribus qui inveniebantur recumbentes habebat quibus[134] de cibis suis caritative[135] mittebat, *et*[136]
os suum ponens in pulvere[137] non numquam scutellas et cibos[138] quas
iam[139] Christi pauperes manibus contrectaverant sibi portari verus
humilis ut inde gustaret faciebat. [6.5] Semel enim dum senem valde
inter dictos tres pauperimos homines non bene manducantem con-
spiceret, scutellam cum cibo que ante se[140] apposita fuerat[141] seni illi
et[142] pauperi apponi precepit, quam postquam ille de ea quantum placuit comederat[143] iterum coram se fecit rex humilis ut inde aliquid
assumeret[144] aportari.[145] Ipsum[146] namque dominum considerans in
paupere,[147] de eius[148] reliquiis nequaquam horruit manducare. [6.6]
Sane cuius interior humilitas spiritus deo erat soli ad honorem, ex-
terior humilitas gestus[149] et habitus omni homini esse poterat ad
edifactionem. Ex quo enim illo inspirante qui humilibus dat gratiam prima vice viam arripuit transmarinam, numquam scarleto[150]

131. domo] palacio BCD
132. C: 227r
133. ac] atque C; *add.* et D
134. quibus] etiam *add.* BCD
135. caritative] caritatem BCD
136. et] tamquam *add.* B *(interlinear)* CD
137. "os suum ponens in pulvere"; cf. Bonaventure, *Legenda Minor,* 1:8. Cf.
Lam. 3.29, "ponet in pulvere os suum si forte sit spes."
138. cibos] vel escas C
139. iam] *om.* C
140. B: 244r; se] ipsum D
141. fuerat] erat C
142. et] atque C
143. placuit comederat] placuerat comedisset C
144. comederat] sumeret BCD
145. aportari] apportari BCD
146. Ipsum] Christum BCD
147. pauper] venerandum *add.* B *[margin]* CD
148. eius] ipsius C
149. gestus] gestas A
150. scarleto] scalleto A

and generously serve 120 poor who were fed daily at his house, and on the vigils of solemn feasts and on certain other days, he would serve dishes to 200 poor guests before he himself would eat.[29] [6.4] At lunch and dinner he always had seated near him three old men who were found among the poor, to whom he would charitably offer food [from his own plate]; and *putting his mouth in the dust,*[30] he sometimes had the dishes and food which the poor of Christ had already touched with their own hands brought to him so that he, truly humble, might eat from them.[31] [6.5] Once, when among three of these poor men he saw one very old man who was not eating at all well, he asked that his own plate of food be put before that poor old man. After the [old man] had eaten as much as he wanted from [the dish], the humble king put [the dish] before himself again so that he might eat something from it since, believing the Lord himself to be in the poor man, [Louis] did not shrink from eating his leftovers.[32] [6.6] Although his inner humility of spirit was for God's honor alone, his outward humility of deeds and habits was for the edification of all men. And thus, inspired by the One who gives grace to the humble, from the time that he first journeyed across the seas, he never wore scarlet or brown or green or fur of any kind.

29. Cf. WSP *vie* 12 (pp. 104–5); BL 4.3.

30. This may be a reference to Bonaventure's vita for Saint Francis, 1:8, in reference to his care of lepers and his kissing of their sores. For the Latin, see Menestò and Brufani, eds. *Fontes Franciscani,* 971. For an English translation, see Armstrong et al., eds., *Francis of Assisi: Early Documents,* vol. 2, 688. The reference is ultimately taken from Lam. 3.29.

31. Cf. WSP *vie* ch. 12 (pp. 104–5), "metant sa bouche ausi comme en la poudre"; BL 4.4.

32. Cf. WC, p. 35; WSP *vie* 14 (p. 105); WSP *sermo* 18 (p. 283); BL 4.5.

seu[151] bruneto, aut viridi[152] nec pellibus variis indutus est. Verum quia vestes quibus usus est postmodum non tantum simplicioris coloris quinimmo minoris valoris comparatione preciosarum quas prius haberat,[153] in detrimentum pauperum quibus semper dabantur cedere videbantur, certam summam pecunie[154] omni anno statuit per suum elemosinarium in recompensationem pauperibus annis singulis erogandam.[155] [6.7] Denique ut humilitatem veram quam exhibuerat vivus doceret et mortuus, voluit et in testamento suo scribi fecit quod[156] sibi[157] sepulchrum humile absque sumptuositate aut curiositate fieret licet ipse predecessoribus suis regibus preciosa sepulchra iuxta quod regia maiestas exigebat prout hodie apparet fieri providisset.

[7.0] De elemosinis eius et operibus misericordie. Septimum capitulum.[158]

[7.1] Porro quia[159] ab infantia[160] secum crevit miseratio [cf. Job 31.18] cepit ab ineunte pueritia super afflictos pauperes caritatis pia[161] gestare viscera[162] cepit et[163] religiosorum facere[164] monasteria.[165] [7.2] Inter[166]

---

151. seu] *om.* BCD
152. viridi] aut alia quamvis veste pomposa aut nimium sumptuosa *add.* BCD; cf. BLQRF 4.
153. haberat] habuerat BC
154. pecunie] peccunie A
155. verum quia vestes quibus . . . annis singulis erogandam] *om.* D
156. quod] sibi *add.* BC
157. sibi] si A
158. De elemosinis . . . capitulum] *om.* D; Septimum capitulum] cap vii B
159. quia] quod C
160. infantia] eius *add.* BCD
161. pia gestare viscera] *add.* semper B
162. viscera] omni tempore *add.* C; necessitatibus omnium prout commode potuit succurrens. Et licet omni indigentisinum misericordie, aperiret tamen divinis et saluti animarum vacantibus maiores et frequentiores elemosinas faciebat] *add.* BD
163. et] ergo B *[margin]* CD
164. facere] construere C
165. monasteria] Et [C: Et nam] licet omni indigentisinum misericordie aperiret, tamen divinis et saluti animarum vacantibus maiores et frequentiores elemosinas faciebat [C: maiorem et frequentiorem elemosinam tribuebat] *add* B *[margin]* C; cf. BLQRF 6.
166. Inter] Interea C

Indeed, not only were the clothes that he wore after his return simpler in color and of less value compared to the expensive ones that he had worn before, but also—since this would result in a detriment to the poor to whom [the expensive clothes] had always been given—he decreed that in compensation every year a certain sum of money would be paid out to the poor by his almoner.[33] [6.7] And finally, so that after his death he might demonstrate the true humility that he exhibited during his lifetime, he wanted written in his testament that a humble tomb without extravagance or frills be made for him, even though he himself, as can be seen today, had provided that expensive tombs befitting of royal majesty be made for his royal predecessors.[34]

[7.0] Chapter 7. On his alms and his works of mercy.

[7.1] Moreover, because mercy grew with him from infancy [cf. Job 31.18], from the onset of boyhood, he endeavored to have a pious heart of love for the afflicted poor, and he began to build monasteries for religious men.[35] [7.2] Among these he took special care in building,

---

33. Cf. GB 8 (p. 6); WSP *vie* 12 (p. 111); BL 4.6.
34. Cf. GB 10 (p. 6).
35. Cf. GB 19 (p. 11).

que[167] specialiter illud preclarum Beate Marie Regalis Montis monasterium cysterciensis ordinis a solo cum ecclesia admirande pulchritu-
dinis edificavit et copiosos redditus assinavit.[168] [7.3] Domum etiam
Dei Parisiensum cum magnis sumptibus ampliavit et augmentavit
redditus, insuper et hospitales domos pauperum[169] in castris Compendii, Pontisare et Vernonis magnis et[170] sumptuosis edificiis a fundamentis perfecit et[171] magnis redditibus dotavit.[172] Fratribus quoque
minoribus et predicatoribus in diversis regni sui partibus, ecclesias,
claustra,[173] dormitoria et ecclesias domos neccessarias[174] quam multas
de toto construxit. [7.4] Nam[175] inceptas ad perficiendum libenter adi-
uvit. Verum horum duorum ordinum conventibus parisiensis quos
pro religione, scientia, ac doctrina precipue venerabatur: solitus[176] erat
circa principium hyemi[177] magnam elemosinam pro vestibus et aliis
necessitatibus elargiri. In estate quoque et alias pluries per annum eisdem ita habunde subvenire:[178] quod uterque conventus centum sexaginta[179] fratres et plus[180] ex regis donariis pro magna parte poterat sustentari.[181] [7.5] Serenoque vultu post illius concessionem elemosine
familiaribus qui aderant dicere solebat: "O Deus quam bene reputo
hanc elemosinam erogatam tot et tantis fratribus qui de toto orbe ad
istos conventus parisiensis[182] pro studio sacre doctrine confluunt.[183]

167. B: 142v; que] *om.* C
168. assinavit] assignavit C
169. pauperum] diversis regni partibus specialiter in *add.* B *[margin]* C; cf.
BLQRF 6.
170. et] *om.* C
171. perfecit et] perfecte et A; perfecit ac C
172. dotavit] ditavit C; Domum etiam dei parisiensum . . . magnis redditibus
dotavit] *om.* D
173. claustra] et *add.* C
174. et ecclesias domos necessiarias] ac ceteras domos *add.* CD
175. C: 227v Nam] et iam *add.* BCD
176. solitus] sollitus A
177. hyemi] hyemis C
178. subvenire] supervenire A; subvenire B; subvenire consuevit C
179. sexaginta] cix C
180. plus] plures C
181. sustentari] sustentare BC
182. parisiensis] parysius C
183. confluunt] profluunt C

from the ground up, the renowned Cistercian monastery of Blessed Mary, Royaumont, along with its outstandingly beautiful church, to which he assigned abundant revenues.[36] [7.3] He enlarged the Hôtel Dieu at Paris at great expense, and he augmented its revenues; moreover, he completed from their foundations the Maisons Dieu for the poor in the towns of Compiègne, Pontoise, and Vernon with great and costly buildings, and he endowed them with great revenues. For the Friars Minor and Friars Preacher in various parts of his kingdom, he constructed *in toto* churches, cloisters, dormitories, and as many ecclesiastical houses as needed.[37] [7.4] He also aided freely in completing [buildings] that had already been started. At the approach of winter he was accustomed to grant many alms for clothing and other necessities to the Parisian convents of these two orders [of friars], which he especially revered for their religion, knowledge, and doctrine. In summer, too, and at many other points in the year, [it was his custom to] so generously support the same [orders] that each convent was able to support more than 160 friars, thanks largely to the king's alms.[38] [7.5] With a serene countenance, after the gift of those alms, he would say to his household: "O God, how important I deem these alms, expended on so many friars who come together from all over the world to these convents in Paris for the study of sacred doctrine. What they

36. Cf. GB 19 (p. 11); BL 6.3.
37. Cf. GB 19 (p. 11); BL 6.7, 6.5, 6.10; WSP *vie* 11 (p. 88). Note also that the later part of this section gets largely adopted from an Anonymous life preserved at the Abbey of Saint Germain des Près (RHF vol. 23, p. 170).
38. Cf. GB 19 (p. 11); BL 6.10.

Et exinde quod[184] de scripturis divinis hauriunt per totum mundum ad dei honorem et animarum salutem effundunt."[185] [7.6] Fratribus[186] Cartursiensis[187] locum aptum iuxta murum parisiensis civitatis providit. Similiter sororibus ordinis[188] sancti dominici monasterium sancti[189] Mathei prope Rothamagum acquisivit, et utrisque redditus assignavit. Cuiuscumque pauperis ordinis[190] religiosi ad eum confugientes, dum tamen eorum ordo approbatus esset a summo pontifice, benigne ab eo suscepti[191] locum[192] ad manendum[193] commodum obtinuerunt.[194] [7.7] Cecis Parisiensis[195] plusquam ccc[196] beghinis[197] cccc cum magnis sumptibus de locis[198] providit miserabilesque[199] mulieres que quandoque pro victus penuria semetipsas exposuerant, in magno numero in domo filiarum dei Parisius congregavit, et ipsis quatuor centum[200]

184. quod] hic *add.* B *(interlinear)* C
185. Verum horum duorum ordinum ... animarum salutem effundunt] *om.* D
186. Fratribus] quoque *add.* BC
187. cartursiensis] carthusiensis B; carthusibus C; carthusiensibus D
188. ordinis] *om.* C
189. sancti] iuxta C
190. ordinis] ordinis pauperis B; *om.* C
191. suscepti] redditus unde sustentarentur et loca *add.* B *[margin]* C ("et loca" is not marginal in B, but the rest is)
192. locum] *om.* C
193. D: 27r
194. obtinuerunt] In quibus mire humilitatis et caritatis officia pluries exercuit, propriis manibus serviendo infirmis humiliter et devote. Unde quando veniebat Parisius. Aut ad alias civitates, hospitales domos in quibus magna infirmorum copia iacebat misericorditer visitans. Nullius infirmi deformitatem vel immundiciam abhominans. Omnibus infirmis pluries propriis manibus et flexis genibus cibaria ministrabat [C: ministravit] . Unde quod est mirabile dictu cuidam monacho leproso abhominabili et horribili iam effecto. Utpote naso et oculis dicti morbi corrosione privato. [D: et] Beatus Ludovicus flexis genibus in quodam eius prandio cibum et potum immittendo [D: immittens] in os eius absque aliqua abhominatione humiliter ministravit, abbate qui aderat et hoc vix videre poterat. In gemitu et lacrimis prorumpente *add.* B *[margin]* CD; cf. BLQRF 6.
195. parisiensis] parisiensibus BCD
196. ccc] trecentis CD, *add.* et D
197. beghinis] benignis A; beghinis [beginis CD] filiabus dei quadringentis B
198. locis] et domibus sibi competentibus quoque C
199. miserabilesque] miserabiles C
200. quatuor centum] cccc B; quadringentas C

drink in from divine scriptures, they pour out throughout the whole world for the honor of God and the salvation of souls."³⁹ [7.6] He provided a fitting place near the wall of the city of Paris for the Carthusian brothers,⁴⁰ and he acquired for the sisters of the Order of Saint Dominic the monastery of Saint Matthew near Rouen, and he assigned revenues to both. When any people from a poor religious order fled to him, provided it was a religious order approved by the pope, he received them kindly, and they obtained a place suitable for living.⁴¹ [7.7] At great expense, he made provisions for places [to live] in Paris for more than three hundred blind people and more than four hundred beguines; and he gathered together in the house of the Filles Dieu in Paris a great number of wretched women who had at one time prostituted

39. Cf. GB 19 (p. 11); BL 6.11.

40. The Carthusian monastery of Vauvert, established by Louis' patronage in 1259.

41. Cf. BL 6.12.

libras de quibus cum laboritio suo viverent annuatim ut eas a peccato retraheret assignavit. [7.8] Ceteras eius *elemosinas* cotidianas et annuas *quas enarrat omnis ecclesia*[201] *sanctorum* [cf. Sir. 31.11] quis enumerare sufficiat? Breviter quicquid[202] pauperibus dabat optime positum estimabat, etcetera[203] vero quasi perdita reputabat.

[8.0] De devocione eius ad sacras reliquias, et ad divinium officium. Capitulum octavum.[204]

[8.1] Capellam[205] speciosissimam deo devotissimus rex mirifico scemate edificavit Parisius[206] in qua sacrosanctam coronam spineam domini, et partem maximam sancte crucis, ferrumque lancee quod latus aperuit salvatoris cum reliquiis aliis multis ac[207] plurimum preciosis, in theca speciosissima ad hoc specialiter elaborata dignissime collocavit. Has siquidem sacras Christi reliquias cum immensis laboribus, et expensis a Constantinopolitano imperatore obtinuit. [8.2] Ad has suscipendas[208] ipse de Parisius cum sollempni ac devotissima processione cleri et populi devote[209] processit, et usque ad ecclesiam beate virginis nudis pedibus hunc sacrum thesaurum propris humeris deportavit. Diem quoque anniversarium qua Parisius recepte sunt, corona scilicet lignum crucis domini,[210] ferrumque lancee et cetera perpetuo sollempnizari instituit.[211] Primum quidem festum per predicatores, aliud per minores.[212] Per fratres enim horum ordinum voluit devotus rex sic cognosci quod obtinuisset hunc thesaurum.[213] [8.3] Omnes horas

201. A: 244v
202. quicquid] quidquid C
203. et cetera] ecclesia A
204. octavum] *chapter title om.* D; vii B; Precipua vero devotione sacrosanctas [D: venerabatur] reliquias et dei cultum et honorem sanctum iugiter augmentabat *add.* B *[margin]* CD
205. Capellam] siquidem *add.* B *[margin]* CD
206. Parisius] in regali suo palacia *add.* B *[margin]* C
207. ac] et C; multis aliis D
208. C: 228r
209. devote] obviam *add.* C
210. domini] *om.* C
211. institui] tria festa in eius solempnitate convertens *add.* B *[margin]* CD
212. minores] 3ᵐ [CD: Tercium] voluit fieri per alios religiosos omnes *add.* B *[margin]* CD
213. thesaurum] magnis ad hoc indulgentiis a sede apostolica impetratis *add.* B *[margin]* CD

themselves for lack of food; and, so that he could bring them back from sin, he assigned to these women four hundred pounds annually so that they might live by their own labor.[42] [7.8] Who could list all the other daily and yearly alms *that the whole church of the saints shall declare* [cf. Sir. 31.11]? In short, whatever he gave to the poor he considered very well spent, and everything else he considered wasted.[43]

[8.0] Chapter 8. On his devotion to sacred relics and the divine office.

[8.1] In a most worthy manner, the king, with the greatest devotion to God, built an extremely beautiful chapel of extraordinary design in Paris, where he brought together the Lord's sacrosanct Crown of Thorns, a very large piece of the Holy Cross, iron from the lance that pierced the Savior's side, and many other very precious relics in a very beautiful reliquary designed specially for this purpose. He acquired these sacred relics of Christ at great labor and expense from the emperor of Constantinople.[44] [8.2] In order to receive these [relics], he went out from Paris in a solemn and most devout procession of clergy and people, and with bare feet he carried this sacred treasure on his own shoulders all the way to Notre Dame [of Paris]. He then instituted the perpetual celebration of the anniversary of the day on which the crown, the wood of the cross of the Lord, the iron of the lance, and the other relics were brought to Paris, the one [feast to be celebrated] by the Dominicans, the other by the Franciscans. For the devout king wished that the treasure that he had obtained be venerated by friars from these orders.[45] [8.3] He always listened to the singing of all the

---

42. Cf. GB 19 (p. 12); BL 6.8.

43. Cf. GB 19 (p. 11); WC, p. 33; BL 6.13.

44. Cf. BL 7.1; GB 24; WSP *vie* 6 (pp. 41–42); WSP *sermo* 22 (p. 286). In this section the author refers to the Ste.-Chapelle, begun in 1239 and consecrated in 1248. The Ste.-Chapelle was part of the palace complex on the Ile-de-la-cité in Paris.

45. Cf. GB 24 (p. 16); BL 7.2; WSP *vie* 6 (pp. 41–42); WSP *sermo* 22 (p. 286). Note that detail about Franciscans and Dominicans being entrusted with the ser - vices appears in WSP *vie* but not in GB or BL.

canonicas[214] de gloriosa[215] virgine cum nota semper audiebat. Submisse tamen easdem inter se et capellanum suum et pro defunctis[216] novem lectiones cotidie dicebat. Et cum semel diceretur sibi quosdam nobilium murmurare quod tot missas cotidie et frequenter valde[217] sermones[218] audiret "forsitan" inquit "si ludendo ad aleas et currendo post feras seu intendendo acupiis[219] plus expenderem de tempore, nemo musicaret."[220] [8.4] Aliquo tempore duxit in consuetudinem media nocte surgere ad confitendum domino completoque nocurnali officio, de capella rediens ad cameram tam diu in oratione ante lectum[221] permanere volebat, quam diu duraverant matutine. Tunc enim non[222] timebat[223] ut quandoque familiariter retulit, si Deus[224] ei aliquam devotionem immitteret, quod impedimentum a supervenientibus pateretur. [8.5] Lacrimarum gratiam quam plurimum[225] affectabat et super harum defectu confessori[226] suo pie et humiliter conquerebatur familiariter ei dicens[227] quod quando in letania dicebatur: "Ut fontem lacrimarum nobis dones." Devote dicebat, "O domine fontem lacrimarum non audeo postulare sed modice lacrimarum stille[228] mihi sufficerent ad cordis mei ariditatem irrigandam." Aliquando confessori suo familiariter recognovit quod quandoque dominus in oratione lacrimas[229] sibi dedit, quas cum sentiret per genas suaviter in os defluere non solum cordi sed et gustui[230] dulcissime sapiebant. [8.6] Dum divinum officium in ecclesia celebraretur, nolebat alicuius colloquio impediri, nisi urgeret aliqua[231] utilitas[232] et

214. canonicas] et. *add.* A
215. gloriosa] eciam *add.* BD
216. defunctis] vigilias *add.* BCD
217. valde] *om.* BCD
218. sermones] quoque *add.* BC
219. acupiis] aucupiis BC
220. D: 27v
221. lectum] in oratione *add.* C (MS repeats the phrase "in oratione" twice)
222. non] *om.* A
223. B: 143r
224. deus] dominus BCD
225. plurimum] cum ieiunia sities, quam *add.* B *[margin]* CD
226. confessori] confessoris A; confessori *in* GB
227. familiariter ei dicens] familiariter ei dicendo A; ei familiariter dicendo C; familiariter ei dicendi D
228. stille] stelle A
229. lacrimas] devotionis *add.* B *[margin]* CD
230. gustui] ori *add.* B *(interlinear)* CD
231. aliqua] aliquas A
232. utilitas] necessitas BCD; WSP *sermo* 23 (p. 286), "neccessitate et breviter"

canonical hours of the Glorious Virgin. Quietly, with his chaplain, he recited these every day, along with the nine lections for the dead. And once, when he was told that certain noblemen were muttering because he heard daily masses so often and listened to sermons so frequently, he said, "Perhaps if I were to spend more of my time playing dice or running after beasts or setting out nets for birds, no one would sing about it [*musicaret*]."[46] [8.4] On occasion he got up in the middle of the night to make confession to God, and when the night office was done, having returned to his bedchamber from his chapel, he would remain in prayer at his bed for as long as morning prayers lasted. For that way, as he explained to friends, he did not worry that if God sent him another prayer, he might have to endure being interrupted if someone entered the room.[47] [8.5] He aspired to [attain] the grace of tears as much as possible and would lament with piety and with humility to his confessor the absence of such tears, saying to him in private the words of the litany, "May you give to us a fount of tears." He would say devoutly, "O Lord, I do not dare to ask for a fount of tears; little drops would suffice for me to irrigate the dryness of my heart." Sometimes, he recollected to his confessor in confidence that whenever the Lord gave him tears as he prayed, and he felt them flowing down his cheeks softly into his mouth, they tasted very sweet to his heart and to his tongue.[48] [8.6] He refused to be interrupted by anyone talking during the celebration of the Divine Office in church unless something important were pressing, and then only briefly and succinctly. He had

46. Cf. GB 21 (p. 13); BL 7.3.
47. Cf. GB 21 (p. 13); BL 7.4; WSP *sermo* 23–24 (pp. 286–87).
48. Cf. GB 21 (p. 14); WSP *vie* 8 (p. 55); WSP *sermo* 24 (p. 287); BL 7.4.

tunc breviter et succincte. Festa annualia[233] ac ceteras sanctorum
festivitates faciebat sollempniter ut decebat celebrari[234] quod et orna-
menta preciosissima[235] haberentur prout diei aut festo congruebat.
[8.7] Insuper cum clericis de capella sua gratiose cantantibus, de
Bonis Pueris vocari aliquos ad officium faciebat, eis que completis
sollempniis denarios erogabat, quibus pro magna parte anni in studio
Parisius poterant sustentari.[236]

[9.0] De[237] amore eius ad fidem et crucem Christi. Novum capitulum.[238]

[9.1] Zelus fidei adeo in[239] corde ipsius fervebat,[240] quod iuramenta
turpia absque horrore audire non poterat.[241] Unde cum de communi

233. annualia] annalia BCD
234. celebrari] de hoc curam habens specialiter *add.* BC
235. preciosissima] tunc *add.* BC
236. festa annualia ac ceteras sanctorum ... parisius poterant sustentari] *om. D*
237. De] Quam prudentia eius in regimine regni et de iusticie equitate in
omni suo iudicio. Capitulum viii. B (142bis–v, inserted folio); de prudentia eius in
regimine et de iusticie equitate in omni suo iudicio. Capitulum novum. C
   Addition: In regimine vero regni ita potenter et prudenter se [sese C] gerebat.
Quod absque personarum acceptione cum diligenti causarum discussione redebat
iudicium et iusticiam unicuique. Consiliarii quoque sui et proceres regni videntes
sapientiam dei esse in illo, cum dilectione sincera ipsum etiam plurimum [*om.* C]
formidabant. Timens autem ne cause pauperum vix ingrederentur ad eos: ad minus
bis in ebdomada ad audiendum conquirentes in loco patenti se [C: 228v] ponebat,
et mediante iusticia plerumque etiam temperante misericordia. Faciebat eos cele -
riter expediri. Et quando negotium fidei per prelatos seu inquisitores deferebatur
ad eum: omnibus aliis postpositis faciebat illud citius expediri. *add.* B (142bis–v,
inserted folio) CD; cf. BLQRF 8.
   Addition: Duella vero tamquam a iure prohibita cuiusquam instancia nullatenus admittebat: sed per aliam viam iuri consonam etiam magnatum malefacta
puniebat. Statuit insuper ad abolendam vorginem usuarum, ut obligatos iudeis aut
publicis usurariis per litteras nullus iusticiarius compelleret ad solvendum. Et sicut
pater eius de hoc etiam habebat graciam specialem, quod inter se discordantes ad
concordiam frequenter revocabat. [B only] Sequitur capitum ix de amore eius ad
fidem christi. *add.* B (142bis–v, inserted folio) C; cf. BLQRF 8.
238. Novum capitulum] Capitulum decimum C. *Chapter title om. in* D. Note
that the numbering is out of sequence for C because of the addition of the chapter
on rule and justice; see introduction to *Gloriosissimi regis.*
239. in] ipsius *add.* BCD
240. fervebat] corde fervebat CD
241. poterat] Opprobia [Obprobria CD] igitur fidei christiane zelando zelum
dei tamquam alter phinees blasphemos et iurantes graviter puniebat. *add.* B [*mar-
gin]* CD; cf. BLQRF 7.

the annual feast days and the feasts of saints celebrated with fitting solemnity with the most precious ornaments, as would befit a ferial or feast day.[49] [8.7] Moreover, while clerics of his chapel were singing beautifully, he would have some of the *bons enfants* called to the service of worship; to these boys, once the solemnities were done, he gave money that allowed them to support themselves at the *studium* [i.e., university] in Paris for the better part of the year.[50]

[9.0] Chapter 9. On his love of the faith and the cross of Christ.

[9.1] Zeal for the faith burned in his heart so greatly that he could not hear foul oaths without horror. Thus, with the unanimous advice of

49. Cf. BL 7.5; WSP *sermo* 23 (p. 286); but not found in WSP *vie.*
50. Cf. GB 21 (p. 14); WSP *sermo* (p. 286). "Bons enfants" or "bonis pueris" were poor university students who lived together in an endowed community. Houses of "Bons enfants" were founded in northern France in the 1240s and 1250s; Louis IX is known to have supported the "bons enfants" who lived near the Victorines. See Reitzel, "Medieval Houses of 'Bons Enfants.'"

consilio prelatorum et principum publice fecisset indici[242] auctoritate domini symonis, tituli[243] Sancte Cecilie tunc presbiteri cardinalis et legati in Francia, postmodum vero summi pontificis, penam statutam contra huiusmodi iuramenta. [9.2] Accidit civem quemdam parisiensem iurando in divinum nomen enormiter blasphemare. Quod ut vir zelotes comperit iuxta edictum regale in peccati sui penam et memoriam illum in labiis ferro candenti ad aliorum exemplum cauterizari precepit.[244] Cumque audiret propter hoc non nullos in se multipliciter maledicta congerere: "vellem" inquit[245] "similiter in labiis meis pati caterium[246] et talem indecentiam quoad vixero sustinere dummodo hoc pessimum iurationis vicium de regno meo penitus tolleretur." [9.3] Dudum quoque ultra mare captus, dum sarraceni interfecto soldano suo[247] cruentatos[248] adhuc gladios tenentes intentendo[249] mortem iuramentum de servando pactum quod cum soldano habuerat[250] exigerent, implicantes quod Christum negasset et fidem si contraveniret, horruit rex pius et in vera fide[251] firmus, et stabilis respondit voce[252] libera: "nunquam sum hoc facturus."[253] Et cum furerent infideles, nam similem conditionem in iurando se servaturos

242. indici] edici C
243. tituli] titulo D
244. precepit] percepti CD
245. A: 245r
246. caterium] cauterium BC
247. suo] *om.* BC
248. cruentatos] cruentos C
249. intentendo] intendendo B; intendando C
250. habuerat] de solvenda pecunia pro sua et suorum liberatione *add.* B *[margin]* C
251. fide] velud alter Eleazarus *add.* B *[margin]* velut alter Eleazarius C
252. voce] vocem A
253. facturus] Quia si corpus occiderent, animam non haberent *add.* B *[margin]* C

prelates and princes, he had a legal penalty for these types of oaths publicly proclaimed, on the authority of Lord Simon, titular priest of Saint Cecilia, who was cardinal priest and legate in France at that time, and then later pope.[51] [9.2] It happened that a certain citizen of Paris blasphemed appallingly by swearing against the divine name. When the zealous man discovered this, he ordered that the man be branded on the lips with a red hot iron according to the royal edict, as an example to others, in punishment for and as a reminder of his sin. And when he heard that on account of this, some people were repeatedly heaping abuse on him, he said: "I would rather suffer this branding and bear this shameful stigma on my own lips as long as I live, so long as this terrible sin of swearing be thoroughly removed from my kingdom."[52] [9.3] Once, when [Louis was] in captivity overseas, the Saracens— having killed their sultan and threatening death while still holding bloody swords—demanded an oath for the upholding of the agreement that [Louis] had made with the sultan. [The oath] stated that [Louis] would deny Christ and the faith if he acted contrary to [the agreement]. The king, pious and firm in the true faith, shuddered and steadfastly responded in a fearless voice, "I will never do this." And so the infidels were angry, for it had been demanded of them that they

51. Cf. GB 32 (p. 19); WSP *vie* 3 (p. 27); BL 8.1. Simon of Brie was legate to France under popes Urban IV, Clement IV, and Gregory X. In 1281 he was named pope, as Martin IV (d. 1285). Prior to this, he was one of Louis IX's chief counselors, including as Chancellor of France and Keeper of the Seal. He was instrumental in the early stages of the papal inquiry into Louis' sanctity.

52. Cf. GB 33 (p. 19); WSP *vie* 3 (p. 27); BL 8.2.

pactum, quod ad eum soldanus habuerat, exacti[254] adiecerant, dicentibus sibi suis qui aderant tam clericis quam laicis quod secure illud poterat dicere[255] cum pactum omnino servare proponeret. "Tantum inquit horreo verbum illud etiam sub conditione audire, quod nequaquam possem illud sono vocis exprimere." Nutu itaque divino flexi pepcerunt[256] sibi sarraceni de hac conditione constanciam fidei et amorem ad deum suum plurimum, admirantes.[257] [9.4] Denique crucis Christi signaculum in tantam[258] habebat[259] reverenciam[260] quod per claustra religiosorum in[261] loca alia ubi cruces super tumulos defunctorum insculpte erant[262] in lapidibus transiens; non tamen[263] calcare desuper verum etiam prope pedem ponere[264] formidabat, unde et a religiosis de quibus confidebat amplius exegit quod de claustris eorum cruces taliter in tumbis insculpte[265] penitus[266] raderentur.[267] [9.5] Quam devote[268] ac reverenter omni anno ad adorandum crucem in Parasceve flexis genibus soluto crine nudis pedibus procederet, testantur illorum[269] oculi qui sine lacrimis ipsum nequaquam poterant intueri.

254. exacti] exasti A
255. dicere] sine peccato *add.* B *[margin]* C
256. pepcerunt] pepercerunt BC
257. admirantes] Ibidem etiam quemdam nobilem saracenum qui recenter soldanum occiderat facere militem omnimodis recusavit: dicens quod nec pro morte nec pro vita infidelem quemcumque baltheo insigniret militari. *add.* B *[margin]* C; cf. BLQRF 7. Dudum quoque ultra mare captus ... deum suum plurimum admirantes] *om.* D
258. tantam] tanta C
259. habebat] habuit BCD
260. reverenciam] reverentia C
261. in] vel B; et C
262. erant] erat B
263. tamen] tantum C
264. ponere] pone C
265. insculpte] inculpte A
266. C: 229r
267. raderentur] Et quod tumulis eorum cruces de cetero non insculperentur *add.* B *[margin]* CD. D: 28r
268. devote] autem *add.* BCD
269. illorum] eorum D

take a similar oath to uphold the pact that the sultan had made with him [Louis]. To those present, both clerics and laymen, [who were] saying that he could safely say [this] since he intended to fulfill the pact in its entirety, Louis responded, "I have such horror of even hearing this that, even under such conditions as these, I could never say this aloud." And thus softened by divine will, the Saracens spared him from the oath, admiring greatly the constancy of his faith and his love for God.[53] [9.4] And finally, [Louis] held the sign of Christ's cross in such reverence that, when he was walking through monastic cloisters and in other places where crosses were carved on the paving stones above the tombs of the dead, he feared not only trampling on [the carved crosses] but even walking near them. And so, he urged that the monks in whom he trusted completely remove the crosses sculpted in this way on the tombs of their cloisters.[54] [9.5] The eyes of all those who could not look at him at all without tears bear witness to how devoutly and reverently he processed every year on Good Friday, on bended knee, hair loosened and feet bare, to adore the wood of the cross.[55]

---

53. Cf. WSP *vie* 3 (pp. 23–34); WSP *sermo* 10 (p. 280); BL 8.3. See also related discussion in Joinville, *Vie de Saint Louis,* §360.
54. Cf. GB 36 (p. 20); BL 8.5.
55. Cf. BL 8.6; WSP *vie* 6 (pp. 39–40).

[10.0] De prima sumptione crucis et liberatione eius de carcere et[270] periculo maris.[271] Decimum Capitulum.[272]

[10.1] Igitur amator fidei et venerator crucis dominice[273] crucem assumpsit dum adhuc esse iuvenis apud pontisarum de desperata quantum inter mortales medicos convalescens infirmitate.[274] Fratresque[275] suos tres comites secum ducens et maiores regni Francie barones ac milites cum exercitu maximo applicuit in Egyptum. [10.2] Occurrerunt pagani valide regi et suis capere volentibus portum. Sed virtutem christiani[276] non ferentes: turpiter in fugam conversi sunt. At nostri ad terram descendentes de navibus famosam illam civitatem que quondam Mempheos[277] nunc Damieta[278] dicitur[279] occuparunt. At non multo post, iusto et[280] occulto dei iudicio, exercitus[281] infirmitate percussus multiplici, corporali morte[282] maioribus mediocribus et minoribus subtractis de medio de triginta duobus milibus numero pervenit ad senarium. [10.3] Volensque pater misericordiarum Dominus omnipotens mirabilem se in suo sancto ostendere [cf. Ps. 76.15], tradidit[283] regem[284] manibus impiorum ut mirabilior appareret, cum posset eum modo inestimabili liberare.[285] Quis enim non cognoscat miraculum

270. et] ac BC
271. maris] mortis BC
272. Capitulum] capitulum xi[iii] C
273. dominice] de manu episcopi parisiensis cum maxime devotione *add.* B *[margin]* CD; cf. BLQRF 5.
274. apud pontisarum de desperata . . . convalescens infirmitate] *om.* D
275. fratresque] fratres quoque C
276. virtutum christiani] exercitus christianorum BCD
277. Mempheos] nempheos A
278. Damieta] demiata A; vero damiata CD
279. dicitur] et circumstantem regionem vi armorum *add.* B *[margin]* CD; cf. BLQRF 5; B: 143v.
280. et] sed CD
281. exercitus] *corr. from* exercuus A; exercitus christianus BCD
282. morte] quam plurimis *add.* B *[margin]* CD
283. traditit] pugilem fidei dominum *add.* B *[margin]* CD
284. regem] in *add.* BCD
285. liberare] Et cum pius rex per navem propinquam evadere potuisset, tamen spontanee se reddidit ut occasione sui suum populum [*C*: populum suum] liberaret *add.* BCD; cf. BLQRF 5. Note that in B this addition is found in the body of the text and not in the margin.

[10.0] Chapter 10. On his first assumption of the cross and his liberation from prison and the danger of the sea.

[10.1] And so, this lover of the faith and venerator of the Lord's cross, while still young, took up the cross when he was at Pontoise, convalescing from an illness which the earthly doctors deemed utterly hopeless. He took with him his three brothers, the counts, along with the great barons and knights of the kingdom of France, and he landed in Egypt with a very large army.[56] [10.2] The pagans put up a strong fight against the king and his men as they tried to take the port, but not possessing the virtue[57] of the Christian [army], they fled in dishonor. Our men, disembarking from their ships, captured that famous city, once called Memphis but now [known as] Damietta. Shortly after, by the just but hidden judgment of God, the army, struck by multiple illnesses, with men of every rank taken from their midst by bodily death, was reduced from thirty-two thousand in number to six thousand.[58] [10.3] And the Father of mercies, the Almighty Lord, wishing to show himself more wondrous in his saint [cf. Ps. 76.15], handed the king over into the hands of the ungodly men so that He might appear even more wondrous, since He would be able to free him in an inestimable

---

56. Cf. WSP *vie* 3 (pp. 22–23); BL 5.1.

57. The Latin "virtus" can mean both "virtue" in our sense, and also courage and strength. Here, the author intends to suggest that Christian virtue is the cause of military strength.

58. Cf. WSP *vie* 3 (pp. 22–23); BL 5.2.

ferocissimam gentem[286] regi quem posse sibi super ceteros mundi principes nocere sciebant parcere eamdemque gentem cupidissimam pro
redemptione[287] minori in parte[288] centupla quam habere potuissent[289]
liberum dimittere? [10.4] Eductus itaque[290] velut Ioseph de carcere
Egyptiaco, non ut fugiens vel timidus[291] statim reversus ad propria, sed
per quinque annorum spatium post modum permansit in Syria. Illo
in[292] tempore captivos christianos qui tunc haberi potuerunt[293] eduxit
de carceribus, sarracenos multos ad fidem venientes clementer suscepit
et baptizari fecit. Cesaream, Ioppen, et Sydonem muris firmavit fortissimis civitatis quoque Achon fortificavit menia et plurimum ampliavit.[294] [10.5] Tandem[295] pie matris ac sibi dilectissime audito transitu
et regno non modicum imminere[296] posse periculum,[297] assensit redire
in Franciam, relictis cum legato multis militibus et expensis in succur-
sum et subsididium terre sancte. [10.6] Nocte vero[298] tercia postquam a
portu Achon recesserat modicum antequam dilucesceret[299] navis subito
ad rupem[300] aut terre lingulam in modum lapidis induratam bina impulsione tam fortiter est collisa, quod vix de centum una posse putabatur, probabiliter sine fractione evasisse. Rex vero devotus spem[301] et

286. gentem] tanto *add.* B *[margin]* CD
287. redemptione] multo *add.* B *(interlinear)* CD
288. parte] ymmo *add.* B *[margin]*; ymmo centesima *add.* CD
289. potuissent] regem ditissimum *add.* B *[margin]* CD
290. itaque] tandem D
291. timidus] est *add.* B *[margin]* CD
292. Illo in] In illo BCD
293. potuerunt] redimens *add.* B *[margin]* CD
294. ampliavit] Tunc enim circa Sydonem multa invenit christianorum corpora [C: corpora christianorum] occisorum iam fetida, et quam [*om.* C] plurima
a bestiis lacerata. Hec propriis manibus cum aliquorum de suis adiutorio qui vix
illorum fetorem sustinere poterant, recollegit et tradidit [*om.* D] ecclesiastice sepulture humiliter et devote [D: traditit] *add.* B *[lower margin]* CD; cf. BLQRF 5.
295. Tandem] vero *add.* B *(interlinear)* CD
296. imminere] incurrere A
297. periculum] baronum suorum consilio *add.* B; considerans baronum
suorum consilio C; baronum suorum consilia consensit D
298. vero] sequente *add.* C
299. A: 245v
300. rupem] rumpem A
301. D: 28v

manner. Who would not recognize the miracle that this fierce people released so great a king, who they knew could harm them more than all the world's princes, and that this same greedy people freed the king for a ransom one-hundredth of what they might have demanded?[59] [10.4] Like Joseph, when released from an Egyptian prison, he did not behave as a fugitive or a fearful man who immediately turns around to go home, but rather he stayed in Syria for five more years [cf. Gen. 40–41]. During that time, he won release from prison for as many captive Christians as he could. And he welcomed with clemency many Saracens who came to the faith and had them baptized. He fortified Caesarea, Joppa, and Sidon with very strong city walls, and also strengthened Acre and greatly enlarged its ramparts.[60] [10.5] Finally, having heard that his pious and beloved mother had died, and that his kingdom could be in great danger, he agreed to return to France; he left many knights and much money with the legate for the aid of the Holy Land.[61] [10.6] On the third night after his departure from the port of Acre, just before daybreak, the ship suddenly hit a rock (or a little slip of land that was hard like a rock), colliding with [it] twice with such force that no one would have believed that even one of a hundred men could have survived the shipwreck. The devout king, having hope and faith in God, woke up and rushed to pray before the holy body of Jesus Christ [i.e., the consecrated host] (which, by a special permission of the

---

59. Cf. GB 25 (p. 16); WSP *vie* 3 (p. 23); BL 5.3.
60. Cf. GB 26 (p. 16); WSP *vie* 11 (pp. 91–92); BL 5.4.
61. Cf. GB 28 (p. 17); BL 5.5; YSD 13 (p. 56).

fidem habens in domino[302] concitus perrexit ad orationem coram[303] sacro corpore Ihesu Christi, quod de speciali licencia legati in altari preciosissime adornato intra navem habebat. Mirum certe! Descendentibus ad fundum marinariis velut desperatis cum lumine, illesa navis omnino est reperta. Et cum aurore lux pene iam noctis tenebras depulisset, excitati sacerdotes et clerici qui circa altare iacebant, viderunt hominem Dei ante altare prostratum deo omnipotenti de tanto beneficio gratias referentem.[304] Fuitque merito firma spes eorum omnium quod dominus eos meritis pii regis et precibus a mortis periculo liberasset.

[11.0] De reditu eius in Franciam et secunda crucis assumptione. Capitulum undecimum.[305]

[11.1] Reversus itaque in Franciam princeps nobilis et cum gaudio effabili[306] susceptus ab omnibus. Licet a puericia sancte conversationis extiterit, ex tunc tamen[307] semper se[308] ipso[309] melior fiebat ut David. Et velut lapis pro celesti edificio multis tribulationum tonsuris[310] quadratus ad tantam vite perfectionem pervenit quod eius deinceps usque in finem conversatio tantum pristinam precessit quantum aurum purissimum optimo etiam prevalet argento.[311] [11.2] Tandem post multorum annorum curricula in quibus se in omni genere virtutum excrevit,[312] videns se[313] fraudatum penitus spe intrande religionis, audiensque calamitates, desolationes, ac pericula terre sancte[314] propositum transfretandi quod

302. C 229v
303. coram] coronam A
304. referentem] agentem C
305. undecimum] xi B; xii[iii] C
306. ineffabili] inestimabilis in *A*; ineffabili BCD estimabili *om.* B
307. tamen] ferrentius de virtutem virtutem [sic] proficiens *add.* B *[margin]* C
308. se] *om.* C
309. ipso] seipso B
310. tonsuris] tonsionibus C
311. semper se ipse melior fiebat . . . etiam prevalet argento] ferventius de virtute in virtutem proficiens semper de ipso melior fiebat D
312. excrevit] exercuit C; in quibus se in omni genere virtutum excrevit] *om.* D
313. se] *om.* C
314. sancte] velut alter mathatias [C: matathias:] cum filiis suis mala gentis christiane et sanctorum ferre non sustinens *add.* BCD; cf. BLQRF 9. Note that the addition in B is not marginal.

legate, he had on board on a most preciously adorned altar). And this was truly wondrous! When sailors, like desperate men, descended below with a light, they discovered that the ship was wholly undamaged. When the light of dawn had barely driven away the shadows of night, the priests and clerics who were near the altar saw in wonder the man of God lying prostrate before the altar, giving thanks to the Almighty God for so great a gift. The hope of all of these men was confirmed because God had released them from this mortal danger through the merits and prayers of the pious king.[62]

[11.0] Chapter 11. On his return to France and his second taking of the cross.

[11.1] When he returned to France, the noble prince was received by all with ineffable joy. Although he stood out for his saintly conduct from boyhood, from this point forward he constantly strove, like David, to become even better. Like a stone squared for a celestial building, he arrived at a life of such perfection through the many cuttings of tribulation that from this point until the end of his life his [new] conduct greatly surpassed his former conduct, just as the purest of gold is of greater worth than even the best silver.[63] [11.2] Finally, after the passage of many years in which he grew in every kind of virtue, having seen himself cheated of his innermost hope of entering the religious life, and having heard of the calamities, hardships, and dangers to the

62. Cf. GB 30 (p. 18); BL 5.6; WSP *vie* 4 (pp. 29–30). Note Joinville's discussion, *Vie de Saint Louis*, §§618–622.
63. Cf. BL 6.1.

inspirante deo conceperat,[315] curavit summo pontifici domino scilicet Clementi quarto per secretissimum ac discretum nuncium aperire. [11.3] Qui tanquam vir prudens in principio reformidans diu que deliberans tandem benigne consensit, et pium propositum multipliciter approbans ad petitionem regis legatum misit in Franciam dominum symonem, tituli[316] sancte Cecilie presbiterum tunc cardinalem, postmodum dominum Martinum quartum divina[317] providencia summum pontificem.[318] [11.4] Convocata igitur multitudine copiosa prelatorum, principum, baronum, ac militum regni Parisius, ipse rex cum devotione multa de manu legati primus crucem accepit, deinde dominus Philippus[319] primogenitus, aliique duo filii,[320] Iohannes comes Nivernensis, ac Petrus, nec non et ceteri magnates, quam plurimi,[321] quorum Deus corda tetigerat per suam inspirationem et per exhortationes multimodas quas[322] ipse eis[323] prudentissime fecerat publice et privatim. [11.5] Preparato vero navigio ad Aquas Mortuas iuxta condictum venerunt[324] ante Sardinam, ibique cum maioribus habito consilio, et certis ac validis rationibus assignatis, de comuni assensu[325] vela direxerunt versus Tunicum. Et enim regem illum qui frequenter se velle baptizari[326] si populum suum non timeret, insinuaverat, tantum desiderabat cum gente sua fieri christianum quod dum semel[327] iudeus quidam famosus apud sanctum Dyonisium in Francia ipso presente baptisimi suscepit lavachrum conversus ad nuncios regis Tunicii

315. conceperat] acceperat D
316. tituli] titulo CD
317. postmodum domino Martinum quartum divina] postmodum domino quartum divina A; postmodum [B: *margin*] dominum videlicet Martinum quarta divina BCD
318. pontificem] anno scilicet domini millesimo ducentesimo sexagesimo nono *add.* BC
319. Philippus] eius BD
320. filii] ipsius *add.* BCD
321. plurimi] plures C
322. quas] rex *add.* C; rex ipse *add.* D
323. eis] *om.* C
324. venerunt] convenerunt CD
325. assensu] consenu BCD
326. baptizari] baptisciri C
327. semel] *om.* BCD

Holy Land, he carefully revealed through a very secret and judicious message to the lord pope, Clement IV, a plan that he had conceived by God's inspiration for crossing the ocean.[64] [11.3] The pope, a prudent man, was at first reluctant, but after deliberating at length, finally consented willingly and approved greatly of the pious proposition. At the king's request, [the pope] sent to France as his legate Simon, titular priest of Saint Cecilia, later cardinal, and finally by divine providence Pope Martin IV.[65] [11.4] Having convoked a great number of prelates, princes, barons, and knights in Paris, it was the king himself who, with great devotion, was the first to take the cross from the hand of the legate. [He was then followed by] Lord Philip, his heir, and his two other sons, John, the count of Nevers, and Peter, and not least as many as possible of the other noblemen whose hearts God had touched through [Louis'] inspiration and through the many exhortations which [Louis] very wisely made to them, both in public and in private.[66] [11.5] Having readied their fleet at Aigues Mortes, according to plan, they arrived at Sardinia. There, after a council with the nobles, during which many strong and worthy arguments were put forth, they agreed by common assent to sail to Tunis. [Louis] made it known that the king [of Tunis] would have frequently proposed being baptized if he were not in fear of his people, and that he desired greatly that he along with his people would become Christians. And so, once, when a certain famous Jew, having been converted, was baptized at St.-Denis in France, in Louis' presence, [Louis] said to the ambassadors of the king of Tunis who

64. Cf. GB 37 (p. 21); BL 10.1. Clement IV (Gui Fouçois), pope between 1265 and 1268, was on the papal throne when Louis began making plans for this second crusade.

65. Cf. GB 23 (p. 21); BL 10.2.

66. Cf. GB 38–39 (p. 21); BL 10.3.

qui tunc[328] presentes aderant[329] "dicite," inquit "domino vestro quod tam vehementer salutem anime eius desidero, quod ego vellem esset[330] in carcere[331] sarracenorum omnibus diebus vite mee ibidem claritatem solis de cetero non visurus dum modo ipse et gens eius ex vero corde fierent christiani." [11.6] Desiderabat quidem rex christianissimus quod fides christiana que tempore beati Augustini et aliorum orthodoxorum in Affrica, et maxime apud Carthaginem tam eleganter floruerat ab antiquo, ibidem ad honorem nominis Ihesu Christi nostris temporibus refloreret.[332] Et cum de terra Tunicii soldano babylonico magnum soleret venire[333] subsidium, cogitabat vir prudentissimus christanis de sancta terra non modicum tollere nocumentum si radix illa pestifera Tunicii posset per francorum exercitum[334] extirpari.

[12.0] De libero ipsius transitu in Affricam et felici illic transitu eiusdem ad dominum. Duodecimam capitulum.[335]

[12.1] Denique navigio cum exercitu libere portum capiente in Affrica illius famose Carthaginis castrum et omnia ad illud pertinentia armorum vi capientes, inter Carthaginem et Tunicum fixerunt tentoria.[336] [12.2] Illic post tot laudabilia virtutum opera, post tot laboriosos agones quos pro fide et ecclesie dilatatione fideliter ac ferventer indefesso animo tolleraverat,[337] disponente domino qui labores illius voluit feliciter consummare, ac ipsi[338] bonorum laborum suorum fructum retribuere gloriosum, febre continua fatigatus lecto decubuit

---

328. B: 144r
329. aderant] ait *add.* D
330. esset] esse D
331. C: 230r
332. D: 29r
333. venire] provenire C
334. A: 246r
335. De libero . . . capitulum] De transitu eius in affricam et felici illic eius obitu. Capitulum xii. B; De transitu eius in affricam: et felici illic eius obitu. xiiii[iii] capitulum. C; *title om. in* D
336. tentoria] ibidem aliquamdiu in moraturi *add.* B *[margin]* CD
337. tolleraverat] toleravit C
338. ipsi] *om.* C

were there: "Tell your Lord that I so strongly desire the salvation of his soul that I would be willing to be in a Saracen jail for all the rest of the days of my life, and not see the light of the sun, if only he and his people would become Christians with a true heart."⁶⁷ [11.6] Finally, the most Christian king desired that the Christian faith, which had flourished so beautifully in Africa since ancient times, and especially at Carthage in the time of the blessed Augustine and other orthodox Christians, would flourish again in our time in the same way for the honor of the name of Jesus Christ. Because the Sultan of Babylon was accustomed to receiving great revenues from the land of Tunis, this most prudent man thought it would be far from harmful to the Christians of the Holy Land if this pestilential root of Tunis could be extirpated by the French army.⁶⁸

[12.0] Chapter 12. Concerning his bold crossing to Africa and his felicitous crossing to the Lord in that same place.

[12.1] And finally, when the fleet, along with the army, had boldly captured the port in Africa, the army, with the force of arms, seized the fortified town of renowned Carthage and everything around it and set up camp between Carthage and Tunis.⁶⁹ [12.2] There, after many laudable works of virtue and many laborious struggles, which he faithfully and fervently tolerated with a tireless soul for the faith and the spread of the church, and tired out by continual fever, he lay down

67. Cf. GB 41 (p. 22), with exact quote.
68. Cf. GB 41 (p. 22); GB 10.4.
69. Cf. GB 42 (p. 22); BL 10.8.

et[339] invalescente morbo sana mente[340] et integro intellectu omnia ecclesiastica sacramenta devotissime suscepit[341] psalmos dicens et sanctos invocans dum sibi ministraretur sacramentum extreme unctionis.
[12.3] Iam vero signis[342] evidentibus proprinquans[343] ad finem; audientibus, qui aderant, et aures ad eius ora, adhibentibus[344] submisse
ut loqui poterat vir deo plenus et vere christianus dicebat, "pro deo
studeamus quo[345] fides catholica predicari possit apud Tunicium et
plantari." [12.4] Cum vero virtus corporis eius ac[346] sermonis paulatim deficeret, non cessebat sanctorum implorare suffragia maxime
autem beati dyonisii specialis patroni sui, cuius se esse hominem
annis singulis dum viveret[347] ex devotione cognoscebat per talenta
quatuor que cadentia de capite suo super altare in ipsius sancti festo si
presens aderat, offerre consueverat. Unde et iuxta assertionem[348] proprius assistentium finem orationis que de ipso beato dyonisio canitur:
"Tribue nobis quesumus pro amore tuo prospera mundi despicere,
et nulla eius adversa formidare,"[349] frequenter cum quodam vocis[350]
iam debilis suavi susurrio repetebat. [12.5] Similiter et pro christiano
exercitu, principium orationis de beato Iacobo. "Esto domine plebi
tue sanctificator et custos,"[351] nicholminus et de sanctis aliis iugem

---

339. et] tunc quedam documenta sancta gallica domino philippo suo primogenito diligenter exposuit et imposuit effaciciter adimplenda *add.* B *[margin]* CD;
cf. BLQRF 9.

340. Sana mente] sanamente A

341. et invalescente . . . devotissime suscepit] Invalescente [*add. interl.* ideo]
morbo sana mente et integro intellectu [*add. in margin:* et auditu] omnia ecclesiastica sacramenta devotissime suscepit B; Invalescente igitur ideo morbo sana mente
ac integro intellectu et intellectu [*sic*] omnia ecclesiastica sa[cramenta] devotissime
suscepit C; decubuit *om.* D

342. signis] *om.* C

343. proprinquans] mortem et *add.* C

344. adhibentibus] adhibentes BCD

345. quo] quomodo BCD

346. ac] et D

347. viveret] vixeret C

348. assertionem] assionem A

349. Oration to Saint Denis: *Saint Andrew Daily Missal,* 1505 (October 9).

350. vocis] *add.* licet BCD

351. Oration to Saint James: *Saint Andrew Daily Missal,* 1573 (July 25).

upon his bed. The Lord wished that his labors be happily brought to perfection and thus rendered to him the glorious fruits of his good labors. With his illness getting worse, [but] of sound mind and his intellect intact, he received all the ecclesiastical sacraments with great devotion. As the sacrament of extreme unction was ministered to him he recited the psalms and invoked the saints.[70] [12.3] And then, when signs made clear that he was approaching the end, this man, who was full of God and truly Christian, could still speak to those around him who leaned over and brought their ears close to his mouth. He said, "Let us work for God, so that the Catholic faith can be preached and implanted in Tunis."[71] [12.4] Although the strength of his body and of his voice was little by little failing, he continually beseeched the intercession of the saints, and especially of blessed Denis, his own particular patron; he had acknowledged that he was a vassal of this saint out of devotion, by the four talents which, dropping them down from off his head and onto the altar, he was accustomed to offer on the saint's feast day when he was present.[72] And thus, according to the testimony of those who were on hand at the end of the prayer that he sang for blessed Denis, he repeated with the sweet whispering of his fading voice: "Grant, we pray, that we may despise the good things of this world for the sake of your love and not fear any of its adversities."[73] [12.5] And likewise, for the Christian army, [he recited] the beginning of the prayer for blessed James: "Lord, be Your people's sanctifier and protector,"[74] and he also

---

70. Cf. GB 44 (p. 23); BL 11.1.

71. Cf. GB 44 (p. 23); BL 11.2.

72. Louis followed the custom of offering four gold byzants to Saint Denis each year on his feast day, which went back at least to the time of Philip Augustus. See Bournazel, "Suger and the Capetian," 62. For a slightly more detailed version of this strange ritual, see WSP *vie* 6 (p. 44); YSD, 51–52.

73. Cf. GB 44 (p. 23); BL 11.3. Translation adapted from *Saint Andrew Daily Missal*, 1505 (October 9).

74. Translation follows *Saint Andrew Daily Missal*, 1353 (July 25).

memoriam faciebat. [12.6] Demum ad extremam horam veniens Christi servus super stratum cinereum recubans extensus in modum crucis et dicens "Pater in manus tuas commendo spiritum meum" [Luke 23.46], felicem spiritum reddidit creatori. Migravit autem de hoc mundo ad dominum in crastino beati apostoli[352] Bartholmei. Anno domini. M. cc. septuagesimo[353] circa nonam. hora[354] videlicet illa qua Dei filius Ihesus Christus pro mundi vita in cruce moriens expiravit. Cui est omnis laus decus et gloria per immortalia secula seculorum. Amen.[355]

Oratio sancti Ludovici

Deus qui beatum Ludovicum confessorem tuum de terreno ac temporali regno ad celestis et eterni gloriam transtulisti; eius quesumus meritis et intercessione regis regum Ihesu Christi filii tui nos coheredes efficias et eiusdem regni tribuas esse consortes.[356] Per eundem.

---

352. apostoli] *om.* C
353. M. cc. setuagessimo] mᵒ ccᵒ lxx B; millesimo ducentesimo septuagesimo C
354. hora] horam C
355. Amen] Corpus vero beati Ludovici delatum fuit ad sepulchrum patrum suorum, apud [C: 230va] sanctum Dyonisium in Francia, ubi et etiam alibi in diversis mundi partibus crebris choruscat miraculis gloriosis. *add.* BCD; de miraculis meritis et precibus beati Ludovici. B *only*; cf. BLQRF 9.
356. consortes] qui tecum vivit et regna in unitate spiritus sancti Deus *add.* C

offered a prayer of perpetual memory to many other saints.[75] [12.6] At last, at the final hour, the servant of Christ, lying atop a bed of ashes, stretched out in the form of the cross, said, "Father, into your hands I commend my spirit" [Luke 23.46] and gave his joyful spirit back to the Creator. He departed from this world on the day after the [feast day] of Blessed Apostle Bartholomew, in the year of our Lord 1270, at the ninth hour [cf. Luke 39.44], that is to say, on that very hour on which the Son of God, Jesus Christ, dying on the cross for the life of the world, breathed his last. For Him, all praise, beauty, and glory for ever and ever. Amen.[76]

75. Cf. GB 44 (p. 23); BL 11.4.
76. Cf. GB 44 (p. 23); BL 11.5–6. The "Oration to Saint Louis" (*Oratio Sancti Ludovici*) appears here in A; it is translated below as 15.13.

APPENDIX: FIFTEENTH-CENTURY ADDITIONS TO *GLORIOSISSIMI REGIS*

A's life ends here. B and C continue as follows (transcription base manuscript is B). Chapter 14, describing Louis' miracles, follows the miracles that were included as the octave readings in BLQRF (themselves partly derived from *Beatus Ludovicus*'s miracles).[357] D includes a highly abbreviated account of the miracles (ch. 14), and includes no material from chapter 15.

There is no "chapter 13" because the insertion of a new chapter taken from BLQRF after chapter 7 made the fifteenth-century version of the original vita thirteen chapters long.

———

[14.0] [BC] De miraculis factis meritis et precibus beati. Capitulum xiiii.[358]

[14.1] [BC] In die autem sepulture beati Ludovici quedam mulier Sagiensis dyocesis, visum quem prius perdiderat, recuperavit omnino meritis et precibus pii regis.

[14.2] [BC] Non multo post quidam iuvenis de Burgundia surdus et mutus a nativitate cum aliis veniens ad sepulchrum beati Ludovici, prout viderat[359] alios facere nutibus exterioribus sancti suffragium implorabat. Et cum aliquamdiu permansisset, virtute divina et meritis sancti regis aperte sunt aures eius et solutum vinculum lingue eius. Et qui nunquam gallicum audierat pure, gallicum optime[360] loquebatur. Et cum audivit primo campanas pulsari, maximo terrore perterritus putabat statim totam ecclesiam supra se ruituram propter sonitum[361] et strepitum campanarum.

---

357. There are only small variants, although miracle 14.8 appears out of order here; it was originally the last paragraph in this section.
358. xiiii] xiii^m B
359. viderat] videatur B
360. optime] aptissime C
361. sonitum] sonicum B

APPENDIX: FIFTEENTH-CENTURY ADDITIONS
TO *GLORIOSISSIMI REGIS*

———

[14.0] Chapter 14. On the miracles done through the merits and prayers of the saint.

[14.1] On the day of the burial of blessed Louis a certain woman from Sées wholly recovered her sight, which she had previously lost, through the merits and prayers of the pious king.[77]

[14.2] Not long after a certain youth from Burgundy, deaf and mute from birth, coming with others to the tomb of blessed Louis, beseeched the help of the saint by a strange bow of the head as he had seen others do. And when he had stayed a little bit longer, by divine virtue and the merits of the saint king, his ears were opened and the chain of his tongue was loosened. And this one, who had never heard French clearly, spoke it perfectly. And when he first heard the church bells ring, he was petrified and believed that the entire church was about to fall down upon him at once on account of the sound and din of the bells.[78]

77. Cf. WC Miracle (hereafter, Mir.) no. 2; BL 12.3; BLQRF Mir. no. 1, RHF vol. 23, 165b–c; Jean de Vignay Mir. no. 1, RHF vol. 23, 69d.
78. Cf. WC Mir. no. 3; BL 12.4; BLQRF Mir. no. 2, RHF vol. 23, 165c–d; Jean de Vignay Mir. no. 2, RHF vol. 23, 69e–f.

[14.3] [BC] Eodem tempore quidam clericus veniens de Britannia Parisius transiens Carnotum,[362] ibidem incidit in tam gravem infirmitatem, quod omnino medici desperabant de eo. Sed emisso voto ad beatum Ludovicum statim sensit divinam adesse virtutem, in tantum quod in crastino iter et votum arripuit et perfecit, meritisque huius sancti[363] pristine restituitur sanitati.

[14.4] [BC] Non multo post magister Dudo phisicus domini regis qui beato Ludovico dum ageret in humanis medicus familiaris fuerat et sibi etiam astiterat in infirmitate qua decessit, febre acutissima Parysius tam graviter patiebatur, quod ipsemet de seipso, et alii medici desperabant. In nocte vero quarte diei sue egritudinis in maximo dolore capitis sompno arreptus, videbat beatum Ludovicum cui se devoverat, sibi assistere, vultum ylarem habentem et quamplurimum gloriosum. Et[364] sibi petenti ab eo in tanta necessitate auxilium et levamen videbatur sibi quod beatus Ludovicus circa ipsum officium cirurgici valde dulciter[365] exercebat. Et statim dictus infirmus excitatus post rigorem fortissimum et sudorem, virtute divina et meritis pii regis, plenarie fuit liberatus. Quod ut dixerunt medici tali die nulla apparenti digestione non potuit contingere per naturam.

[14.5] [BC] Eodem tempore apud castrum Lupere Parisius Petrus de Lauduno cambellanus[366] quondam beati Ludovici, tunc custos puerorum domini regis Philippi, cum in brachio suo dolorem intolerabilem pateretur, rex apposuit ad locum doloris capillos beati Ludovici quos apud se cum magna devotione servabat. In tercia vero appositione fuit

362. Carontum] *om.* C; B *under-dotted for expulsion*
363. B: 144v
364. Et] sibi *add.* C
365. dulciter] diligenter C
366. cambellanus] cambellarius BC

[14.3] During that same period, a certain cleric coming from Brittany to Paris, going through Chartres, fell into such a great illness that the doctors totally despaired for him. But, having sent a prayer to the blessed Louis, he immediately felt divine power to be near, to such a degree that the following day he took up and fulfilled both his journey and his vow, and was restored to his former health by the merits of the saint.[79]

[14.4] Not long after, Master Dudo, the doctor of the lord king [Philip III], who, while Louis was still living, had also been his familial doctor and attended him in the infirmity by which he died, suffered so badly from a very high fever in Paris that he himself and all other doctors despaired for him. On the night on the fourth day of his illness, with a great pain of his head, he was wrested from sleep, and he saw blessed Louis, to whom he had made a vow, attending him and having a extremely joyful and glorious countenance. And it seemed to him, who was asking Louis for help and relief in such great adversity, that blessed Louis sweetly exercised the duties of a surgeon on his behalf. Immediately the said patient was raised up after the strongest stiffness and sweat, by divine power and the merits of the pious king, having been fully liberated. The doctors said that at such a time this could not have happened by any obvious natural process of healing.[80]

[14.5] At the same time, at the palace of the Louvre in Paris, Peter of Laon, formerly the chamberlain of blessed Louis, and at that time guardian to the sons of the Lord King Philip, suffered an intolerable pain in his arm.[81] At the location of the pain, the king[82] placed some hairs of the blessed Louis that he had kept with him with great devotion.

79. Cf. WC Mir. no. 4; BL 12.5; BLQRF Mir. no. 3, RHF vol. 23, 165e; Jean de Vignay Mir. no. 3, RHF vol. 23, 69g.

80. Cf. WC Mir. no. 5; BL 12.6; BLQRF Mir. no. 4, RHF vol. 23, 165f–g; WSP *mir* no. 38; Jean de Vignay Mir. no. 4, RHF vol. 23, 69h–k.

81. Peter of Laon was in fact Louis' chamberlain; see WSP *vie* 6 (pp. 132–33). The fourteenth century texts read "cabellanus"; see RHF vol. 23, 165, and BNF Lat. 911, 29v.

82. This is a misreading. The miracles to BLQRF read here "ter apposuit." The copyist who produced B misread this as "rex apposuit," and this reading was then replicated in C.

plenarie liberatus, cum tamen prius suum non posset levare brachium nec ex eo aliquod operari.

[14.6] [BC] Eodem anno quedam mulier de Rothomago lumine oculorum privata adducta ex devotione ad sepulchrum sancti regis eiusdem meritis et precibus visum recuperavit omnino.

[14.7] [BC] Eodem anno sed diversis[367] diebus sibi succendentibus aliquibus interpositis intervallis, quinque mulieres et duo viri persone bene note probis et fide dignis, usum recte et bene incedendi quem ex diversis infirmitatibus et variis languoribus amiserant, beati Ludovici implorantes suffragia recuperaverunt ad sepe dictum sepulchrum eiusdem sancti meritis[368] et precibus gloriosis.[369]

[14.8] [BCD] Anno quo beatus Ludovicus fuit assumptus sanctorum cathalogo confessorum, in diversis mundi partibus ad invocationem ipsius, eius meritis et precibus,[370] multa contigerunt miracula laude digna. Ebroicis namque quadam die mercurii per quindecim[371] dies ante festum Ascensionis Domini, videlicet ultima tunc die aprilis,[372] contigit quemdam puerum quatuor annorum vel circa prope quoddam molendinum fuisse submersum, et per longum tempus, et post plura experimenta, a magna multitudine populi concurrente mortuum iudicatum; et post multas orationes et[373] invocationes Dei et beate Marie ac aliorum sanctorum nullum penitus in ipso sensum vel motum aut[374] vite vestigium[375] appareret.[376] Tandem omnipotenti Deo[377] misericorditer

367. diversis] temporibus et *add.* C
368. C: 231r
369. ch. 13: De miraculis factis meritis . . . sepulchrum eiusdem sancti meritis et precibus gloriosus] *om.* D [i.e., D omits the first seven miracles entirely]
370. in diversis mundi . . . meritis et precibus] *om.* D
371. D: 29v
372. aprilis] apprilis A
373. et] ac C
374. ipso sensum vel motum aut] *om.* D
375. vestigium] in ipso *add.* C
376. appareret] apparentem C; apparebat D
377. Deo] Domino C

And truly on the third application he was fully healed, whereas before he could not raise his arm or do anything with it.[83]

[14.6] In that same year a certain woman from Rouen, having lost the light from her eyes, and being led out of devotion to the tomb of that saintly king, because of his merits and prayers, recovered her sight entirely.[84]

[14.7] In that same year, but on different days that followed one another by a period of time, five women and two men, all well known for their probity and worthy of faith, who had lost the power of walking upright and well due to different infirmities and a variety of illnesses, asking help from blessed Louis, recovered at the often-mentioned tomb, through the merits and glorious prayers of that very same saint.[85]

[14.8] In the year that blessed Louis was raised into the catalogue of the confessor saints [1297], in various parts of the world and at the invocation to him, many miracles worthy of praise occurred through his merits and prayers. At Evreux, on a certain Wednesday about fifteen days before the feast of the Lord's Ascension, that is, on the last day of April, it happened that a certain boy of about four years of age had been submerged near a certain mill. For a long time and after many efforts, he was thought to be dead by the great number of people who had gathered around. And after many prayers and invocations to God and to blessed Mary and other saints, it appeared that there was no interior feeling, or movement, or sign of life in him. Finally, the Almighty God having mercifully arranged to exalt His saint in that crowd

---

83. Cf. WC Mir. no. 6; BL 12.7; BLQRF Mir. no. 5, RHF vol. 23, 165h; Jean de Vignay Mir. no. 5, RHF vol. 23, 70a–b. Note that in all other versions, it is Peter himself, not the king, who touches the hairs to the forearm.

84. Cf. WC Mir. no. 7; BL 12.8; BLQRF Mir. no. 6, RHF vol. 23, 165j; Jean de Vignay Mir. no. 6, RHF vol. 23, 70c.

85. Cf. BLQRF Mir. no. 7, RHF vol. 23, 165k; Jean de Vignay Mir. no. 7, RHF vol. 23, 70d.

disponente mirificare sanctum suum in illa turba populi, insonuit vox cuiusdam persone, ut dictus puer nominee Iohannes[378] devoveretur beato Ludovico, quod quedam matrona statim fecit cum candela de proprio lucro. Et matri dicti pueri desolate dicebant quamplures, ut statim deferretur ad ecclesiam fratrum predicatorum in honorem beati Ludovici noviter dedicatam. Mira res. Nam protinus,[379] facto voto, cepit puer gemere et portatus ad dictam ecclesiam,[380] plenarie fuit resuscitatus et restitutus pristine sanitati.

[14.9] [BC] Publicata vero in Francia canonizatione beati Ludovici quantus fuerit iubilus gaudii et exultationis unanimiter apud omnes nullus posset sufficienter referre. Tunc enim fides catholica cepit omni instantia constantissime roborari, spes firmissime erigi ad superna et caritas ferventius dilatari, et ad beatum Ludovicum fidelium devotio sollicitius excitari. Unde tunc temporis[381] in episcopatu Belvacensi quidam operarii decem vel circa fuerunt oppressi in quadam lapidicina,[382] et super cadente maxima gleba terre, fere per diem et noctem sic steterunt. Tandem quidam clericus, virtuteque[383] scientia, et honestate famosus iter faciens iuxta locum, audivit gemitum predictorum. Et appropinquans ac sic considerans miserabilem casum, et recolens beati Ludovici recentem canonizationem, confidens de eius meritis et precibus, descendens[384] de equo, cum fletu et lacrimis prostravit se ad adorationem,[385] specialiter beati Ludovici suffragium implorando.[386] Et cum diutius in oratione permansisset, assumpta fiducia de miraculo affuturo, surrexit, et homines a longe transeuntes vocavit. Et deponens[387] vestimenta cum aliis ad suffodiendum et succurrendum viriliter

378. nominee Iohannes] *om.* D
379. protinus] *om.* C
380. ecclesiam] portatus *add.* C
381. Publicata vero . . . tunc temporis] *om.* D
382. lapidicina] lapicidina B
383. virtuteque] virtute B
384. descends] que *add.* C
385. ad adoratione] in oratione C
386. implorando] impetrando C
387. deponens] reponens D

of people, someone's voice rang out that the boy, named John, be dedicated to blessed Louis, which a certain matron immediately did with a candle she bought with her own money. And many people were saying to the boy's mother [who had been deprived] of the said boy that the body be immediately carried to the Dominican church that had newly been dedicated in honor of blessed Louis.[86] Wondrous event! Straight away, after the vow had been made, the boy began to groan, and having been carried to the said church, was fully resuscitated and restored to his previous health.[87]

[14.9] The canonization of blessed Louis having been made public in France, there was such a great shout of joy and exultation by everyone that it cannot be sufficiently described. Then the Catholic faith began in every instance to be very steadfastly strengthened, hope for the heavens to be very firmly aroused, charity to be very fervently magnified, and devotion of the faithful to blessed Louis more eagerly stirred up. At that time, in the episcopacy of Beauvais, about ten workers were trapped in a quarry when a great clod of earth fell from above, and they were stuck there for nearly a day and night. Finally a certain cleric, well known for his virtue and knowledge and honesty, while journeying near this place, heard the groaning of these men. And approaching and considering this miserable accident, remembering the recent canonization of blessed Louis, and trusting in his merits and prayers, he got down from his horse and prostrated himself in weeping and tears in adoration, while imploring specifically the help of blessed Louis. And when he had remained for a while in prayer, with faith that a miracle would occur, he got up, and called to men who were traveling some distance off. And taking off his vestments with the others he courageously

---

86. The Dominican church of Saint Louis at Evreux was the first foundation to be dedicated to Louis after his canonization; a series of miracles recorded there for the year 1299 is published in RHF vol. 23, 41–44. On the foundation, see Chapotin, *Histoire de Dominicains de la Province de France*, 756–57.

87. Cf. BLQRF Mir. no. 15, RHF vol. 23, 167c–f; Jean de Vignay Mir. no. 8, RHF vol. 23, 70e–h.

hortabatur. Quid plura? Operante virtute divina per merita beati Ludovici, exigente eorum fide et[388] devotione, omnes fuerunt extracti, incolumes et illesi.[389]

[14.10] [BC] Fama autem predicti miraculi per patriam discurrente, contigit quosdam antiquos cophinos per Belvacum deportari, qui dicebantur beati Ludovici, ad quorum tactum cum fide et[390] devotione plures infirmi a variis languoribus sunt curati.

[14.11] [BC] Eodem tempore, rex Philippus reversus de Flandria, devotissimus avo suo, quoddam nobile monasterium sororum inclusarum ordinis fratrum predicatorum instituit fieri in honore Dei,[391] et gloriosissimi confessoris beati Ludovici, apud pysiacum, ubi predictus sanctus extitit oriundus. In cuius monasterii constructione plura antiqua edifica oportuit dirimi, ut ad hoc platea competens haberetur. Et cum quidam paries deberet cadere, clamantibus operariis qui eam suffoderant, et dicentibus quod omnes fugerent, contigit quemdam puerum musicantem a supercadente pariete quasi in medio deprehendi. Mira res! Stupefactis omnibus et dicentibus mortuus est, et nescientibus ex qua parte deberent puerum extrahere, quem mortuum iudicabant, quasi in medio illius parietis apparuit quedam fissura per quam mittentes brachia sua dictum puerum extraxerunt vivum penitus et illesum; et multitudo magna que aderat testimonium perhibuit veritati.

[14.12] [BC] In eadem villa postea satis cito ad fontes ubi beatus Ludovicus fuerat baptizatus in ecclesia beate Marie cepit fidelium devotio beati Ludovici suffragium implorare et impetrare frequentius beneficia

---

388. et] ac C
389. illesi] Et multitudo populi que aderat testimonium perhibuit veritati D. D *ends here.*
390. B: 145r
391. C: 231v

urged them to dig down and rescue [the men]. What more to say? By the work of divine power and through the merits of blessed Louis, with their faith and devotion urgent, they were all extracted, safe and unharmed.[88]

[14.10] The report of the aforesaid miracle spreading throughout the country, it happened that some old baskets which were said to have belonged to blessed Louis were being carried through Beauvais, at the touch of which, with faith and devotion, many people infirm from various illnesses were cured.[89]

[14.11] In that same time, King Philip [IV], returning from Flanders, extremely devoted to his grandfather, had arranged that, in honor of God and of the most glorious confessor blessed Louis, a noble monastery for cloistered Dominican women be built at Poissy, where the said saint had been born. In the construction of this monastery, it happened that many old buildings had to be torn down to make a suitable road. When the workmen who were undermining a certain wall that had to come down were shouting, saying that everyone ought to flee, it happened that a certain boy playing music [there] was buried, right, as it were, in the middle of the falling wall. Wondrous thing, this! While everyone, stunned, was saying that he was dead and that they did not know from which part they should pull out this boy who, they thought, was dead, just then a crack appeared in the middle of that wall through which, reaching their arms in, they dragged out the boy, fully alive and uninjured. And the great multitude who were there testified to this truth.[90]

[14.12] In that same town, quite soon after this, at the font in the church of the Blessed Mary where Louis had been baptized, devotion led the faithful to begin to entreat the help of blessed Louis and to obtain more frequently the miracles of health. And many glorious miracles

---

88. Cf. BLQRF Mir. no. 8, RHF vol. 23, 165k–166c; Jean de Vignay Mir. no. 9, RHF vol. 23, 70j–71b.

89. Cf. BLQRF Mir. no. 9, RHF vol. 23, 166d; Jean de Vignay Mir. no. 10, RHF vol. 23, 71c.

90. Cf. BLQRF Mir. no. 10, RHF vol. 23, 166e–f; Jean de Vignay Mir. no. 11, RHF vol. 23, 71d–h. On Poissy, see note 100 below.

sanitatis. Unde presente domino rege et regina cum sua nobili comitiva, contigerunt ibidem eodem anno plura miracula gloriosa.

[14.13] [BC] Quedem enim mulier de sancto Germano nota pluribus de curia regis, percussa sacro igne in multis partibus sui corporis, venit cum fide et[392] devotione ad predictum vas baptismale, et fusis ibidem lacrimis habunde, gloriosi regis devote patrocinium implorabat. Mox vero ut tetigit illos fontes, cepit illa nigredo et morbus predicti ignis abscedere[393] a toto corpore predicte[394] mulieris, exceptis digitis manus sinistre, in quibus illa nigredo et morbus[395] diutius apparebat. Et assistente ibi multitudine populi ac etiam pluribus de curia regis, paulatim et[396] visibiliter cepit dicta mulier digitos movere et tendere,[397] sicque morbus ille totaliter discessit, in tantum quod nullum penitus vestigium eius apparebat. Hoc autem miraculum plures de curia fide digni clarissime probaverunt, qui ad predictos fontes beati Ludovici sepedictam mulierem eodem modo, quo dictum est, infirmam et[398] postea omnino sanatam cum diligenti perscrutatione propriis oculis conspexerunt.

[14.14] [BC] Ibidem feria secunda sequente vir quidam de sancto Germano moribus honestus et in temporalibus sufficiens,[399] sibi ipsi multo tempore pedum ac crinium infirmitate depressus, in tantum quod ire non poterat nisi cum duabus[400] ligneis potentiis et cum maxima difficultate. Hic cum fide et[401] devotione ad predictos fontes beati Ludovici fusa oratione et facta oblatione, protinus[402] allevatum se[403]

392. et] ac C
393. abscedere] abcedere C
394. predicte] prefate C
395. et morbus] *om.* C
396. et] ac C
397. redere] extendere C
398. et] ac C
399. sufficiens] sufficies C
400. duabus] duobus C
401. et] ac C
402. protinus] penitus C
403. se] *add.* protinus C

occurred there that very year, when the king and queen with their noble retinue were present.[91]

[14.13] A certain women from Saint Germain known to many at the royal court was struck by the Holy Fire[92] in many parts of her body. She came with faith and devotion to the aforementioned baptismal font, and with abundant tears flowing, she devoutly begged the patronage of the holy king. And then, as soon as she touched the font, that blackness and the sickness of that fire began to depart from this woman's entire body, with the exception of the fingers of her left hand, where that blackness and disease lasted a while longer. And in the presence of the multitude of people there, and even of several members of the royal court, that woman began visibly to move and spread her fingers, and so the disease departed completely, to such an extent that no vestige at all was apparent. And many trustworthy persons of the court testified with great clarity to this miracle, who with careful scrutiny observed with their own eyes, at the aforementioned font of St. Louis, this oft-mentioned woman ill, and then afterwards, totally healthy in precisely the way described above.[93]

[14.14] On the following Monday in the same place, a certain man from Saint Germain, of honest character and sufficient wherewithal, was cast down for a long time by an illness of feet and hair to such an extent that he could not walk without two wooden crutches and with the greatest difficulty. This man, with faith and devotion, pouring out prayers and making oblations at blessed Louis' font, immediately felt relieved, and, throwing aside his crutches, he began to walk through

91. Cf. BLQRF Mir. no. 11, RHF vol. 23, 166g; Jean de Vignay Mir. no. 12, RHF vol. 23, 71g–k.
92. Known elsewhere as "Saint Anthony's Fire"; erysipelas.
93. Cf. BLQRF Mir. no. 12, RHF vol. 23, 166h–k; Jean de Vignay Mir. no. 12, RHF vol. 23, 71g–k.

perceperat, et dimissis potentiis cepit ire per ecclesiam potenter et recte sine adminiculo cuiuscumque. Et sic meritis et precibus beati Ludovici restitutus fuit pristine sanitati.

[14.15] [BC] Eodem modo, quidam serviens armorum, nomine Henricus de Bituricas qui usum incedendi gravi languore amiserat, cum magno labore et adminiculo potentiarum adductus, cum magna devotione beati Ludovici, cuius serviens fuerat, suffragium implorabat. Et cum ibi devotam orationem fudisset, satis cito meritis et precibus gloriosi regis fuit propriis viribus restitutus. Et ibidem etiam plura alia contigerunt et frequenter contingunt[404] miracula meritis et precibus beati Ludovici ad laudem et gloriam redemptoris, cui honor et gloria per[405] infinita seculorum secula. Amen.

[15.0] [BC] De translatione corporis sancti Ludovici. Capitulum xv^m.[406]

[15.1] Beatus Ludovicus multorum annorum spatio regni francorum regimini discrete et pacifice prefuit. Hic cum tricesimum quartum etatis sue[407] attigisset, in terre sancte subsidium cum copiosa exercitus multitudine transfretavit. Cumque ad partes ultramarinas venisset, post Damiate captionem ab exercitu christiano, subsecuta ipsius exercitus generali egritudine, in manus soldani et sarracenorum incidit, illo permittente qui de malis bona novit elicere, et facere cum temptatione proventum. Nam soldano ipso post cito a suis interempto, predictus rex fuit non sine divini ut pie creditur operatione miraculi[408] liberatus. [15.2] In partibus illis vir sanctus pro Christo tot et tantos agones habuit,[409] tam virtuosos actus exercuit, tanta sancte edificationis exempla prebuit, quod lingua[410] vix sufficeret enarrare. Inde vero

404. et frequenter contigunt] *om.* C
405. C: 232r
406. B: no chapter number
407. sue] annum *add.* C
408. miraculi] *om.* C
409. B: 145v.
410. lingua] carnis *add.* C

the church, strongly and upright, without anyone's support. And so, through the merits and prayers of the blessed Louis, he was restored to his former health.[94]

[14.15] In the same way, a certain sergeant at arms named Henry of Bourges, who had lost the ability to walk through a serious illness, was brought forward with great effort and the help of crutches, and with great devotion he implored the aid of blessed Louis, whose sergeant he had been. And when he had poured out there a devout prayer, he was quite quickly restored to his own strength, through the merits and prayers of the glorious king. And there also many other [miracles] occurred and frequently continue to occur, through the merits and prayers of blessed Louis, in praise and glory of the Redeemer, to whom honor and glory, for ever and ever. Amen.[95]

[15.0] Chapter 15. On the translation of the body of Saint Louis.[96]

[15.1] Blessed Louis for a space of many years oversaw the rule of the kingdom of France with discretion and in peace. This man, when he had reached his thirty-fourth year, in the aid of the Holy Land crossed the sea with the great multitude of an army. When he had arrived at these overseas lands, after the capture of Damietta by the Christian army, and following a general illness of that army, he fell into the hands of the Sultan and the Saracens—the One permitting who knows how to elicit good things from evil and to make a good outcome from a trial. For the sultan was killed a short while later by his own men, and thus the aforesaid king was freed by the work of a divine miracle, as is piously believed. [15.2] In those regions, the saintly man endured many and great agonies for Christ; he performed so many virtuous deeds, and he

94. Cf. BLQRF Mir. no. 13, RHF vol. 23, 166l–167a; Jean de Vignay Mir. no. 13, RHF vol. 23, 71l.

95. Cf. BLQRF Mir. no. 14, RHF vol. 23, 167b; Jean de Vignay Mir. no. 14, RHF vol. 23, 72b.

96. Sections 15.1–15.11 are taken from the original lections composed for the translation of Louis' head in 1306. The text survives in BNF Lat 14511, 179r–182r. See Gaposchkin, *Making of Saint Louis*, 205.

morte sue matris audita, reversus in Franciam sic sanctitatis insistebat operibus, quod ut ipsius ieiunia, vigilias, et disciplinas multimodas pretereamus plura monasteria et[411] pauperum hospitalia construxit, infirmos et decumbentes inibi visitando personaliter, et manibus propriis ac flexo genu cibaria eis ministrando. Hoc autem humilitatis immense ministerium leprosis quibusdam legitur impendisse. [15.3] Sic autem ad incrementum fidei et liberationem terre sancte votis ardentibus anhelabat,[412] assumpto denuo signo crucis ad partes[413] rediit cum immenso exercitu transmarinas. In quibus post captionem Carthaginis in castris ante Tunicium gravis infirmitatis violentia superatus, sacramenta ecclesiastica cum summa devotione, premissa sui salutari successorium admonitione, suscepit. Instante vero verisimiliter hora mortis, verba que Christus moriens protulisse legitur ista videlicet "in manus tuas domine commendo spiritum meum" devotus[414] exprimens, suum spiritum suo reddidit Creatori. [15.4] [BC] Cum vero vite presentis functus curriculis, verius viveret quam vixisset, noluit Dominus eius mundo supprimi sanctitatem. Nam cui meritorum pluralitate prefulsisse contulerat,[415] miraculorum diversitate multimode clarere concessit.[416] Contractis siquidem artuum extensione subvenit, curvis terram ferme tangentibus stare plene ac recte incedere[417] restituit, strumosis beneficium liberationis impendit,[418] quam pluribus etiam aliis qui diversis languoribus tenebantur subvenit, plena reddita sanitate.

411. et] par *add.* C

412. terre sancte vocis ardentibus anhelabat] terre sancte anhelabat votis ardentibus C

413. partes] denuo *add.* C

414. devotus] devote C

415. contulerat] concesserat C

416. concessit] contulit C

417. incedere] dedit *add.* C

418. impedit] *om.* C

offered so many examples of saintly teachings, that it is scarcely possible for the tongue to relate them. After he heard about the death of his mother and had returned to France, he then set about pursuing saintly works, and granted that we pass over his many and varied fasts, vigils, and disciplines, he built many monasteries and hospitals for the poor, and he visited the infirm and bedridden in those places, and ministered food to them with his own hand while on bended knee. This man is even said to have devoted the ministry of his immense humility to certain lepers. [15.3] Then he so desired with ardent vows the advancement of the faith and the liberation of the Holy Land, and having assumed anew the sign of the cross, he returned to the lands across the sea with an immense army. There, having been overcome by the violence of a grave illness in the camp outside of Tunis after the capture of Carthage, he took the ecclesiastical sacraments with the greatest devotion, having sent his salvific advice to his successors. Truly, with the hour of his death imminent, devoutly expressing the words that Christ is said to have uttered as he was dying—"Into your hands, Lord, I commend my spirit" [Luke 23.46]—he rendered his spirit unto his Creator. [15.4] Indeed, when he had discharged the course of this present life, in order that he might live [even] more truly than he had lived, God did not want his sanctity concealed in this world. To him whom He had given the ability to shine forth with so many merits, He thus made gleam with a diversity of many kinds of miracles. He [Louis] succored the palsied by stretching out their joints, he restored to those bowed over and almost touching the earth the ability to stand fully and walk upright, he extended the benefits of freedom to those with scrofula, and he helped as many others as possible who were afflicted by all kinds of illnesses, returning them to full health.

[15.5] Propter que romane sedi presidens Bonifacius scilicet[419] octavus, curiose ac solempnis inquisitionis diligentia, et districti examinis discussione premissis, de communi cardinalium et prelatorium omnium tunc apud sedem eundem existentium consilio et assensu, sanctorum hunc cathalogo sollempniter asscripsit. [15.6] Facta est autem beati Ludovici canonizatio anno domini millesimo ducentesimo nonagesimo septimo, tercio idus Augusti. Eodem vero anno octavo kalendas Septembris qui dies fuit revolutis viginiti septem[420] annis natalis ipsius, de loco in quo per dominum Philippum regem Francie eius filium sepulchrum sibi fuerat cum patribus suis prout magnificentiam regalem decuit gloriose constructum, per dominum regem Philippum predicti domini Philippi filium, fuit venerabile[421] corpus ipsius reverenter extractum et sollempniter elevatum, sollempnibusque[422] processione ac predicatione premissis, in capsa argentea sursum sita e regione corporis sanctissisimi[423] patris[424] et patroni regum francie beati Dyonisii collocatum. Interfuerunt autem elevationi predicte una cum domino rege archiepicopi, episcopi et[425] abbates, duces, comites, et barones regni Francie, et[426] religiosorum et popularum multitudine[427] copiosa. [15.7] Canonizationem beati Ludovici, quam mater ecclesia meritis et miraculis eius approbatis ediderit, sponsus ecclesie Christus rationabiliter approbandam ostendit. Nam cum antea magnis et mirabilibus miraculis claruisset ex tunc maioribus et mirabilioribus choruscavit. [15.8] Cecis quidem visus, claudis gressus, surdis auditus, loquela mutis reddita sunt ad ipsius invocationem in plerisque regni partibus restituta, nonnullos etiam mortuos specialiter duos, unum in Remensi et alium in Eboracensi dyocesi suscitavit. De tot et de tantis miraculis unicum hic videtur[428] merito recitandum.

---

419. scilicet] *om.* C
420. septem] xcvii B
421. C: 232v
422. sollempnibusque] solemp [sic] sollempnibusque C
423. corporis sanctissimi] *om.* C
424. patris] sanctissimi *add.* C
425. et] *om.* C
426. et] ac C
427. multitudine] multitudo C
428. miraculis unicum hic videtur] miraculis unum videtur et unicum hic C

[15.5] On account of this, Pope Boniface VIII, after the diligence of a careful and solemn inquest and with an investigation of strict inquiry by men who had been sent ahead, and with the assent and advice of the community of cardinals and all prelates present at the papal see, solemnly ascribed [Louis] into the catalogue of saints. [15.6] The canonization of blessed Louis was done on the third ides of August in the year 1297.[97] In that same year, on the eighth calends of September, twenty-seven years having passed since the year he was born into Heaven,[98] from the place where his glorious tomb had been built by his son, Louis Philip [III], King of France, along with his forefathers as befits the royal majesty, his venerable body was reverently exhumed and solemnly elevated by the Lord King Philip [IV] (son of the aforesaid King Philip [III]).[99] With solemnities, a procession, and a sermon having been performed, he was placed in a silver reliquary, located up near the body of the most blessed father and the patron of the kings of France, blessed Denis. Present at this elevation together with the lord king were archbishops, bishops, dukes, counts, and the barons of the kingdom of France, a great many religious men, and a great multitude of ordinary people. [15.7] Christ, the bridegroom of the Church, revealed that the canonization of blessed Louis, which the Mother Church had proclaimed once his merits and miracles had been confirmed, had indeed been rightly confirmed. For, since beforehand he had shone with great and wondrous miracles, from that point on he gleamed with ever greater and more miraculous ones. [15.8] Sight to the blind, footsteps to the lame, hearing to the deaf, and speech to the mute were returned at the invocation of [Louis], these same things restored in many parts of the kingdom. And he even revived some from the dead, two in particular, one in Reims and the other in the diocese of Evreux. Of so many and such great miracles, one in particular must be recounted.

97. The third ides, that is, August 11, in the Roman Calendar.

98. The author is mistaken here. The translation ceremony took place only in 1298, a year later. He is correct that it occurred on August 25, the anniversary of Louis' death (which was referred to as the *dies natalis*, the birth day, since this is the day the saint was "born" into Heaven).

99. On the tomb of Saint Louis, see Wright, "The Tomb of Saint Louis" and "The Royal Tomb Program in the Reign of St. Louis"; also Brown, "The Chapels and Cult of Saint Louis at Saint-Denis."

[15.9] Cum enim dominus rex Philippus huius sancti nepos, apud Pysiacum unde sanctus ipse traxit originem, monasterium sollempne sororum[429] ordinis sancti Dominici, construi faceret in honore ipsius, ipso rege tunc in castro Pysiaci existente, mulier quedam igne sacro per totum brachium accensa, tactu vasis lapidei in quo sanctus baptizatus fuerat, plenam ibi recuperavit perceptibiliter sanitatem. Qui hoc vidit cum aliis quampluribus utriusque sexus mirantibus, et inde Deo et[430] beato Ludovico laudes acclamantibus testmonium perhibuit; et hec ad futuri temporis edificationem fidelium in scripto[431] redegit. [15.10] Sanctus autem iste dum vitam in humanis ageret, ad sacrosancta dominice passionis insignia ceterasque reliquias, quas[432] Parisius in capella palacii cum summa reverentia collacaverat, sedulam semper et specialem devotionem habebat.[433] [15.11] Ob hoc igitur et ut fidelium augeretur ad ipsum devotio, in cor regis immisit Dominus ut[434] ad capellam ipsam venerandum dicti sancti caput, cum omni solempnitate que fieri debet in talibus convocatione generali prelatorum et principum propter hoc facta, specialiter transferretur.[435] Decens siquidem esse conspexit, ut ubi caput est tocius regni Francie, ibi caput illius qui francis tam gloriose prefuit, et profuit cum ingenti reverentia collocatum veneratione condigna in perpetuum coleretur ad laudem et honore[436] domini nostri Ihesu Christi,[437] qui cum[438] patre et spiritu sancto vivit et regnat[439] secula seculorum. Amen.[440]

[15.12] [B only] Ora pro nobis beate confessor Ludovice, ut digni efficamur promissione Christi.[441] [15.13] [B only] Collatione. Deus qui

429. sororum] *om.* C
430. et] ac C
431. scripto] commendando *add.* C
432. quas] *om.* C
433. B: 146r
434. ad] domini sit ut *add.* C
435. transferretur] trans C
436. et honore] *om.* C
437. Christi] eiusque honorem *add.* C
438. cum] deo *add.* C
439. regnat] trinus et unus per infinita *add.* C
440. Amen] Explicit vita sanctissimi Ludovici. Confessoris quondam francorum regis incliti de stripe karolidarum. *add.* C
441. Christi] Oremus *add.* C

[15.9] When once the Lord King Philip [IV], this saint's grandson, was building in [Louis'] honor an illustrious monastery for Dominican nuns at Poissy where the saint was born,[100] while the king himself was residing in the castle in Poissy, a certain woman whose entire arm was aflame with holy fire,[101] at the touch of the baptismal font where the saint had been baptized, there clearly recovered her full health. He [Philip] saw this along with many others of both sexes and offered witness to those acclaiming praise to God and blessed Louis, and he set these things down in writing for the edification of the faithful in future times. [15.10] This saint while he was living always had a particular and special devotion for the sacrosanct insignia of the Lord's Passion and the other relics which, with the greatest reverence, he had placed in the palace chapel in Paris. [15.11] On account of this and in order to increase the devotion of the faithful toward [Louis], the Lord sent into the heart of the king that the head of this saint be venerated at that very chapel with all the solemnity due in such things, and with a general convocation of prelates and princes held on account of this, be specially transferred. Indeed, He further deemed it fitting that where the head of the entire kingdom of France is, there the head of that one who so gloriously ruled over and benefited France should be placed with great reverence, [and] shall be forever worshipped with worthy reverence for the praise and honor of our Lord Jesus Christ, who lives and reigns with the Father and the Holy Spirit, forever and ever and ever. Amen.

[15.12][102] Pray for us blessed Louis confessor, that we may become worthy of the promise of Christ. [15.13] Collect: O God who brought

---

100. Louis was born on April 25, 1214 (or perhaps 1215) at the royal residence of Poissy (about twenty miles from Paris) and was baptized in the local parish church, which was dedicated to the blessed Virgin. After Louis' canonization, Philip IV founded a monastery for Dominican nuns in Louis' honor at Poissy. Work on the monastery began immediately after Louis' canonization and it is assumed that Philip had begun these plans well before August 25, 1297. On the history and the building, see Erlande-Brandenburg, "La Priorale Saint-Louis de Poissy" and "Art et politique."

101. See note 92 above.

102. This was the standard collect for Louis' feast day.

beatum Ludovicum confessorem tuum de terreno ac temporali regno ad celestis et etiam regni gloriam transtulisti eius quesumus meritis et intercessione regis regum Ihesu Christi filii tui nos coheredes efficias, et eiusdem regni tribuas esse consortes, per eundem dominum nostrum Ihesum Christum filium tuum[442] qui tecum vivit et regnat in unitate spiritus sancti deus per omnia secula seculorum. Amen.

[15.14] [BC] Explicit vita ac conversatio[443] beatissimi Ludovici confessoris quondam francorum regis incliti deo gratiae.[444]

---

442. Per eum de domini . . . filium tuum] *om.* C
443. ac conversatio beatissimi] sanctissimi C
444. deo gratie] de stripe karolidarum C

blessed Louis your confessor up from the earthly and temporal king-dom to the glory of the heavenly kingdom, we beseech You through his merits and through the intercession of the King of kings, Jesus Christ your son, to make us co-inheritors and grant that we share in the same kingdom, through Him, our Lord Jesus Christ, your son, who lives and reigns with you, in unity of the Holy Spirit, God, forever and ever. Amen.

[15.14] Here ends the life and the conduct in that life of the most blessed Louis confessor, formerly the illustrious king of the French by the grace of God.

2

BEATUS LUDOVICUS

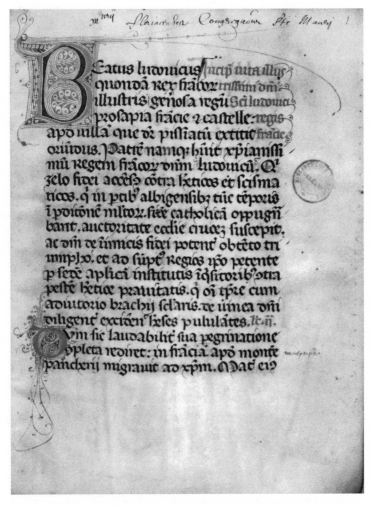

Orleans BM 348 [siglum O], 1r. Courtesy of the Bibliothèque municipale d'Orleans.

Beatus Ludovicus (BHL no. 5043b), like *Gloriosissimi regis,* was written shortly after the canonization. As with *Gloriosissimi Regis,* it echoes William of Saint-Pathus' *Vie* and was probably based on the canonization proceedings. Unlike *Gloriosissimi Regis,* however, its author also had access to William of Chartres' life of Louis, and he incorporates some of William's themes pertaining to Louis' royalty. Our evidence for the early date of *Beatus Ludovicus* comes from its anterior relationship to the liturgical vita BLQRF. *Beatus Ludovicus* is not a polished text, but it is important for the history of the construction of Louis' sanctity, both because it represents one of the earliest post-canonization efforts to synthesize the story of Louis' saintly life and, critically, because it formed the basis of the liturgical vita BLQRF, which was the single *most* widely known hagiographical text of Louis in the Middle Ages. Additionally, as the reader will see, its materials and content are in tune with and often resonant with *Gloriosissimi regis,* indicating, it appears, mutual influences and the same well of sources. But they are different texts, not mutually dependent, and they evince different interests and emphases.

Beatus Ludovicus comprises twelve chapters and includes a list of seventeen miracles. The anonymous author's access to William of Chartres' little-known or little-disseminated De *vita et actibus,* together with the text's emphasis on the Dominican role in the education of Louis, suggests a Dominican cleric in the ambit of the royal court as its author.

The text of *Beatus Ludovicus* survives in a single manuscript, Orleans BM 348 (siglum O), which probably dates to the second quarter of the fourteenth century.[1] This manuscript is an odd collection of liturgical and paraliturgical texts. It is not a lectionary or a breviary per se, but rather a kind of *libelli,* or "shrine book"—that is, a manuscript that includes a series of texts important to a particular institution but that does not follow the liturgical year. A note in the manuscript indi-

---

1. It has been dated anywhere from "after 1297" (based on the date of Louis' canonization) to the fifteenth century. It must date before 1424, at which time the chapel of Notre-Dame des Miracles, founded by John XXII in 1320, was defunct. The pen flourishes of the incipit "B" on fol. 1 indicate a date of the first half of the fourteenth century.

cates that it was owned at one time by a cleric associated with the chapel of Notre-Dame des Miracles in Avignon, and may have been copied for the chapel, and it later showed up in the library of St.-Benoît (Fleury).[2] In addition to the texts for Louis (fols. 1–22r), MS 348 includes a vita of Saint Margaret (fols. 22v–37) and offices for the dedi - cation of a church (fols. 37–41), the conception of the Blessed Virgin (fols. 41–44), the dedication of the Church of Santa Maria Maggiore in Rome (fols. 44–50), Saint Gaudens martyr (fols. 50–61), and Saint Bernard Commingnes (fols. 61–76v).

The section devoted to Louis is written in a different hand from the rest of the manuscript and was added later. It includes *Beatus Ludovicus* (fols. 1–18), our text here, and also the unique witness to an early redaction of a liturgy for Louis (fols. 18–22). The latter is the secularized version of the Cistercian office for Louis, *Lauda celestis,* which was then the basis for the liturgical office in use at St.-Denis and St.-Germain-des-Près in Paris.[3] The vita itself runs from fol. 1 to fol. 14v; the miracles run from fol. 14v to fol. 18.

2. Mostert, *The Library of Fleury,* 183; Samaran and Marichal, *Catalogue des manuscrits en écriture latine,* vol. 7, 497.

3. On the liturgical tradition for *Lauda celestis,* see Gaposchkin, "The Mo - nastic Office," 143–74.

BEATUS LUDOVICUS

[1.0] Incipit vita illustrissimi domini sancti Ludovici regis Francie.

[1.1] Beatus Ludovicus quondam rex francorum illustris generosa regum prosapia Francie & Castelle apud villam que dicitur pissiacum extitit oriundus. Patrem namque habuit christianissimum regem francorum dominum Ludovicum, qui zelo fidei accensus contra hereticos et scismaticos, qui in partibus albigensibus tunc temporis in perditionem multorum fidem catholicam oppugnabant, auctoritate ecclesie crucem suscepit, ac Deum de inimicis fidei potenter obtento triumpho et ad sumptus regios ipso petente per sedem apostolicam institutis inquisitoribus contra pestem heretice pravitatis, qui omni tempore cum adiutorio brachii secularis, de vinea domini diligenter exciderent hereses pululantes.[1] Dum sic laudabiliter sua peregrinatione[2] completa rediret in Franciam apud Montem[3] Pancherii migravit ad Christum. [1.2] Mater eius[4] domina Blancha[5] regina quondam [regis[6]] Castelle filia viro suo ac domino sic orbata, beatum Ludovicum adhuc puerum, diligentissime enutrivit. Et bonis et religiosis viris precipue fratribus ordinis predicatorum in sanctitate ac sciencia scripturarum tradidit imbuendum, de quo ordine quo advixit habuit confessorem. Cum et aliis probis viris, frequenter de scripturis & pertinentibus ad salutem, dulci ac devoto fovebatur alloquio, ex verbis et exemplis sanctorum semper proficiens *de virtute in virtutem* [Ps. 83.8]. Et dum ipse sub tutela domine matris sue decurreret puerilem etatem, ipsam strenue potenter ac iuste administravit. Iura regni et contra plures adversarios,

---

1. pululantes] *in red,* lectio ii, appears within original text but as modification. The chapter titles seem to be original to the text.
2. perigrinatione] *corr. from* pegrinatione
3. montem] *right margin, later hand:* Montpanyra
4. 1v
5. Blancha] *left margin* Blancii
6. regis] *absent in* MS, but consistent with other traditions.

BLESSED LOUIS

[1.0] Here begins the life of the most illustrious lord saint Louis, king of France.

[1.1] Blessed Louis, the illustrious late king of the French, was born in Poissy, of the noble lineage of the kings of France and Castile. His father, Lord Louis [VIII], most Christian king of the French, who, burning with the zeal of faith against the heretics and schismatics who were besieging the Catholic faith at the time [and] bringing many to ruin in the Albigensian regions, took up the cross with the authority of the church. Having achieved a decisive triumph for God against the enemies of the faith at royal expense, he asked the apostolic see to institute inquisitors to thereafter counter the pestilence of heretical depravity,[1] [and] aided by the secular arm, they diligently weeded out the heresies sprouting in the vineyard of the Lord. At Montpencier, as he was returning to France, his pilgrimage laudably complete, he departed to Christ.[2] [1.2] [Louis'] mother, the late Lady Queen Blanche, daughter of [the king of] Castile, bereaved of her husband and lord, raised the blessed Louis from boyhood with the greatest care. So that he be educated in sanctity and the knowledge of scripture she entrusted him to good and religious men, especially those of the Order of the Preachers; he had a confessor from this order as long as he lived. And, also [along with] other honest men, he was frequently nourished with sweet and devout encouragement in the scriptures in those things pertaining to salvation, and by the words and examples of the saints, [so that] he progressed always from virtue unto virtue [Ps. 83.8]. He traversed his youth under the care of his mother, who oversaw this stage with vigor, strength, and justice. She defended with her skillful foresight the laws of

---

1. Louis VIII (r. 1223–1226) participated in the Albigensian Crusade in 1219 and again in 1226. The Albigensian Crusade, called by Pope Innocent III, began in 1209 and was directed against heretics of southern France, often called Cathars or Albigensian heretics. The so-called "inquisitors of heretical depravity" were appointed by the pope, with royal support, beginning in the early 1230s.

2. Cf. GB 3 (p. 4); WSP *vie* 1 (pp. 12–13); GR 1.2.

qui tunc apparebant, solerti providencia defensavit. [1.3] Insuper et beatum Ludovicum Deum timere ab infancia et abstinere ab omni peccato quam plurimum affectantem ipsam sibi pluries dixi[sse][7] seipso referente didicimus in laudem pie matris. Dicebat "inquit de me, quod pre cunctis mortalibus diligebat[8] quod si infirmarer ad mortem, et sanari non possem nisi facerem tale quid quo peccarem mortaliter, plus vellet me mori, quam si meum offenderem creatorem." [1.4] Quod videlicet verbum bone matris cordi devoti filii sic adhesit, et letalis criminis contagium divina se protegente gratia numquam sensiit, prout firma discreta et sancta confessorum suorum assertione monstratur.

[2.0] Capitulum ii. De devoto sue puerilis instructione.[9]

[2.1] Puerilibus igitur annis innocenter transactis, providencia carissime & matris, procerum ac sapientum regni, uxorem duxit primogenitam[10] comitis Provincie dominam videlicet Margaritam. [2.2] Qui ambo in domo dei ambulantes unanimiter cum consensus [cf. Ps. 54.15]; prolem nobilissimam genuerunt, quam vir sanctus summo opere religiose studuit educare, et ad amorem dei contemptumque mundi et cognitionem sui salutaribus monitis et exempli sepius informare. Volebat siquidem quod pueri sui et singuli litteras addiscerent; et quod horas de beata[11] virgine integraliter dicerent; et quod non solum missam set ad matutinas divinasque & horas canonicas cum cantus devote audiret; et quod frequenter predicaretur coram eis publice et privatim. [2.3] Serta quoque de rosis seu capellos quosque eos portare sextis feriis [prohibebat[12]] propter coronam spineam tali die impositam capiti Salvatoris.

---

7. Original manuscript read "dixit," with a scribal emendation adding "isse" interlinearly. It is not clear whether the scribe intended "dixisse" or "dixisset"—we are choosing the latter.
8. 2r
9. rubric in red
10. *in right margin, later hand,* Margareta uxor Ludovici
11. 2v
12. prohibebat] *om. in* MS, added here

the kingdom against the many adversaries who appeared at this time.[3] [1.3] Moreover, we learned (because Louis himself spoke of it in praising his pious mother) that she herself had spoken many times to him, desiring that Louis fear God from infancy and abstain from all sin as much as possible. He said, "She used to say about me, because she loved me above all other mortals, that if I were sick unto death and I were not able to get well except by committing a mortal sin, that she would prefer that I die than that I should offend the Creator."[4] [1.4] The devout son took to heart this saying of his good mother and, as demonstrated by the irrefutable, distinguished, and saintly testimony of his confessors, protected by divine grace, he never felt the contagion of mortal sin.[5]

[2.0] Chapter 2. On the devout instruction of his children.

[2.1] Having passed his boyhood years in innocence, he, owing to the solicitude of both his very dear mother and the wise noblemen of the kingdom, married the eldest daughter of the Count of Provence, namely, the Lady Marguerite.[6] [2.2] These two walked in the house of God in fellowship and in harmony [cf. Ps. 54.15]; they engendered most noble offspring, whom this saintly man greatly desired to educate religiously and instruct very often in the love of God, contempt for the world, and self-knowledge through salutary admonitions and examples. He wanted each of his sons to learn letters, say the hours of the Blessed Virgin in their entirety, hear devoutly not only mass but also matins and the singing of the divine and canonical hours, and hear sermons frequently both in public and in private.[7] [2.3] Further, [he forbade] them to wear either wreaths of roses or hats of any kind on Fridays on account of the crown of thorns that had been placed on the head of the Savior on that very day.[8]

---

3. Cf. GB 4 (p. 4); WSP *vie* 1 (p. 13); GR 1.3.
4. Cf. GB 4 (pp. 4–5); WSP *vie* 1 (p. 13); GR 1.4.
5. Cf. GR 1.5.
6. Cf. GR 2.1.
7. Cf. GB 13 (p. 7); GR 3.1–2.
8. Cf. GB 13 (p. 7); GR 3.3.

[3.0] Capitulum iii.[13] De suis penitentiis & corporis afflictione.[14]

[3.1] Ac vero deo placere cupiens, corpus suum castigans et in servitutem redigens [cf. 1 Cor. 9.27], ipsum spiritui servire cogebat. Multo
enim tempore in adventu domini et quadragesima et in vigiliis beate virginis, clam ad carnem cilicio utebatur. Sed eius confessor tandem considerans quod huiusmodi asperitate cilicii nimium[15] gravabatur, et quod
eius valitudo esset neccessaria toti ecclesie maxime regno Francie, vix
cum instancia obtinuit quod vir sanctus uti cilicio pretermisit. In cuius
tamen recompensationem volebat quod idem confessor suus illis diebus
suis quibus portare cilicium consueverat, quadraginta solidos[16] parisientium secreto pauperibus erogaret. Nec et hiis contentus, nonnumquam
in quadragesima quadam fascia de cilicio se cingebat. [3.2] Ieuinabat
enim omni tempore sextis feriis, quarta quoque feria a carnibus abstinebat. Aliquamdiu et hoc idem fecit die lune. Sed hanc abstinenciam
secunde ferie dimisit, inductus concilio medicorum.[17] Pane et aqua tantummodo in Vigiliis Beate Marie virginis, et in parasceve et in aliquibus
aliis per annum solennitatibus ieiuniis utebatur. Sextis quodque feriis in
quadragesima et in adventu a piscibus et fructibus abstinebat, nisi quod
interdum propter debilitatem corporis accipere, saltem[18] de uno genere
piscium et fructuum acquiescere suo confessore suadente solebat.

[4.0] Capitulum iiii. De eius vera humilitate.[19]

[4.1] Omnium virtutum decor humilitas adeo refulgebat in eo, ut tam
magnum considerantes et semetipsum tam humilem exhibentem &
magni et parvi, qui prorumperent in lacrimas continere non possent.
[4.2] Quolibet namque sabbato consueverat[20] flexis genibus in loco secretissimo pauperum quorumdam abluere pedes et post ablutionem

13. iii] *corr. from* iiii
14. rubric in red
15. nimium] *corr. from* ninium
16. 3v
17. Concilio medicorum] cf. WC 35, in the same context
18. saltem] *corr. from* salte
19. rubric in red
20. 3v

[3.0] Chapter 3. On his penitence and the mortification of his flesh.

[3.1] Desiring to please God, [Louis] forced his body to submit to his spirit by castigating it and reducing it to servitude [cf. 1 Cor. 9.27]. Often in Advent and Lent and on the vigils of the Blessed Virgin, he would secretly wear a hair shirt. His confessor, thinking that the harshness of the hair shirt was too great a burden, since the whole church and especially the kingdom of France depended on his good health, insisted that the saintly man desist from wearing it. In compensation for this, [Louis] proposed that on those days that he had been used to wearing the hair shirt, his confessor would secretly distribute forty Parisian *solidos* to the poor. But not content with even this, in Lent he would still sometimes wrap [himself] in a strip of hair shirt.[9] [3.2] He fasted throughout the year on Fridays, and he abstained from meat on Wednesdays. For a time, he did this also on Mondays, but on the advice of his doctors, he stopped this Monday abstinence. On the vigils of the Blessed Virgin Mary, on Good Friday, and on other solemn days of the year, he fasted on bread and water. He also abstained from fish and fruit on Fridays during Lent and Advent, except on occasion when, because of an infirmity of the body, he let himself be persuaded by his confessor to eat at least one type of fish or fruit.[10]

[4.0] Chapter 4. On his true humility.

[4.1] Humility, the glory of all virtues, shone in him so much that men, both great and small, seeing [Louis] at once so mighty and so humble, could not refrain from bursting into tears.[11] [4.2] Indeed, sometimes on Saturdays he would, on bended knee, in a very secret place, wash the feet of some poor men, and, after washing them, would dry and

---

9. Cf. GB 17–18 (p. 10); WSP *vie* 14 (p. 122); GR 5.2.

10. Cf. GB 18 (pp. 10–11); WSP *vie* 14 (p. 121); WSP *sermo* 26 (p. 287); GR 5.3; WC, p. 35.

11. Cf. WSP *vie* 12 (p. 104); GR 6.1.

tergere ac humiliter osculari. Similiter aquam devote fundebat eorum manibus abluendis, et postmodum cuilibet eorum cum osculo manus certam denariorum summam porrigebat. [4.3] Quandoque etiam centum viginti pauperibus qui cotidie in domo eius reficiebantur habundanter ipsemet serviebat. Et in vigiliis solemnibus ac quibusdam certis diebus per annum ducentis pauperibus discumbentibus priusquam ipse comederet, manu propria quandoque fercula ministravit. [4.4] Semper enim in prandio et cena prope se tres senes pauperes recumbentes habebat, quibus de cibis sibi appositis caritative mittebat. Et quandoque scutellas et ciphos quos Christi pauperes manibus contrectaverant ut exinde gustaret sibi faciebat portari.[21] [4.5] Unde semel contingit quod unus de illius tribus pauperibus senex valde male comederet, et rex pius eidem compatiens offas quas libenter comedebat cum scutella et[22] transmisit eidem. Ac ille pauper offas illas modo istam modo illam manibus contrectans, quantum voluit comedit, licet parum. Quod sanctus Dei conspiciens scutellam eandem cum residuis offis ut adhuc de eis commederet, ante se readportari [sic] precepit Christum dominum considerans in paupere de cuius reliquiis nequaquam horruit manducare. [4.6] Nec enim solum verbis et factis, sed etiam in exteriori habitu vestium, humilitatem maximam pretendebat. Nam scarleto aut bruneto seu viridi, non utebatur, nec pellibus variis, aut aliis nimium sumptuosis.

[5.0] Capitulum v. De eiusdem prima transfretatione.[23]

[5.1] Dilitationem vero fidei ferventi desiderio cupiebat. Unde tam - quam amator fidei et zelator, adhuc esset iunior apud Pontisaram de gravi infirmitate convalescens, crucem accepit. Fratresque suos tres comites secum ducens, ac maiores regni barones & milites cum exercitu maximo aplicuit in Egyptum. [5.2] Occurrerunt pagani valide regi et

---

21. *in* MS, vii *added,* in middle of the line in red
22. 4r
23. rubric in red

humbly kiss them. And then he would devoutly pour water on their hands to wash them, and afterwards, with a kiss to the hand, would extend to whomever among them a certain sum of money.[12] [4.3] Sometimes he would himself generously serve the 120 poor who were given meals in his household each day. On solemn vigils and on certain other days of the year he would, with his own hands, serve dishes to 200 poor guests before he would himself eat.[13] [4.4] At lunch and at dinner he always sat three poor old men next to him, to whom he would charitably offer the food served to him. He might also have dishes and bowls that these poor of Christ had touched with their own hands brought to him so that he could eat from them.[14] [4.5] Once it happened that one of these three old men had eaten very little, and the pious king, pitying him, sent over some food that he was enjoying eating. And the poor man, picking at bits and pieces of food, ate of it what he wanted, though this was very little. The saint of God, looking at the dish with its leftovers, asked that it be brought back to him to eat, for he believed that Christ the Lord was in the poor man and did not shrink from eating his leftovers.[15] [4.6] He demonstrated the greatest humility, not only in words and deeds, but also in the outward style of his dress. He wore neither scarlet, nor brown, nor green, nor mixed-color furs, nor indeed anything at all that was too extravagant.[16]

[5.0] Chapter 5. On his first trip across the sea.

[5.1] He sought with fervent desire to spread the faith. When this lover and zealot of the faith was still young, although convalescing at Pontoise from a serious illness, he took up the cross. He led his three brothers, the counts, along with the great barons and knights of the kingdom, and he landed in Egypt with a very large army.[17] [5.2] The pagans put

12. Cf. GB 9 (p. 6); WSP *vie* 12 (p. 104); WSP *sermo* 18 (p. 283); GR 6.2.

13. Cf. GB 11 (p. 19); WSP *vie* 12 (pp. 104–5); GR 6.3.

14. Cf. WSP *vie* 12 (pp. 104–5); WSP *sermo* (p. 283); GR 6.4.

15. Cf. WC p. 35; GR 6.5; WSP *vie* 12 (p. 105); WSP *sermo* 18 (p. 283); and see also YSD 7 (p. 52).

16. Cf. GB 8 (p. 6); WSP *vie* 12 (p. 111); GR 6.6.

17. Cf. WSP *vie* 3 (pp. 22–23); GR 10.1.

suis volentibus capere portum, sed virtutem exercitus christiani non ferentes,[24] turpiter in fugam versi sunt. Ac nostri ad terram descendentes de navibus, famosam illam civitatem, que quondam Nepheas, nunc Damiata dicitur occuparunt. At non multo post, iusto sed occulto dei iudicio, exercitus infirmitate percussus multiplici, corporali morte, maioribus minoribus et mediocribus subtractis de medio, de triginta duobus milibus, pervenit ad senarium. [5.3] Volensque pater Dominus misericordiarum in sancto suo se mirabilem ostendere [cf. Ps. 76.15], pugilem fidei Dominum regem tradidit manibus impiorum, ut mirabilior appareret. Quis enim non cognoscat miraculum, gentem ferocissimam parcere tanto regi, quem super omnis principes mundi si posse nocere[25] sciebant, et eandem gentem cupidissimam, regem liberum dimittere pro redemptione minori in parte centuplum quod habere potuisset? [5.4] Eductus itaque velud Ioseph de carcere Egipciaco, non ut fugiens vel timidus statim reversus ad propria, sed per v^e annorum spacium postea permansit in Syria.[26] In illo tempore captivos christianos qui tunc haberi potuerunt eduxit de carceribus. Multosque sarracenos ad fidem venientes clementer suscepit et & baptisari fecit. Cesaream[27] Iopem & Sydonem muris firmavit fortissimis. Civitatis quoque Achon fortificavit menia et plurimum ampliavit. [5.5] Tandem pie matris ac sibi dilectissime audito transitu et regno non modicum posse iminere periculum assensit redire in Franciam relictis cum legato multis militibus et expensis in subsidium terre sancte. [5.6] Nocte vero tercia postquam a portu Achonensi recesserat aliquantulum ante diem, navis subito ad rupem, aut terre lingulam in modo lapidis induratam, bina impulsione tam fortiter est collisa quam vix de centum una absque

24. 4v
25. *corr. from* noscere
26. 5r
27. *corr. from* Iesaseam

up a strong fight against the king and his men as they tried to take the port, but not possessing the virtue[18] of the Christian army, they fled in dishonor. Our men, disembarking from their ships, captured that famous city, formerly called Memphis but now [known as] Damietta. Shortly after, by the just but hidden judgment of God, the army, struck down by multiple illnesses, with bodily death taking men of all ranks from its midst, was reduced from thirty-two thousand in number to six thousand.[19] [5.3] The Lord Father of mercies, wishing to show Himself wondrous in his saint [cf. Ps. 76.15], handed this lord king, this fighter for the faith, over into the hands of the ungodly men, in order that He might appear even more wondrous. Who would not recognize the miracle that this very fierce people released so great a king, whom they knew could harm them more than all the world's princes, and that this same very greedy people freed the king for a ransom one-hundredth of what they might have demanded?[20] [5.4] Just like Joseph, when freed from an Egyptian prison, [Louis] did not immediately turn around and go home as if a fugitive or fearful man, but rather stayed in Syria for five more years.[21] During this time, he secured the release from prison of as many captive Christians as possible. Mercifully, he welcomed the many Saracens who came to the faith and had them baptized. He fortified Caesarea, Joppa, and Sidon with very strong city walls, and also strengthened Acre and greatly enlarged its ramparts.[22] [5.5] In the end, when he heard that his pious and beloved mother had died and that his kingdom was in great danger, he agreed to return to France, leaving many knights and much money with the legate for the support of the Holy Land.[23] [5.6] On the third night after his departure from the port at Acre, just before daybreak, the ship suddenly hit a rock (or a little slip of land that was hard like a rock), colliding with [it] twice with such force that no one would have

---

18. Cf. GR 10.2, n. 57 of the translation, on the word *virtus*.

19. Cf. GB 41 (p. 22); GR 10.2; WSP *vie* 3 (pp. 22–23): "par le jugement de Nostre Seigneur droiturier et secré."

20. Cf. GB 25 (p. 16); WSP *vie* 3 (p. 23); GR 10.3.

21. Cf. Gen. 39–40.

22. Cf. GB 26 (p. 16); WSP *vie* 11 (pp. 91–92); GR 10.4.

23. Cf. GB 28 (p. 17); GR 10.5; YSD 13 (p. 56).

fractione potuisse evadere probabiliter putabatur. Rex vero Deo devotus semper fiduciam habens in domino concitus perrexit ad orationem coram sancto corpore Ihesu Chrisi, quod de speciali licencia legati intra navem habebant in altari speciosissime adornato. Mirum certe! Descendentibus[28] ad fundum marinariis velud desperatis cum lumine illesa fuit navis omnino reperta. Tunc vero sacerdotes et clerici qui circa altare iacebant tanta concussione navis et commotione huiusmodi excitati et valde attoniti pre timore surrexerunt, et viderunt hominem dei ante altare prostratum, Deo omnipotenti de tanto bene - ficio gratias referentem. Fuitque firma fides eorum omnium, quod Dominus eos meritis pii regis et precibus a predicto mortis periculo liberasset.

[6.0] Capitulum vi. De suarum elemosinarum largitione.[29]

[6.1] Reversus itaque in Franciam princeps nobilis et cum gaudio inestimabili susceptus ab omnibus. Licet a puericia sancte conversationis extiterit, ex tunc tamen semper seipso melior fiebat, ut David. Et velud lapis pro celesti edificio multis tribulationum tonsuris quadratus ad omnimodam vite perfectionem pervenit. [6.2] Licet enim ab infancia semper creverit in eum miseratio [cf. Job 31.18], ex tunc tamen evidencius cepit super afficitos et pauperes pia gestare viscera et religiosorum facere monasteria et semetipsum sollicicius in perfectione[30] humilitatis et caritatis operibus exercere. [6.3] Fecit namque illud prec - larum Beate Marie Regalis Montis monasterium Cisterciensis ordinis, in quo pluries mirande humilitatis et caritatis officia exhibebat, ser - viendo proprius manibus humiliter et devote. [6.4] Unde etiam cuidam

28. 5v
29. rubric in red
30. 6r

believed that even one out of a hundred men could have survived the shipwreck. Devoted to God and always faithful in the Lord, the king woke up and rushed to pray before the holy body of Jesus Christ [i.e., the consecrated host], which, by a special permission of the legate, he had on board on a most preciously adorned altar. This was truly wondrous! When the sailors, like desperate men, descended below with a light, they discovered that [the ship] was completely undamaged. The priests and clerics who were sleeping near the altar were awakened by the great shock to the ship and the ensuing commotion; struck dumb with fear, they got up to see this man of God prostrate before the altar, giving thanks to Almighty God for so great a gift. And everyone's faith was strengthened because God had released them from mortal danger on account of the merits and prayers of the pious king.[24]

[6.0] Chapter 6. On the generosity of his alms.

[6.1] When he returned to France, the noble prince was received with ineffable joy by all. Although from boyhood he stood out for his saintly conduct, from this point forward he, like David, strove constantly to become even better. Like a stone made square for a celestial building, [Louis], chiseled by his many tribulations, reached a life of full perfection.[25] [6.2] Although compassion flourished in him continually from infancy [cf. Job 31.18], from this point onwards he more visibly bore himself with a pious heart toward the afflicted and the poor, building monasteries for religious [men or women], and [becoming even] more solicitous in perfecting his own humility and charity through his works.[26] [6.3] He built the renowned Cistercian monastery of the Blessed Mary, Royaumont, where he often wondrously performed the obligations of humility and charity by ministering humbly and devoutly with his own hands.[27] [6.4] Once, at dinner, blessed Louis

<hr>

24. Cf. GB 30 (p. 18); GR 10.6; WSP *vie* 4 (pp. 29–30); Joinville, *Vie de Saint Louis*, §§618–622.

25. Cf. GR 11.1.

26. Cf. GB 19 (p. 11); WSP *sermo* 14 (p. 282); GR 7.1.

27. The Cistercian Abbey of Royaumont was founded at royal expense and consecrated in 1236. Cf. GR 7.2.

monacho leproso, omnibus abhominabili iam effecto, ut pote naso et occulis ipsius morbi corrosione privato, ipse beatus Ludovicus flexis genibus in quodam eius prandio servivit, cibum et potum immittendo in os eius, prout eidem melius placere credebat, in gemitus et lacrimas prorumpente abbate (qui aderat) et plurimum admirante quando vir sanctus talia faceret absque nimio gravi abhominationis horrore. [6.5] In civitate[31] Silvacensi infra castri sui menia, de ordine beati Maurecii monasterium et conventum fundavit, et bonis regalibus habundanter dotavit. Hospitales vero domos pauperum in castris Compendii, Pontizare et Vernoni magnis et sumptuosis edificiis prout decebat magnificenciam regiam[32] a fundamentis perfecit, et eisdem perpetuo et magnos redditus assignavit. [6.6] Similiter et sororibus inclusis ordinis fratrum predicatorum monasterium sancti Mathei iuxta Rothomagum acquisivit, conferendo eisdem in perpetuum pro quinquaginta soro - ribus redditus competentes. [6.7] Domum etiam Dei Parisius cum magnis sumptibus ampliavit, et redditibus augmentavit. Cecis autem Parisius ut commode possent vivere plus quam trecentis, beguinis[33] vero plus quam quadringentis cum magnis sumptibus de locis providit.

31. *add. in* MS: etiam Belvacensi [Beavais] alias. We have elided this as the reference to Beauvais is anomalous, and the wording makes little sense.

32. 6v.

33. beguinis] *corr. from* benignius

himself, on bended knees, ministered to a certain leprous monk who, because the corrosive disease had gnawed away his eyes and nose, was disgusting to everyone. [Louis] placed food and drink directly into his mouth, believing that by doing so he would better please the leper, with the abbot (who was there) breaking out into groans and tears, greatly admiring the holy man for doing such things without being excessively horrified by such an abomination.[28] [6.5] In the city of Senlis he founded a monastery and convent of the order of blessed Maurice within the walls of his palace, and he endowed it with abundant royal goods.[29] Within the walls of Compiègne, Pontoise, and Vernon he built, from the ground up, Maisons Dieu for the poor, great and sumptuous buildings as befits royal magnificence, and he assigned to them substantial rents in perpetuity.[30] [6.6] Likewise, for the cloistered sisters of the Dominican Order, he acquired the monastery of Saint Matthew near Rouen and conferred on them in perpetuity rents suitable for fifty nuns.[31] [6.7] And at great expense he enlarged the Maison Dieu at Paris and augmented its revenues.[32] With the great rents from his estates he provided for 300 blind people and more than 400 beguines in Paris in order that they could live comfortably.[33]

28. Cf. WSP *vie* 11 (pp. 94–96).

29. The Priory of St.-Maurice in Senlis was established by a foundation of Louis IX in 1261 for relics acquired from the monastery of St.-Maurice d'Aguane (in modern Switzerland). See Édouard Aubert, *Trésor de l'Abbaye de Saint-Maurice d'Agaune,* vol. 1, 57, and vol 2, *piéce justificatives* no. 24. Cf. WSP *vie* 6 (pp. 45–46); WSP *sermo* 20 (p. 284).

30. "Maisons Dieu" were charitable hospitals for the poor. Cf. GB 19 (p. 11); GR 7.3; WSP *vie* 6 (pp. 45, 47) and 11 (p. 88).

31. Founded between 1258 and 1264. See Chapotin, *Histoire de Dominicains de la Province de France,* 327–28; Hallam, "Aspects of Monastic Patronage," 381. Cf. GB 19 (p. 11); GR 7.5.

32. The largest such institution in Paris was called uniquely the Hôtel Dieu. It had existed on the Ile-de-la-cité (next to the Cathedral of Notre-Dame) since well before the year 1000. Cf. WSP *vie* 11 (p. 88).

33. The author refers here to the hospital for the blind known as the Quinz-Vingt, which Louis founded around 1260, and to the Beguinage, a house for women who took a vow of voluntary poverty but did not enter a monastic order, which he founded before 1264. Cf. GB 19 (pp. 11, 12); GR 7.3, 7.6; WSP *vie* 11 (p. 87).

[6.8] Miserabilesque mulieres que quandoque pro victus penuria semetipsas exposuerant, in magno numero in domo filiarum dei Parisius
congrevavit et ipsis quadrigintas libras, de quibus cum laboricio suo
viverent annuatim ut eas a peccato retraheret assignavit. [6.9] Fratribus quoque predicatoribus et minoribus in diversis regni sui parti -
bus ecclesias, claustra, et dormitoria, et ceteras domos necessarias
construxit et specialiter Compendiensium, Masticonensium, Cado -
niensium conventus ordinis fratrum predictorum, plures etiam ordinis
fratrum minorum fundavit[34] ex toto. [6.10] Et licet omnibus conventibus predicatorum ordinum immediate sue ditioni subiectis magnam
elemosinam faceret. Annuatim tamen conventibus Parisiensibus quos[35]
pro religione scientia et doctrina precipue venerabatur solitus erat circa
festum sancti Michaelis pro suis neccesitatibus procurandis multo
maiorem elemosinam elargiri. In estate quoque et alias pluries per
annum eisdem ita habunde subvenire solebat, quod uterque conventus centum sexaginta fratres et plus ex regis donariis pro magna parte
poterant sustentari. [6.11] Et multociens dixit. "O domine quam bene
ponitam reputo istam elemosinam, tot et tantis fratribus qui de toto
orbe ad istos duos conventus Parisius pro studio sacre scripture confluunt. Et ex inde quod de divinis scriptures hauriunt, pro totum mundum ad dei honorem et animarum salutem effundunt." [6.12] Fratribus
etiam Carturciensis[36] locum aptum bonis redditibus dotavit, iuxta
murum[37] parisiensis civitatis donavit. Sed ut cuiuscumque paup[er]is

34. 7r
35. quos] *corr. from* quo
36. MS *reads* Caturciensis
37. MS *reads* munerum

[6.8] At the house of the Filles Dieu in Paris he brought together a great number of wretched women who had at one time or another prostituted themselves for want of food, and he assigned to these women four hundred pounds annually from which they might live by their own labor that he might bring them back from sin.³⁴ [6.9] For the Friars Preachers and Minors in various parts of his kingdom he built churches, cloisters, and dormitories, and other necessary buildings, and especially in Compiègne, Mâcon, and Caen, he founded and funded convents for the Dominican Order and also several for the Franciscans.³⁵ [6.10] Although he gave great alms to all the convents of the Order of Preachers that were subject to his immediate jurisdiction, he would nonetheless offer even greater alms around the Feast of St. Michael to the convents in Paris, which he held in special veneration because of their religion, knowledge, and teaching, to take care of their needs. And in the summer and often at other points of the year, he would give so much to these same convents that each of the convents was able to support more than 160 friars, mostly through the king's gifts.³⁶ [6.11] Many times he said: "O Lord, how well-appointed I think these alms, expended on so many great friars who come to these two convents in Paris from around the world for the study of holy scripture. What they drink in from divine scriptures they pour out throughout the whole world for the honor of God and the salvation of souls."³⁷ [6.12] He also gave the Carthusian brothers a suitable place with good rents, next to the walls of the city of Paris.³⁸ When religious from any poor order fled to him (provided that the religious order

34. The community of the Filles Dieu was founded in 1226 as a haven for reformed prostitutes by the bishop of Paris; Louis, however, was a generous early patron. See Hallam, "Aspects of Monastic Patronage," 255. Cf. GB 19 (p. 11); GR 7.6.

35. Louis assisted in the foundation of Dominican convents at Compiègne (1257 or 1258), Mâcon (ca. 1239, certainly by 1246), and Caen (date uncertain, maybe by 1246). Chapotin, *Histoire de Dominicains de la Province de France*, 499–501, 472–73, and 194–96, respectively. Note that the author is not specific about Franciscan houses. Hallam, "Aspects of Monastic Patronage," 220–83 and 381. Cf. GB 19 (p. 11); GR 7.3. WSP discusses only Compiègne and Caen, *vie* 11 (pp. 86, 88).

36. Cf. GR 7.3.

37. Cf. GB 19 (p. 11); GR 7.5.

38. See GR 7.6, n. 40 of the translation.

ordinis religiosi ad ipsum confugientes, dum tamen eorum ordo esset a sede apostolica approbatus; benigne ab eo suscepti locum pro seipsis optinuerunt commodum ad manendum.³⁸ [6.13] Quando veniebat Parisius aut alias civitates semper religiosis pauperibus pitancias faciebat et hospitales domos in quibus magna multitutudo infirmorum iacebat misericorditer visitans cum magna humilitate et devotione et assistentium edificatione omnibus infirmis pluries propriis manibus cibaria ministravit. Ceteras autem huius helemosinas cotidianas et annuas quis sufficeret enarrare? Breviter quicquid pauperibus dabat optime positum extimabat.

[7.0] Capitulum vii. De sanctarum reliquiarum veneratione et eius ferventi devotione.³⁹

[7.1] Precipua vero devotione venerabatur reliquias unde capellam speciosissimam mirifico scemate Parisius edificavit. In quam sacrosanctam Coronam Domini spineam, et maximam partem sancte crucis, ferrumque lancee quod latus aperuit salvatoris, cum multis aliis reliquis ac plurimum preciosis in theca preciosissima adhoc specialiter fabricata dignissime collocavit. Has siquidem sacras Dei reliquias cum immensis laboribus et expensis a Constantinopolitano imperatore obtinuit. [7.2] Ad has suscipiendas ipse de Parisius⁴⁰ cum solemni et devotiossima processione cleri et populi obviam processit; et usque ad ecclesiasm beate virginis nudis et pedibus hunc sacrum thesaurum propriis humeris deportavit. Diem quoque anniversarium quo predicte reliquie Parisius sunt recepte in capella regia regalis palacii perpetuo solemnizari instituit duo festa in huius solemnitate connectens.

38. 7v
39. rubric in red
40. 8r

was approved by the papacy), he would receive them with kindness and obtain suitable living places for them.[39] [6.13] When he came to Paris or [went to] other cities he would always give pittances to the religious poor, and he would compassionately visit with great humility and devotion hospitals where a great many sick people lay, and for the edification of those who were present there, he would often serve dinner with his very own hands to all the sick.[40] Who would be able to detail fully the rest of his daily and annual alms? In short, he thought that whatever he gave to the poor was well spent.

[7.0] Chapter 7. On the veneration of saintly relics and his fervent devotion.

[7.1] He revered with special devotion relics for which he built in Paris an extremely beautiful chapel of most extraordinary design.[41] In this [chapel] he, to his great credit, brought together the Lord's sacrosanct Crown of Thorns, the greater part of the Holy Cross, iron of the lance that had pierced the Savior's side, and many other relics and very precious items in an extraordinarily precious reliquary that had been specially made for this purpose. He acquired these sacred relics of God with great labor and expense from the emperor of Constantinople.[42] [7.2] He went out from Paris to receive these relics in a solemn and most devout procession that included both clergy and people, and on bare feet he carried this sacred treasure on his own shoulders all the way to the church of Notre Dame [of Paris]. For the anniversary of the reception of these relics at the royal chapel of the royal palace in Paris, he instituted two feasts that were to be celebrated in perpetuity, connecting [them] in the solemn observance of the

39. Cf. GB 19 (p. 12); GR 7.5.
40. Cf. WSP *vie* 11 (p. 83); WSP *sermo* 19 (p. 283).
41. The author here refers to the Ste.-Chapelle. See GR 8.1, n. 44 of the translation.
42. Cf. GB 24 (p. 15); GR 8.1; WSP *vie* 6 (pp. 41–42); WSP *sermo* 22 (p. 286).

[7.3] Omnes horas canonicas et de gloriosa virgine cum nota semper audiebat; submisse tamen inter se et quondam capellanum suum, et pro defunctis novem lectiones dicebat, omni die nisi alicuius festi solemnitas aut nimis magna et perutilis occupacio impediret. Unde quibusdam nobilibus super hoc murmurantibus, quod tot missas, tot sermones audieret et tot orationes diceret, respondet, "Si ludendo, inquit ad aleas vel currendo post feras, seu aucupiis intendendo, plus expenderem de tempore, nullus forsitan loqueretur." [7.4] De nocte et pluries surgebat ad orationem, considerans quod si Deus tunc sibi aliquam orationem immitteret impedimentum a supervenientibus non haberet. Confessori suo quandoque pie etiam familiariter conquerebatur, super lacrimarum, quarum non fontem sed stillas[41] pluviarum affectabat. Unde confessori suo aliquando familiariter dicebat quod quandoque dominus in oratione lacrimas sibi dabat quas cum sentiret per genas suaviter in os defluere, non solum cordi, sed et gustui dulcissime sapiebant. [7.5] Et ne devotio sua a quoquam impediretur dum in ecclesia celebrarentur divina, non admittebat cuiusquam colloquium, nisi urgeret neccesitas aut evidens utilitas et tunc breviter et succincte.

[8.0] Capitulum viii. De zelo fidei et eius firma adhesione.[42]

[8.1] Zelus vero fidei adeo in ipsius corde fervebat, quod iuramenta turpia absque horrore audire non poterat. Unde publico et solemni edicto de consilio prelatorum et principum, et etiam domini Symonis tunc legati in Franciam, turpiter sic iurantes et blasphemantes puniri

41. 8v
42. rubric in red

[feasts].[43] [7.3] He always listened to the singing of all the canonical hours and [the hours of] the Glorious Virgin; quietly, with his chaplain, he would recite nine lections for the dead every day except for times that the celebration of another feast or some great and important business prevented this. Once, when some noblemen were muttering about this—muttering that he listened to so many masses and so many sermons and that he said so many prayers—he responded: "Perhaps if I were to spend more of my time playing dice or hunting beasts or setting nets for birds, no one would say a thing."[44] [7.4] He got up many times during the night to pray, thinking that if God were to send him a prayer he would not be hindered by people interrupting him. He sometimes complained, piously and in private, to his confessors about tears; of these he aspired not to a fountain but to mere drops of rain. And to his confessor he once revealed in confidence that God gave tears to him as he prayed, and, when he felt them flowing down his cheeks softly and into his mouth, they tasted very sweet to his heart and to his tongue.[45] [7.5] And lest his own devotions be interrupted by someone while the divine office was being celebrated in church, he allowed no conversation unless the need were quite evident, and then only briefly and succinctly.[46]

[8.0] Chapter 8. Concerning his zeal and his firm adherence to the faith.

[8.1] Zeal for the faith burned in his heart so greatly that he could not hear foul oaths without horror. For this reason, by a public and solemn edict, on the advice of prelates and princes and of Lord Simon, who was then legate in France,[47] he ordered that those who swore foully or

---

43. WSP *vie* 6 (p. 42) states that Louis instituted three new feasts on this occasion. This account conforms to GB 24 (p. 15), which tells of twice-yearly feasts instituted to commemorate the two occasions on which relics arrived. There were, in fact, three separate shipments of relics. The Crown of Thorns arrived in 1239. A second group of relics, including a piece of the True Cross, arrived in 1241, and a third, including the Holy Lance, in 1242. See *Le trésor de la Sainte-Chapelle*, 37–41. Cf. GB 24 (pp. 15–16); GR 8.2; WSP *vie* 6 (pp. 41–42); WSP *sermo* 22 (p. 286).

44. Cf. GB 21 (p. 13); GR 8.3; WSP *sermo* 23 (p. 286; absent from WSP *vie*).

45. Cf. GB 21 (pp. 13–14); WSP *vie* 8 (p. 55); WSP *sermo* 24 (p. 287); GR 8.4–5.

46. Cf. GB 21 (p. 13); WSP *sermo* 23 (p. 286; absent from WSP *vie*); GR 8.6.

47. On Simon of Brie, see GR 9.1, n. 51 of the translation.

statuit gravi pena. [8.2] Et quemdam civem Parisiensem qui iuramento enormiter blasphemaverat, iuxta edictum regale in peccati sui penam et aliorum terrorem candenti in labiis suis cauterizari precepit. Cumque audiret propter hoc[43] aliquos a maledicto nolle corrigi, ait: "vellem" inquit "quoad vixero[44] in labiis meis talem indecenciam sustinere, dum modo hoc pessimum iuracionis peccatum de regno nostro penitus tolleretur." [8.3] Similiter dum in carcere sarracenorum ultra mare teneretur, petentibus sarracenis ut in quadam pactione facta super sua liberatione adderent quod Christum negaret si pactum non teneret, constanter hoc facere denegavit. Etiam si sua liberatio debet propter hoc impediri, et clericis et laicis qui sibi aderant dicentibus quod secure illam conditionem poterat opponere cum pactum omnino servare proponeret, respondit "tantum" enim inquit "horreo verbum de neganda fide etiam sub conditione audire quod nequaquam possem illud sono vocis[45] exprimere." Nutu itaque divino flecti sarraceni sibi pepercerunt a predicta conditione constanciam fidei et amorem ad Deum suum plurimum admirantes. [8.4] Ibidem etiam quidam nobilis sarracenus, qui ex conspiratione multorum soldanum occiderat adhuc tenens gladium cruentatum, accessit ad regem carceri mancipatum, instanter requirens ut ipsum faceret militem, quasi mortem intentans si ipse facere denegaret. Ipse vero attendens catholice[46] fidei dignitatem, constanter respondit, quod numquam nec pro morte nec pro vita infidelem quemquam insigniret balteo militari. Sed si ille vellet[47] fieri christianus ipsum non solum militem sed eciam divitem et honorabilem faceret in partibus gallicanis. [8.5] In tantam denique reverenciam habebat signaculum crucis Christi, quod quam poterat desuper calcare cavebat, et a pluribus religiosis exegit ut in claustris

---

43. Hoc] *absent in* MS; emended in accordance with the tradition in GR and BLQRF

44. 9r

45. sono vocis] sola voce *in* MS; emended in accordance with the tradition in GR and BLQRF

46. 9v

47. vellet] *corr. from* vellem

blasphemed in this way be punished severely.[48] [8.2] Thus, in compliance with this royal edict, he ordered that a certain citizen of Paris who had blasphemed outrageously by swearing be branded on his lips with a red hot iron in punishment for his sin, as an example to others. When he heard that some men did not want to be so punished for their cursing, he said, "I would endure this shameful stigma on my own lips as long as I live so long as the dreadful vice of swearing could be entirely eradicated from our kingdom."[49] [8.3] In the same vein, during the time that he was incarcerated overseas by the Saracens, when a stipulation was added to the treaty [that was being negotiated] to secure his liberty that he would deny Christ if he failed to keep to the agreement, he steadfastly refused to do so even though his freedom depended on it. And when the clerics and laymen who were with him said that he could safely pledge this condition since he fully intended to keep the pact in its entirety, he responded, "I have such horror of even hearing a word about denying the faith that, even under these conditions, I could never say this aloud." And thus softened by divine will, the Saracens, admiring very much the constancy of his faith and his love for God, spared him from this oath.[50] [8.4] At that time the Saracen nobleman who had killed the sultan in a conspiracy involving many others, and who was still holding a bloody sword, came to free the king from prison and vehemently demanded that [Louis] make him a knight, threatening to kill him if he refused.[51] Protective of the dignity of the Catholic faith, [Louis] responded steadfastly that he would die before he would bestow the belt of knighthood on an infidel, but if this man should wish to become a Christian then he would make him not only a knight but also rich and honorable throughout France.[52] [8.5] Finally, [Louis] held the sign of Christ's cross in such great reverence that, as much as possible, he took care to not tread upon it, and in many

48. Cf. GB 32 (p. 19); GR 9.1.
49. Cf. GB 33 (p. 19); GR 9.2.
50. Cf. WSP *vie* 3 (pp. 23–24); WSP *sermo* 10 (p. 280); GR 9.3. See also related discussion in Joinville, *Vie de Saint Louis,* §360.
51. The Ayyubid Sultan Turanshah was overthrown and murdered in a palace coup during Louis' captivity in 1250, inaugurating Mamluk rule in Egypt.
52. Cf. WSP *vie* 3 (pp. 24–25); WSP *sermo* 11 (p. 280).

eorum in tumbis huiusmodi cruces non insculperentur de cetero et insculpte penitus raderentur. [8.6] Quam etiam devote et reverenter omni anno in Parasceve ad adorandum lignum crucis flexis genibus resoluto crine ad nudis pedibus procederet, testantur illorum occuli qui ipsum sine lacrimis non poterant intueri.

[9.0] Capitulum nonum. De eius diligenti iusticiae[48] et pacis conservatione.[49]

[9.1] In regimine vero regni et subditorum tam potenter at prudenter se gerebat, quod absque aliqua personarum acceptione cum diligenti et sollicita causarum discussione reddebat iusticiam unicuique. Et conciliarios[50] suos quandoque sublimes aut aliis magnatibus faventes minus iuste quando poterat in hoc eos deprehendere, valde dure redarguebat, dicens: "In hoc solum vos reputo mihi servire; vel[51] infideles esse si vel pro me vel contra me seu contra quoscumque semper quod iustum est non discernatis." [9.2] Timens etiam ne cause pauperum vix ingrederentur ad eos, et ne populus suus per officiales suos aut alios opprimeretur iniuste, frequenter ad minus bis in ebdomada ad audiendum conquerentes in loco patente se ponebat. Et ipso presente cum bona diligencia faciebat celerius expedire. Et si quandoque negocium fidei inquisitores seu prelatos sibi defereba[tur][52] pro celeri expeditione, volebat illud pre aliis omnibus negociis quantumcumque arduis anteponi. [9.3] Consuetudines vero iniquas quantumcumque[53] longevas faciebat quantum poterat aboleri. Unde in dominio suo cuiuscumque instancia non admittebantur duella. Sed per aliam viam iuri consonam maleficia puniebat. Preposituras autem suas[54] et alia officia suum populum deprimencia non vendebat, pie considerans et attendens quod

---

48. MS abbreviation unclear: iustici⁻
49. rubric in red
50. 10r
51. We don't know what to do with this "vel."
52. *corr. from* defereba
53. MS *adds* iniquas quantumcumque [repeated in MS twice]
54. 10v

monasteries he ordered that crosses of this sort not be sculpted on the tombs of their cloisters, and furthermore, that those that had [already] been sculpted be completely removed.[53] [8.6] The eyes of all those who could not look at him without tears bear witness to how devoutly and reverently he processed every year on Good Friday, on bended knee, hair loosened and feet bare, to adore the wood of the cross.[54]

[9.0] Chapter 9. Concerning his dedicated preservation of justice and peace.

[9.1] In his rule of the kingdom and of his subjects he conducted himself with such force and wisdom that, with favoritism to no one, he rendered justice to each individual after careful and thoughtful inquiry into their cases. If he discerned that his own high counselors were unjustly showing favoritism to other noblemen, he would reproach them very harshly, saying: "It is my feeling that in this alone [i.e., justice] you serve me. If—whether in my interests or against my interests—you do not always render judgment according to what is just, you are unfaithful."[55] [9.2] Fearing lest the cases of the poor be only rarely brought before [the high counselors], and lest his people be unjustly oppressed through his officials or others, he frequently, at least twice a week, stationed himself in an accessible place to hear plaintiffs. With great diligence, he would have these cases expedited more quickly in his presence.[56] And if a matter of faith was brought before his inquisitors or prelates for a quick decision, he wished it to be considered before all other matters, however pressing.[57] [9.3] He tried as much as possible to abolish unjust customs, however long-standing they might be. Therefore, in his own lordship duels were not allowed under any circumstance whatsoever. Rather, he punished crimes in other ways consonant with the law. He did not sell his prevostships or the other offices

53. Cf. GB 36 (p. 20); GR 9.4.

54. Cf. GR 9.5; WSP *vie* 6 (pp. 39–40).

55. Cf. WC, p. 34. But note that this quotation is unknown from other sources.

56. A version of this was famously told by Joinville, *Vie de Saint Louis*, §§59–60, although this text is not specifically related to Joinville.

57. Cf. WC, p. 34.

predicta officia ementes carius et super hiis expensas splendidas ac donaria facientes, totum ab humili populo nequiter extorquebant. [9.4] Iudeos vero fenerantes super pignora, etsi pro neccesitate humilis plebis ad persuasionem aliquorum de suo concilio tolerabat, tamen super litteris christianorum periuria et coactiva ministeria usurarie pravitatis, non permittebat eos ipsos nec alios publicos usurarios fenerari. Et ne huius litteras facerent compleri suis officialibus districtius prohibebat. Magnates vero delinquentes punire mediante iusticia minime formidabat, quandoque pena corporali quandoque pecuniaria quam semper in helemosinam convertebat. [9.5] Sic de cuiusdam magni condempnatione edificata fuit Parisius ecclesia fratrum minorum, et similiter dormitorium fratrum predicatorum, cum sumptibus valde magnis. Et quia pacem operatur iusticia, ideo ipsi iusticiam sic operanti non solum ad Deum, sed etiam ad seipsum. Dedit Deus pacem et[55] tranquillitatem super omnes reges, nec disponente omnipotente deo molestabatur ab aliquo. Set inter se discordantes, quodam spirituali dono divine gratie ut communiter ad pacis concordiam reducebat.

55. fol. 11r

[in ways that] oppressed his people; he piously believed and was worried that those [people] selling offices at a high price and, even worse, demanding extravagant payments and gifts, were wickedly extorting everything [they could] from humble people.[58] [9.4] For the need of ordinary people, at the request of others of his council, he permitted Jews to take interest on pledges. Nevertheless, he did not permit them or any other obvious usurers to exact interest based on the lies and forced impositions of depraved usury in Christians' bonds. And he strictly prohibited his own officials from enforcing such bonds.[59] He in no way feared punishing delinquent noblemen through justice, sometimes with a corporal punishment and sometimes with a fine, which he always converted into alms.[60] [9.5] And thus the church of the Friars Minor in Paris was built from [the fine from] the verdict against a certain nobleman, and so too the dormitory of the Friars Preachers [was built] at very great expense.[61] Because he brought about peace through justice, in this same way he brought about justice not only for God but also for himself. God gave peace and tranquility to him above all kings, and by the arrangement of the almighty God, he was troubled by no one. Through this spiritual gift of divine grace, [Louis] reconciled those fighting among themselves to the harmony of peace.

58. Cf. WC, p. 33: "Consuetudines siquidem iniquas et pravas quantumcumque longaevas, ut commode poterant, aboleri, et exactiones indebitas amoveri jubebat"; see also WC's discussion of duels (p. 34).

59. We are greatly indebted to William Jordan for help in translating this passage. Jordan, *The French Monarchy and the Jews*, 128–54, is helpful for the context of this paragraph.

60. Cf. WC, p. 34.

61. Cf. WSP *vie* 18 (p. 139). This is a reference to the episode involving Enguerrand de Coucy, who summarily hanged three young noblemen for hunting on his lands, and who was brought before Parliament for royal judgment. Louis imposed a hefty fine of, depending on the source, either 10,000 or 12,000 *livres*. The episode is known from WSP *vie* 17, the continuator of William of Nangis, RHF vol. 20, 399–401, and Viard, *Grandes chroniques de France,* vol. 7, 190–93. Only the *Grandes chronique,* the source for the 10,000 *livres* amount, indicates that the sum was used for building the "meison Dieu de Ponthoise . . . et si en fist fere le dortoir aus Freres Preecheeurs de Paris, et du remenant fist fere le moustier aus Freres Meneurs de Paris" (p. 193).

[10.0] Capitulum x. De sancta crucis assumptione et primogeniti sui sancta eruditione.[56]

[10.1] Tandem post multorum annorum curricula quibus se in omni genere virtutum exercuit, audiens calamitates desolationes ac pericula terre sancte; propositum secundo transfretandi quod deo inspirante conceperat, summo pontifici domino Clementi quarto per secretum discretum nuncium insinuare curavit. [10.2] Quod discretus et pius pater primo reformidans sed plenam deliberationem multipliciter approbans ad petitionem regis legatum misit in Franciam, ad predicandum crucem in subsidium terre sancte. [10.3] Cruce signatis igitur ipso domino rege cum domino Philippo primogenito suo, et duobus aliis filiis suis, videlicet domino Iohanne comite Nivernensi, et domino Petro Comite Alenzonis, ac multis aliis magnatibus et nobilibus regni et communis[57] populi multitudine copiosa, preparato navigio secundum condictum ad Aquas Mortuas convenerunt. [10.4] Ibique inito concilio quod rex Tunicii soldano Babilonico multa subsidia faciebat, et quia pluries insinuaverat se fieri christianum si suum populum non timeret, et pro fide Christi ibi renovanda, que dudum ibidem tempore beati Augustini et aliorum orthodoxorum tam eleganter floruerat, vela versus Tunicium direxerunt.[58] [10.5] Et postquam devoti filii et dominum genitorem suum ad navem deduxerunt suas sibi preparatas postea ascensuri[59] de navi sua sanctus pater inferius filios in barca prospiciens, ait, "Placeat, dilecti filii, quod usque huc veneritis me aliquantulum audire antequam vos equorum spaciis et fluctibus committamus." [10.6] Et tunc ad dominum Philippum primogentium specialius sermonem dirigens, sic ait: [10.7] "Considera fili quod ego sic grandevus

---

56. rubric in red
57. 11v
58. di[re]xerunt] *corr. from* dixerunt
59. ascensuri] *corr. from* ascensii

[10.0] Chapter 10. On his saintly assumption of the cross and the saintly instruction of his eldest son.

[10.1] Finally, after the passage of many years, in which he grew in every kind of virtue, hearing of the calamities, hardships, and dangers to the Holy Land, he took pains to reveal to the lord pope, Clement IV,[62] through a secret and judicious messenger, a plan that he had conceived of by God's inspiration for crossing the ocean a second time.[63] [10.2] The judicious and pious pope was at first reluctant, but then, after full deliberation, he approved of the king's request, and sent his legate to France to preach the crusade in support of the Holy Land.[64] [10.3] The lord king having been signed by the cross, along with his eldest son, Lord Philip, two of his other sons, Lord John, the count of Nevers, and Lord Peter, the count of Alençon, many other counts and nobles of the kingdom, and a great abundance of common people, they all convened according to plan at Aigues Mortes once the fleet was ready.[65] [10.4] And there, counsel having been undertaken, because the king of Tunis had made an agreement to give much aid to the Sultan of Babylon and because [the King of Tunis] had hinted many times that he would become a Christian if only he did not fear his own people, and also so that the faith of Christ would be renewed in the place where it had for such a long time so beautifully flourished in the time of blessed Augustine and other orthodox Christians, they set their sails for Tunis.[66] [10.5] And when his devoted sons had led their lord father to the ship and were themselves about to embark on their own readied ships, the saintly father, looking down from his ship at his sons on the barge below, said, "Please, beloved sons, because you have come this far, listen to me before we commit ourselves to the expanse and waves of the sea."[67] [10.6] And then, directing his speech in particular to Lord Philip, his eldest son, he said the following: [10.7] "Consider, son, that

---

62. See GR 11.2, n. 64 of the translation.
63. Cf. GB 37 (p. 21); GR 11.2.
64. Cf. GB 37 (p. 20); GR 11.3.
65. Cf. GB 38 (p. 21); GR 11.4.
66. Cf. GB 41 (p. 22); GR 11.5–6).
67. Cf. GR 4.2–3 (where the story is in the first person).

pro Christo alias transfretavi, et regina mater tua iam processerit in diebus suis, et quod regnum nostrum favente Deo possedimus pacifice[60] et quiete diviciis deliciis ac honoribus temporalibus quam libuit et licuit habundantes. Te quoque ac fratres tuos et sorores prolem genuimus generosam. Vide igitur quod pro fide Christi et eius ecclesiae nec mee parco senectuti nec matris tue desolate misereor, delicias et honores relinquo ac expono pro Christo divicias, te quoque qui regnaturus es ac fratres tuos et sororem primogenitam. Duco etiam quartum adduxissem filium si annos pubertatis attigisset. Que idcirco te audire[61] volui ut post obitum meum cum ad regnum parveneris, pro dei ecclesia et fide catholica sustinenda et defendenda nulli rei paveas [sic] nec uxori nec liberis nec et regno. Tibi enim et fratribus tuis do exemplum ut si opus fuerit similiter faciatis." [10.8] Currente igitur navigio versus Tunicum ac exercitu christiano libere portum capiente in Affrica illius famose Cartaginis castrum et omnia ad illud pertinencia capientes vi armorum inter cartaginem et tunicium fixerunt tentoria, ibidem aliquandiu moraturi.

[11.0] Capitulum xi.[62] De eius felici ad Christum migratione. Lectio.[63]

[11.1] Illic enim beatus Ludovicus post tot et laudabilia virtutum opera, post tot laboriosos agones quos pro fide Christi et ecclesia tam fideliter et ferventer indefesso animo toleraverat. Disponente Domino qui labores illius voluit feliciter consumare, ac ipsi bonorum laborum suorum fructum retribuere gloriosum, lecto decubuit febre continua fatigatus, et invalescente morbo sua mente et integro aspectu et auditu psalmos dicens, sanctos invocans devotissime suscepit omnia ecclesiastica sacramenta. [11.2] Iam vero signis evidentibus apropinquans ad finem; audientibus qui aderant prout submisse loqui poterat

60. 12r
61. *corr. from* audiri
62. 12v
63. rubric in red

I, now aged, have crossed the sea another time for Christ and that your mother the queen is far advanced in years. We have possessed our kingdom through God's favor peacefully and quietly, enjoying temporal riches, honors, and pleasures as was good and right. We bore noble offspring, both you and your brothers and sisters. See how for faith in Christ and his church I neither spare my old age, nor do I take pity on your forsaken mother. I relinquish delights [and] honors, and, for Christ, I offer my wealth. I lead you who are about to reign, and your brothers, and your firstborn sister, with me, and I would even have brought my fourth son, if he were of age. Therefore I wish that you listen, so that after my death, when you attain the kingdom, you spare nothing for the preservation and defense of the church of God and of the Catholic faith—neither yourself, nor what belongs to you—not your kingdom, not your wife, not even your children. I give this example to you and your brothers so that, if need be, you will all do the same."[68] [10.8] The fleet sailed to Tunis, and the Christian army boldly captured the harbor in Africa and with the force of arms seized the city of renowned Carthage and the lands around it. They pitched their tents between Carthage and Tunis, where they would stay for some time.[69]

[11.0] Chapter 11. Of his felicitous departure to Christ.

[11.1] There, after many laudable works of virtue and many laborious struggles, which he had faithfully and fervently borne with a tireless soul for the faith of Christ and his church, and tired out by continual fever, blessed Louis lay down on his bed. The Lord wished that his la - bors be happily brought to perfection and thus granted to him the glorious fruit of his good labors. With disease gaining the upper hand, [but] with mind, appearance, and hearing intact, he recited the psalms and invoked the saints with great devotion, [and] received all the ecclesiastical sacraments.[70] [11.2] When, as it became evident that he was approaching the end, this man, full of God, was able to speak to

68. Cf. GR 4.4.
69. Cf. GB 42 (p. 22); GR 12.1.
70. Cf. GB 44 (p. 23); GR 12.2; YSD 13 (p. 56). (This ultimately goes back to the letter sent out by Philip III from Tunis announcing Louis' death.)

vir deo plenus dicebat. "Pro deo studeamus quomodo fides cathlica predicari possit apud Tunicum et plantari." [11.3] Cum vero virtus corporis eius ac sermonis paulatim deficeret, non cessabat Dei et sanctorum implorare suffragia maxime autem beati Dyonisii specialis patroni sui, cuius sancti se esse hominem ex devotione recognoscebat,[64] per talenta quatuor que cadencia[65] de capite suo super altare in ipsius sancti festo si presens aderat annis singulis offerebat. Unde et iuxta assertionem propius assistentium finem orationis que de beato Dyonisio cantatur: "Tribue nobis quesumus pro amore tuo prospera mundi despicere, et nulla eius adversa formidare,"[66] frequenter cum quodam[67] vocis iam debilis suavi[68] eloquio repetebat. [11.4] Similiter et de beato Jacobo: "Esto domine plebi tue sanctificator et custos."[69] Et de pluribus aliis sanctis iugem memoriam faciebat. [11.5] Demum vero ad extremam horam veniens Christi servus, super stratum cinerum recubans in modum crucis extensus verba ultima proferens. "Pater in manus tuas commendo spiritum meum," [Luke 23.46] felicem animam suo reddidit Salvatori. Corpus vero ad sepulcrum patrum suorum delatum fuit in Franciam apud sanctam Dyonisium, ubi cum magna veneratione et devotione fidelium non longe a sanctorum martyrum Dyonisii, Rustici, et Eleutherii corporibus adoratur. In quo loco crebris coruscat miraculis. Et ex diversis mundi partibus oppressi[70] variis infirmitatibus devotione, qua oportet, beati Ludovici suffragium implorantes, salutem recipiunt, et frequenter eiusdem sancti meritis et precibus beneficium sanctitatis. [11.6] Migravit autem beatus Ludovicus de hoc mundo ad dominum, in crastino beati Bartholomei apostoli,

64. 13r
65. cadencia] candencia *in* MS
66. Oration to Saint Denis: *Saint Andrew Daily Missal,* 1505 (October 9)
67. quodam] *corr. from* quondam
68. suavi] *corr. from* suam
69. Oration to Saint James: Dumas, *Liber Sacramentorum Gellonesis,* 165 (rbc: 1247); Deshusses, *Le Sacramentaire Grégorien,* vol. 1, p. 699. For English translation, *Saint Andrew Daily Missal,* 1573 (July 25).
70. 13v

those around him who were leaning over and listening. He said, "Let us work for God, so that the Catholic faith can be preached and implanted in Tunis."[71] [11.3] Although the strength of his body and of his voice was failing little by little, he did not cease imploring the intercession of God and of the saints, and especially of blessed Denis, his particular patron; he had acknowledged that he was a vassal of this saint out of devotion, by the four talents which, dropping them down from off his head and onto the altar, he offered each year on the saint's feast day in the years that he was present.[72] And thus, according to the testimony of those who were present nearby, he said again and again with a certain sweet eloquence in his now fading voice the prayer sung for blessed Denis: "Grant, we pray, that we may despise the good things of this world for the sake of your love and not fear any of its adversities."[73] [11.4] Likewise [he said] to blessed James "Lord, be Your people's sanctifier and protector,"[74] and further offered a prayer of perpetual memory to many other saints.[75] [11.5] At last, at the final hour, the servant of Christ, lying atop a bed of ashes, stretched out in the form of the cross, said, "Father, into your hands I commend my spirit" [Luke 23.46] and rendered his joyful spirit back to his Savior. His body was then carried back to the resting place of his fathers in France, at St.-Denis, [and was entombed] not far from the bodies of the martyr-saint Denis, Rusticus, and Eleutherius, where it was venerated with the great reverence and devotion of the faithful. At this place [he] shone with frequent miracles. From diverse parts of the world, those overwhelmed by various maladies, praying for the intercession of blessed Louis with fitting devotion, frequently received deliverance and the favor of his sanctity because of the merits and prayers of that same saint.[76] [11.6] Blessed Louis departed from this world to the Lord on the day following that of blessed Bartholomew, the apostle, in

71. Cf. GB 44 (p. 23); cf. GR 12.3. See also YSD 13.

72. See GR 12.4, n. 72 of the translation.

73. Translation adapted from *Saint Andrew Daily Missal*, 1505 (October 9). Cf. GB 44 (p. 23); GR 12.4; YSD 13 (p. 56).

74. Translation follows *Saint Andrew Daily Missal*, 1353 (July 25).

75. Cf. GB 44 (p. 23); WC, p. 36; GR 12.5; YSD 13 (p. 57).

76. Cf. GB 44 (p. 23); WSP *vie* 20 (p. 155); WSP *sermo* 28 (p. 288); GR 12.6.

anno domini M° cc° lxx°, circa horam nonam. Videlicet quam hora dei filius dominus Ihesus Christus pro mundi vita in cruce moriens expiravit.

[12.0] Capitulum xii. De eius migratione et operatione.[71]

[12.1] Et sicut sol inter mundi principes quadam prerogativa solus lucens, et omnibus dans lucem omnimode bonitatis ac vite, custos gratie salutaris, quasi occidit in prima eius transfretatione per sarracenorum captionem et multimodam iniuriarum et carceris oppressionem. Sed ad locum suum reversus fuit per eius miraculosam liberationem, et iterum *giravit per meridiem* [cf. Eccles. 1.6] per secundam eius transfretationem, et reflexus est ad aquilonem per sui sanctissimi corporis de Tunicio apud sanctum Dyonisium in Franciam deportationem, ubi velut sol rutilans minime latuit sub[72] nubilo, ymmo; operante Dei clemencia crebris cepit coruscare miraculis infra scriptis.

[12.2] Antequam enim de eius obitu essent rumores in Francia pro - palati, quadam famosa matrona Parisius, cuius vir domino regi erat familiaris et carus, divinitus ammonita in sompnis, beatum Ludovicum vidit capa purpurea indutum valde spendidum et gloriosum iunctis manibus ad altare capelle regie palicii Parisiensi, accendens quasi super illud aliquod sacrificium oblaturus, magna circumstantium concomitatante caterva, et postmodum versus chorum multum erigens, omnium astantium letificabat aspectum. Stabat et quidam alius aliquantulum distancius ab altari in consili habitu tamen minus splendidus, iunctis manibus quasi orans. Et quia regem cum filiis ultra mare sciebat cum aliis astantibus plurimum mirabatur predicta matrona.

71. rubric in red
72. 14r

the year of our lord 1270, at about the hour of None,[77] which is the exact hour that the Son of God expired from the life of this world as he died on the cross.[78]

[12.0] Chapter 12. On his departure [to God] and his [miracle] works.

[12.1] Just like the sun, Louis, shining alone among princes of the world by special right and giving the light of every kind of goodness and life to all, was the guardian of the grace of salvation. He set like the sun from the various hardships of injuries and imprisonment on his first voyage when he was captured by the Saracens, but, through miraculous liberation he returned to his place [in the heavens], and *wheeled round southwards* [cf. Eccles. 1.6] again on his second voyage, and was then turned again to the north with the return of his most saintly body from Tunis to St.-Denis in France, where, just as the shining sun is hardly hidden behind a cloud, so by God's mercy he began to shine forth with the frequent miracles, which are written about below.[79]

[12.2] Even before the news of his death was known in France, a certain noted lady of Paris, whose husband was a familiar of and dear to the lord king, warned from heaven in her sleep, saw blessed Louis splendidly and gloriously dressed in a purple cape, his hands joined, at the altar of the palace's royal chapel in Paris, approaching as if about to offer a sacrifice upon it, surrounded by a great crowd of bystanders. After a while, rising up toward the great sanctuary, he made glad the countenance of all who were standing around. Another man in the dress of an advisor (though less splendid) was standing a short distance from the altar with his hands joined as if praying. And because the said matron knew that the king was overseas with his sons, she

77. None, literally, "the ninth hour of the day," was one of the canonical hours. The ecclesiastical service of None was generally celebrated at 3:00 in the afternoon, which was the hour that Christ was thought to have died.

78. Cf. GB 44 (23); GR 12.6. WSP *vie* 20 (pp. 52–55) proceeds somewhat differently.

79. These miracles closely follow William of Chartres' miracle account, with one exception (BL 12.17). See WC, pp. 37–40. Note that WC 37 also includes a (less elaborate) comparison between Louis and the sun in his transition for Louis' vita to Louis' miracles.

Crastina vero die postquam illa fuerat ad ecclesiam et de dicta capella redierat ad domum invenit virum suum lamentantem pro dolore mortis regis domini sui quam[73] statim recenter[74] audiverat, ipsa hoc penitus ignorante, et ad eius consolationem predictam referens visionem pie interpretationi adhibens fidem pleniorem, quam in predicta visione sibi Deus ostenderat beatum Ludovicum et eius filium qui cum eo decesserat Comitem Nivernensem in celesti patria gloriosos.

[12.3] In die vero sepulture sacri corporis beati Ludovici apud sanctum Dyonisium quadam mulier Sagiensis diocesi, que dudum visum quasi totaliter amiserat, recuperavit omnino, quod clare probatum fuit testibus fide dignis.

[12.4] Non multo post autem contingit quod quidam iuvenis quasi vigintiquinque annorum a nativitate surdus et mutus, de ultimis finibus Burgundie venit cum quibusdam peditibus ad sepulcrum beati Ludovici ibidem plorans et eiulans cum gemitibus et suspiriis Deum et sanctum regem orans corde prout poterat et sciebat. Tandem vero divina virtute et meritis pii regis ob cuius devotionem venerat, aperte sunt aures eius et solutum est vinculum lingue eius et loquabatur recte coram omnibus ipsum cognoscentibus, in admirationem nimiam[75] versum est et stuporem. Ipse etiam postmodum enarrabat quod quando primo audivit campanas ecclesie pulsari, tantus timor et tremor invasit eum, quod credebat statim super eum totam ecclesiam ruituram, hoc testati sunt vir nobilis dominus Joahnnis Capilonensis, et eius familia cum qua per plures annos dictus iuvenis conversatus fuerat ser - viens in conquina solum innuens et intelligens per signa corporalia et indicia mute[76] voluntatis.

73. 14v
74. recenter] recentem *in* MS
75. 15v
76. *MS reads*: mutue

marveled greatly with the others standing with her. The following day after she had been to church and returned from that said chapel, she found her husband at home grieving on account of the sorrow of the death of the king his lord, of which he had just learned; she had been completely unaware of this, and she told him of the aforesaid vision in order to console him, offering the fuller faith in pious interpretation, which was that in her vision God had shown her blessed Louis and his son, the Count of Nevers, who had died with him, glorious in the celestial homeland.[80]

[12.3] On the day of the burial of blessed Louis' sacred body at St.-Denis, a certain woman from the Diocese of Seés, who had for some time almost completely lost her sight, recovered it fully, which was proven clearly by witnesses worthy in faith.[81]

[12.4] Not long after, it happened that a certain young man who was about twenty-five years old, deaf and dumb from birth, came from the outermost territories of Burgundy to the tomb of blessed Louis with some travelers. He wept and wailed with groans and sighs, praying to God and the saintly king with his heart as far as he could and knew how to. And then, by divine power and the merit of the pious king in whose devotion he had come, his ears were opened, the chain on his tongue was loosened, and he spoke correctly, and all who knew him were astonished that he and his stupor had been so changed. And he later recounted that when he first heard the church bells ringing, a great fear and tremor came over him because he thought the entire church was about to fall down upon him. The witnesses to this were the nobleman Lord John of Châlons and his family, with whom this young man had lived for many years, serving in the kitchen and understanding things only through nods and bodily signals and the signs of his unspoken needs.[82]

---

80. Cf. WC Miracle (hereafter, Mir.) no. 1.

81. Cf. WC Mir. no. 2; GR 14.1; BLQRF Mir. no. 1, RHF vol. 23, 165b–c.

82. Cf. WC Mir. no. 3; GR 14.2; WSP *vie* 15; BLQRF Mir. no. 2, RHF vol. 23, 165c–d; Jean de Vignay, RHF vol. 23, 69e–f.

[12.5] Eodem tempore contigit quod quidam clericus de Britannia natus, cum pluribus fide dignis veniens Parisius transiens per Carnotum, graviter infirmaret ibidem in tamen quod de eius salute medici desperarent, at vero aliquibus pie suggerentibus votum vovit Deo et beato Ludovico, quod eius sepulcrum devotissime visitaret si suis meritis et precibus sibi sospitatem corporis impetraret. Mirum certe et omni gratiarum actione, dignum statim sensit divinam adesse virtutem, in tamen quod in crastino surgens, iter propositum ac votum arripuit et perfecit, restitutus totaliter pristine sanitati.

[12.6] Parum post sepulturam beati Ludovici magister⁷⁷ Dudo⁷⁸ physicus et clericus domini regis qui eidem beato Ludovico diu servierat, et sibi etiam institerat in infirmitate quasi decessit. Febre acuta in festo pentecostes cepit gravissime egrotare, in tamen quod ipse morbus invaluit ipse de seipso at et alii medici penitus desperabant. Quarto vero die sue egritudinis sentiens dolorem capitis vehementem, dominum suum beatum Ludovicum cepit totis affectibus invocare in hunc modum. "Domine mi rex beate Ludovice ego fui clericus vester; et credo vos esse sanctum. Succurrite mihi obsecro in hac necessitate et votum facio quod per noctem ante vestrum tumulum vigilabo." Quo dicto profundo sompno arreptus, videbat⁷⁹ se stare ante sanctum Dyonisium, ante tumulum beati Ludovici super quem tumulum altum cernebat feretrum et desuper regem Ludovicum habentem in manu sceptrum regium indutum dalmatica alba longa usque ad pedes cum fimbriis deauratis insertisque lapidibus preciosis et habens coronam auream in capite suo pulcrior quod nusquam fuerat dum vivebat et hilarior, et verbis⁸⁰ latinis dicebat infirmo ecclesie. "Assum quid vis? multum enim vocasti me." Cui dictus infirmus lacrimando respondit: "Domine, pro Deo succurratis mihi." At ille dixit: "ne timeas, quia ab ista infirmitate curaberis. Sed humor corruptus venenosus et obscenus

77. 15v
78. Dudo] *corr. from* duco
79. Videbat] videba *in* MS
80. 16r

[12.5] At the same time it happened that a certain cleric from Brittany, coming to Paris with many trustworthy men, when traveling through Chartres became so gravely ill that the doctors despaired of his heath, but at some people's suggestion he vowed to God and to blessed Louis that he would devotedly visit his tomb if by [Louis'] merits and prayers [the cleric] might be granted bodily health. Wondrous to say, and worthy of all thanks, he immediately felt that divine power was with him, so much so that the following day he got up, and he undertook and finished the proposed journey and vow, having been totally restored to his former health.[83]

[12.6] A short time after blessed Louis' entombment, Master Dudo, the doctor and cleric of the lord king [Philip III], who had also for a long time been in blessed Louis' service, was himself threatened by an illness as if about to die. On Pentecost he began to languish grievously with an acute fever. The disease became so violent that both he and the other doctors gravely despaired for him. On the fourth day of his illness, feeling a violent pain in his head, he began to call on his lord blessed Louis with great conviction in this way: "My Lord, blessed King Louis, I was once your cleric and I believe that you are a saint. I beg of you to help me in this time of need, and I vow that I will stand vigil at your tomb throughout the night." Having said this, he was overcome by a deep sleep, and he saw himself at St.-Denis, before blessed Louis' tomb, upon which tall tomb he saw a tall bier and on it King Louis holding in his hand the royal scepter, dressed in a long white dalmatic [deacon's vestment] that went down to his feet with a golden fringe, studded with precious stones, wearing a golden crown on his head, and more handsome and more joyful than at any time when he was alive. And [Louis], speaking in Latin to the ailing man of the church, said: "I am here; what do you wish? For you have been calling for me a lot." The ill man responded to him, weeping: "Lord, for God's sake, help me!" And [Louis] said: "Fear not, because you will be cured of this illness. But the corrupt, venomous, repulsive, and foul humor that you have in your brain is the cause of your illness, and does not permit you to recognize your Creator as you should." Louis promised to remove that said evil humor,

83. Cf. WC Mir. no. 4; GR 14.3; BLQRF Mir. no. 3, RHF vol. 23, 165e.

ac fetidus quam habes in cerebro est causa infirmitatis tue, nec permittit ut debes te tuum cognoscere Creatorem." Et promittens amovere dictum malum humorem, ut dicto physico videbatur scidit eum inter nasum et supercilium sinistre partis immitens pollicem cum alio digito sequente, extraxit de dicto humore ad quantitatem unius nucis magne, dicens "quod quamdiu hoc in capite habuisses numquam sanitatem haberes." Excitatus vero dictus infirmus assistentibus dixit se esse curatum et ipsiis putantibus ipsum esse alienatum ipsa nocte quarte diei post rigorem fortissimum et sudorem, fuit dei virtute ac meritis sancti regis, plenarie liberatus. Quod ut dixerunt medici tali die et in illa apparenti digestione non potuit contingere per naturam.[81]

[12.7] Apud castrum Lupere Parisius dominus Petrus de Lauduno miles, condam cambellanus beati Ludovici, tunc custos puerorum domini regis Philippi, cum in dextro brachio suo dolorem intolerabilem pateretur, capillos beati Ludovoci quos apud se honorifice et cum devotione servabat ter apposuit ad locum doloris et in trina appositione fuit plenarie liberatus, cum prius non posset suum levare brachium nec ex eo aliud operari.

[12.8] Eodem tempore quadam mulier de Rothomago, quasi omnino visum amiserat occulorum, adducta ex devotione apud sanctam Dyonisium ad sepulchrum beati Ludovici, ibidem visum recuperavit, meritis et precibus sancti regis.

[12.9] Eodem anno feria tercia post festum beati Urbani pape quadam mulier de Cambeliaco nomine Amelina ita curva cum adiutorio parvi baculi incedebat quod capud suum ultra pedem et dimidium non poterat elevare, hec veniens ad sepulcrum beati Ludovici, fusa oratione devota usum recte incendendi recuperavit omnino; hec mulier[82]

81. 16v
82. 17r

and it seemed to the said doctor that [Louis] split open [his head] on the left side between his nose and eyebrows, using his thumb and forefinger, and extracted from the humor something the size of a big walnut, saying: "As long as you had this in your head, you would never be healthy." Having awoken, the sick man said to those who were attending to him that he had been cured. And to those people who thought that he was about to be given up that night, the fourth day after his great numbness and sweat, [he said that] he, by the power of God and the merits of the saint king, was fully liberated. The doctors said that such a thing could not have happened on that day [the fourth day of his illness] simply through natural causes, given the state of his bodily imbalance.[84]

[12.7] At the palace of the Louvre in Paris, Lord Peter of Laon, a knight and previously blessed Louis' chamberlain, and then guardian to the sons of the Lord King Philip [III], was suffering from an intolerable pain in his right arm. Three times he touched to the site of the pain hairs of blessed Louis that, in honor and with devotion, he had preserved at his house, and with this triple application was fully healed, even though previously he was not able to lift up his arm nor do anything with it. [85]

[12.8] At that same time a certain woman from Rouen, having lost nearly all the sight of her eyes, out of devotion was led to St.-Denis and to blessed Louis' tomb, and right there and then recovered her sight by the merits and prayers of the saint king.[86]

[12.9] In that same year, three days after the feast of the blessed pope Urban, a certain woman from Chambly called Amelina, who was so crooked that she used to walk with the aid of a little cane because she could not lift her head up more than a foot and half off the ground, came to the tomb of blessed Louis and, pouring forth in devout prayer, wholly recovered her ability to walk upright. This woman, so crooked

84. Cf. WC Mir. no. 5; GR 14.4; BLQRF Mir. no. 4, RHF vol. 23, 165f–g; WSP *mir* no. 38; Jean de Vignay, RHF vol. 23, 69 h–k.

85. Cf. WC Mir. no. 6; GR 14.5; BLQRF Mir. no. 5, RHF vol. 23, 165h.

86. Cf. WC Mir. no. 7; GR 14.6; BLQRF Mir. no. 6, RHF vol. 23, 165j.

et sic curva multo tempore et postmodum erecta, in utroque statu cognita fuit a quam pluribus fide dignis.

[12.10] Feria vero sexta subsequente, quadam puella Petronilla nomine qua numquam ire potuerat nisi trahendo se cum pedibus et manibus super terra veniens ad sepulcrum beati Ludovici, recuperavit usum membrorum et plenam corporis sanitatem.

[12.11] Eodem anno aliquantulum postea, quadam[83] mulier de Parisius nomine Agnes Lamaquina, in cimiterio sancti Innocentii dum audiret sermonem, percussa fuit paralisi, que adducta ad locum sepe dicti sepulcri virtute divina, et per ipsius gloriosi regis merita, partis infirme recuperavit plenissime sanitatem.

[12.12] Item eodem anno quadam mulier de Villataneuse nomine Hodierna, per duodecim annos continue gravi infirmate afflicta, de lecto surgere non valens nisi cum magna difficultate, per quinque annos solum in paschate apodians se cum baculo et cum aliorum adiutoriuo ad ecclesiam veniebat. Tandem cum magna devotione, perducta ad sepulcrum beati Ludovici, meritis pii[84] regis, restituta fuit pristine sanitate.

[12.13] Item eodem anno paulo post Michael dictus Samiage,[85] commorans Parisius in parochia sancti Pauli, qui sine duabus potenciis ire non poterat per sex annos, veniens ad sepulcrum beati Ludovici, per merita ipsius perfectam et integram optinuit sanitatem.

[12.14] Item eodem anno die dominica ante festum beati Barnabe apostoli, Aelis filia Roberti dicti Pilum,[86] qua toto tempore vite sue

---

83. quadam] quada *in* MS
84. 17v
85. Cf. version in WC, *Hamiage* or *Sauvage* (p. 40, note 5).
86. The name in WC's account is Robert dictus Peclecoc.

for so long, and afterwards upright, was observed in both states by many men of good faith.[87]

[12.10] Six days later a certain girl called Petronilla, who had never been able to go without dragging herself over the ground with her feet and hands, came to the tomb of blessed Louis and recovered the use of her limbs and the full health of her body.[88]

[12.11] A little later that same year a certain woman from Paris named Agnes Lamaquina, while she was listening to a sermon in the cemetery of the Holy Innocents, was struck by paralysis. Repeatedly brought to the location of the aforesaid tomb, she, by divine power and by the merits of that glorious king himself, completely recovered the health of her ailing parts.[89]

[12.12] In that same year there was a certain woman from Villetaneuse named Hodierna who had for twelve years been afflicted by a grave malady. Unable to get out of bed without great difficulty, for five years she came to church only on Easter and only by pressing herself forward with her walking stick and with the help of others. At length, having been led to the tomb of blessed Louis, with great devotion and by the merits of the pious king, she was restored to her former health.[90]

[12.13] A little later that same year, Michael, called Savage, dwelling in Paris in the parish of Saint Paul, who for six years had been unable to walk without the help of two crutches, came to the tomb of blessed Louis and, by the merits of that same one, obtained perfect and complete health.[91]

[12.14] In the same year on the Sunday before the feast of Barnabas, the blessed Apostle, Aelis, daughter of Robert of Pilum, who had for

87. Cf. WC Mir. no. 8; WSP *mir* no. 5; William of Nangis, RHF vol. 20, 464b.
88. CF. WC Mir. no. 9; WSP *mir* no. 54.
89. Cf. WC Mir. no. 10; WSP *mir* no. 44.
90. Cf. WC Mir. no. 11; WSP *mir* no. 32.
91. Cf. WC Mir. no. 12; WSP *mir* no. 48.

manum habebat recurvam nec etiam usque ad pectus levare poterat, nec super genua inclinare sine adiutorio alterius manus, veniens ad predicti sancti sepulcrum, per eius merita gloriosa, de infirmitate sua rediit liberata et multi alii, etc.

[12.15] Eodem die Iohannis dictus Camos de parochia sancti Mederici Parisius, qui per quatuor annos nisi apodiando se manibus super genua incedere non valebat, ad sepulcrum dicti sancti, recuperavit modum et usum debitum incedendi.

[12.16] Ibidem die martis ante festum predictum, Gila de Salvaneto commorans Parisius in parochia sancti[87] Pauli per quatuor annos sine potenciis ire non potuerat, per merita beati Ludovici perfectam optinuit sanitatem.

[12.17] Et in vigilia dicti festi scilicet beati Barnabe quadam Ioheneta dicta de Porta Bandoier, que per plures annos sine potenciis gressum non habuerat, eiusdem sancti meritis incedendi modo debito recuperavit virtutem.

[12.18] Die vero sabbati immediate sequenti, Emmelina Lambreita, uxor Iohannis Angelici de Parisius, que a festo beati Martini yemalis unam de tibiis suis quasi totaliter amiserat, ita quod paralitica[88] videbatur, ad sepulchrum predictum veniens, integre recuperavit pristinam sanitatem.

[12.19] Et alia multa contingunt miracula, meritis et precibus beati Ludovici, ad laudem et gloriam Redemptoris, cui est honor et gloria per infinita secula seculorum. Amen!

---

87. 18r
88. paralitica] *corr. from* parelitica

her entire life a crooked hand, which she could not even lift to her breast or stretch out over her knees without the aid of the other hand, came to the tomb of the aforementioned saint, and afterwards, by his glorious merits, she went away, freed from her infirmity and much else.[92]

[12.15] That same day, John Camos, from the parish of Saint Medard in Paris, who for four years was not strong enough to walk without pushing himself by his hands upon his knees, recovered the means and use necessary for walking at the tomb of the said saint.[93]

[12.16] In that same place one day in March, before the aforesaid feast, Gila of Senlis, dwelling in Paris in the parish of Saint Paul, unable to walk without crutches for four years, obtained perfect health through the merits of blessed Louis.[94]

[12.17] And on the vigil of the said feast, that is, of blessed Barnabus, a certain Johanneta, said to be of Porta Baudéer, who for many years was not able to walk without crutches, recovered the strength needed to walk by the merits of that same saint.[95]

[12.18] On the Saturday immediately following, Emmelina Lambre-ita, wife of John Angelici of Paris, who since the winter feast of blessed Martin had lost almost entirely the use of one leg, such that she seemed paralyzed, went to the foresaid tomb and entirely recovered her former health.[96]

[12.19] And many other miracles occurred through the merits and prayers of blessed Louis, for the praise and glory of the Redeemer, to whom honor and glory, forever and ever, through the ages. Amen.

92. Cf. WC Mir no. 17.
93. Cf. WC Mir. no. 14.
94. Cf. WC Mir. no. 16.
95. Cf. WC Mir. no. 13.
96. Cf. WC Mir. no. 15; WSP *mir* no. 52.

3

OFFICE AND MASS TEXTS

Paris BNF Lat 911, 3r. *Ludovicus decus.* Courtesy Bibliothèque
nationale de France.

One of the most important ways in which a community celebrated and remembered a saint was through liturgical devotion. What follows is the most popular liturgical office in honor of Louis, *Ludovicus decus regnantium,* and the mass in honor of Louis, *Gaudeamus omnes,* as they were celebrated in Paris.

Ludovicus decus regnantium was probably commissioned by Louis IX's grandson, Philip the Fair, and compiled by a well-known liturgist, Pierre de la Croix, after Louis' canonization. It is based on a liturgical office, *Nunc laudare,* that was written shortly before by Dominicans, and adopts a number of its texts. The lections (readings for Matins, compiled a few years later, which constitute the text referred to here as BLQRF) were drawn from *Beatus Ludovicus,* but they were edited and shortened in such a way as to create a tightly composed, elegant vita, which was later disseminated independently of the office. An updated set of miracle stories was added for the octave reading, including miracles that occurred after 1297. (These miracle accounts are not translated here, since they are essentially identical to those added to *Gloriosissimi regis* in the fifteenth century, translated in the appendix to GR as chapter 14.) The octave prayers and readings were added to *Ludovicus decus regnantium* soon afterward; most of the antiphons were drawn from other offices that had been composed by that time.

Liturgical offices followed a specific format, based on the ecclesiastical hours of the day. What we do not necessarily see when we read through a saint's office is the underlying substructure of the recitation of psalms, which constituted the core of the *Opus Dei* and on which the proper prayers (that is, prayers specific to Louis) were built. It is useful to think of the proper office as an appendage to the set singing of the psalms and other fixed liturgical items that varied according to the day (in that the appendage would be different for the feast day of, say, Saint Francis, or on Christmas). Proper texts also had the effect of linking the greater themes of the psalms to the individual lives of the saints being celebrated. The essential themes of any proper saint's office were the honoring of the saint and the entreaty to him or her as intercessor.

It is useful, as one reads through *Ludovicus decus,* to keep in mind that most of these items were sung, and that they were communal rituals for which the religious community of clerics gathered together in celebration. As with so much that has to do with the liturgy, practice varied greatly, and the same office might be performed differently in

different churches. But in general, the liturgical office is structured by the liturgical day and the recitation of the psalms. Proper items are principally made up of Antiphons, Responsories, Hymns, and Lections (readings). The participating clergy would be divided into two halves, each sitting on opposite sides of the choir. Antiphonal and responsorial singing meant that different parts of the choir sang different parts of the office. Antiphons are proper chant items that are paired with specific psalms. They introduce and follow the reading of a psalm or canticle, and they were sung antiphonally—that is, by alternating halves of the choir. In many cases the antiphons would take up or play with an image, word, phrase, or idea from the psalm that they introduced. In this way, the antiphons associated the themes of scripture to the life of the saint and used scripture to explicate his or her sanctity. Responsories have two parts, the respond and the verse. The great responsories that followed the readings (lections) of Matins may have been sung by the choir, with a soloist (or two) then singing the verse; or, in large congregations, the respond and the verse each may have been sung by a small group of soloists. Lections were simply the hagiographical readings that were intoned (recited using a repetitive, chant-like, melodic formula) during the Matins service. Here, the lections (BLQRF) are uncharacteristically long. Often, however, these might be truncated to hasten the performance of the service. An office would also generally include three proper hymns. Hymns are stanzaic songs of praise that were sung at First Vespers, Matins, and Lauds, and that would often, as in *Ludovicus decus,* pick up the narrative and symbolic themes of the office. Other items, such as the little hours, or the canticles (often taken from or adapted from a scriptural text), were either intoned (that is, chanted) or sung throughout the day.

Ludovicus decus is an elegant example of a rhymed office—a genre that became increasingly popular after about 1100. As such, antiphons, responsories, and hymns followed a specific rhyming and beat pattern. A reader should be aware that the liturgy is essentially musical poetry. Consider the opening antiphon of First Vespers:

Ludovicus decus regnantium
transit felix ad celi solium,
cuius prece cetus fidelium
summi regis intret in gaudium.

Each line of the antiphon comprises ten beats and ends with a word finishing with "ium." This antiphon would have been followed by the recitation of a psalm (dictated by the day of the week).[1] A translation that aims primarily for fidelity to the language loses much of the feeling of the text, as, for instance, with this version:

> Louis, glory of rulers,
> Happily crosses to the throne of the heavens,
> By whose prayer the assembly of faithful
> May enter into the joy of the highest king.

Instead, in the translation offered here, with its eight beats per line and final words ending alike, we have tried to capture some of the original poetic and rhythmic tone of the liturgy. In this instance, we have rendered a looser translation but one that, we hope, better evokes the aesthetic, rhythmic affect of the Latin:

> Glory of all kings who reign
> Happy to heaven's throne he came,
> Louis, by whose prayer and name
> All men of faith may God's joy gain.

Likewise, we have tried to maintain, in some measure, the thematic relationship between the antiphons and the psalms with which they were paired. For example, the second antiphon for Matins introduced the second psalm, which includes the verse, "But I am appointed king by him over Sion, his holy mountain, preaching his commandment" (Ego autem constitutus sum rex ab eo super Syon, montem sanctum eius predicans preceptum eius). The antiphon plays with the image of Louis being "constituted king over Sion"; a literal translation would be:

> Having obtained the throne of the kingdom,
> He surrendered himself to humility,

---

1. On the psalms used for First Vespers, see "Vespers" in the *New Grove Dictionary of Music and Musicians,* 2nd ed., ed. Stanley Sadie (New York: Grove, 2001), also available online by subscription as the "Oxford Music Online."

And appointed in Sion,
He shone in service to the Lord.

In order to maintain both the rhyming aesthetic of the original and its relationship to Psalm 2, we have translated this as:

Even on the royal throne
He ever kept a humble look.
In worshipping his God he shone,
For Sion's was the rule he took.

The antiphon would normally be followed by the recitation of an entire psalm, which was generally identified by its incipit. In the Latin text we have listed the psalm by chapter and verse to reflect the sources, which offered only the incipit, but in the translation we have cited the entire psalm, to reflect the fact that the psalm was to be recited in its entirety at this point.

The long readings during the service of Matins (the lections), which here constitute a liturgical vita (BLQRF), are an edited, sharpened, and polished version of *Beatus Ludovicus*. Most manuscript versions of the office would include shorter versions still, since these readings were the least important and thus the most expendable elements of the divine office. But the liturgical vita also circulated independently, often as part of a collection of saints' lives, and was sometimes included in later compilations of Jacob of Voraigne's popular *Golden Legend*. It is offered here as an element of the office, but also, when compared to *Beatus Ludovicus*, as an example of how liturgical texts evolved in this fluid environment.

Included here as well are the texts for the Mass of Saint Louis. Like the office, this mass included texts specifically composed for use on August 25, in conjunction with the mass itself; the core items of this central ritual, such as Canon of the Mass and the Lord's Prayer (not reproduced here), were constant. Items that were proper to the individual day could vary but might include the Introit, Gradual, Alle - luia, Sequences (akin to hymns), Offertory, and Communio. The performance of the mass also varied greatly, but in the later Middle Ages a proper mass for an important feast day would be celebrated in the

sanctuary, with a chief celebrant presiding at the altar and the other participants singing in the choir. As with the office, a number of items were intoned (as in the collect, or scriptural readings such as the Epistle), and other items were sung in the choir. Sequences, sometimes called prosae, were like hymns in that they constituted musical poetry, sung antiphonally either by alternating sides of the choir or by individual groups of soloists. The gradual can be compared to the great responsories of the Matins service of the office in that they were sung "responsorially" between a soloist (or two) and the choir, or by groups of soloists.[2]

2. For a full explanation of the medieval mass and office in context, see John Harper, *The Forms and Orders of Western Liturgy from the Tenth to the Eighteenth Century: A Historical Introduction and Guide for Students and Musicians* (Oxford: Clarendon Press, 1992). For those interested in the musical aspect, see David Hiley, *Western Plainchant: A Handbook* (Oxford: Clarendon Press, 1993). Enormously helpful for clarifying individual aspects of the mass and office is the *New Grove Dictionary of Music and Musicians*.

LUDOVICUS DECUS REGNANTIUM:

OFFICE IN HONOR OF SAINT LOUIS

LUDOVICUS DECUS REGNANTIUM: OFFICE IN HONOR OF SAINT LOUIS

Ad I Vesperas
Antiphonae
1. Ludovicus decus regnantium
transit felix ad celi solium,
cuius prece cetus fidelium
summi regis intret in gaudium.

2. Gaude regnum Francie,
cui dedit rex glorie
tam excellens donum,
quod tu regem proprium
habes in subsidium
in celis patronum.

3. Te dum ipse viveret
ac coronam regeret,
tamquam rex deffendit,
nunc particeps glorie
factus tue venie
diligens intendit.

4. Plebs ergo francigena,
non tanquam gens advena,
Christo refer laudes,
in cuius palatio
tui patrocinio
quondam regis gaudes.

5. In terris regimine
ac sub eius nomine
protecta fuisti
modo tibi gratiam
impetret ac veniam
in conspectu Christi.

LOUIS, THE GLORY OF ALL KINGS:
OFFICE IN HONOR OF SAINT LOUIS
Verse translation by Phyllis B. Katz

First Vespers
Antiphons
1. Glory of all kings who reign;
Happy to heaven's throne he came.
Louis, by whose prayer and name,
All men of faith may God's joy gain.

2. O realm of France, rejoice and sing,
For you on high the Glorious King,
Your own king to the sky has raised
To be your guardian and your aid,
A perfect gift for you God made.

3. While he lived with earthly men,
Louis wore the diadem
And kept you safe as king.
Now he shares in heaven's glow,
And works to pardon you below.

4. O denizens of France's lands,
No foreign ground is in your hands.
Give praise to Christ your King.
Rejoice that in His royal home
Your former king sits by His throne
And to you safety brings.

5. On earth his rule protected you
As did his royal name.
And so before Christ's heavenly face
For you he garners pardon's grace
And frees you from sin's blame.

Capitulum
Benedictus Dominus Deus patrum nostrorum qui dedit hanc volun-
tatem in cor regis clarificare domum suam que est in Iherusalem. Deo
gratias. [Cf. Ezra 7.27]

Responsorium
Cum esset in accubitu,
rex interne dulcedinis,
arcens potenti spiritu
pestes carnis et sanguinis
bonorum septus ambitu,
sceptro fulsit regiminis.

[v] David regis
sedit in solio,
Salomonis utens
iudicio

Hymnus
Gaude mater ecclesia
nove laudis preconio
quam Ludovici gloria
solenni replet gaudio.

De regno terre vehitur
ad regni celi solium,
cuius vita dignoscitur
forma virtutum omnium.

Fide purus, spe paciens
et caritate fervidus,
omni petenti largiens,
pius, pudicus, providus.

Fraus, furor, violentia
relegantur a subditis;
signa choruscant varia
virtutum eius meritis.

Scriptural Reading
Blessed Lord God of our fathers who gave this will into the heart of
the king to glorify His house, which is in Jerusalem. [Cf. Ezra 7.27]

Responsory
Even when he went to sleep
The king's sweet nature watch did keep.
Radiant with his ruler's scepter
He drove away all evil specters,
Lusts of the body or the blood,
Protected by a wall of good.

[v] A David sitting on the royal throne,
A judgment like to Solomon's he owned.

Hymn for Vespers
Rejoice in celebration new,
Praise, O mother church, for you;
For Louis' glory fills you through
With festive joy that is your due.

From his kingdom's earthly home
He moved to heaven's royal throne.
His virtues bear all beauty's hues
And set his life apart for you.

Patient, kind, and faithful too,
He burns with love to aid the poor.
Modest in his goodness true,
He gives to all before his door.

From his subjects he sends far,
Fraud, violence, and rage;
Examples of his goodness are
Through merits shining made.

Pro corona iusticie
iam coronatus gloria;
nostre memor miserie
celi procuret premia.

Trino Deo et simplici
Laus, honor, virtus, gloria,
qui nos regis mirifici
coronet per suffragia.

Ad Magnificat antiphona
Magnificat gesta clarissima
sancti Ludovici
divino cultui
devotum hodie
presens collegium,
cuius sancta conscendit anima
sub fine felici
regni perpetui
cum sanctis patrie
sublime solium.

Oratio
Deus qui beatum Ludovicum confessorem tuum de terreno ac temporali regno ad celestis et eterni gloriam transtulisti; eius quesumus meritis et intercessione regis regum Ihesu Christi, filii tui, nos coheredes efficias et eiusdem regni tribuas esse consortes.

Ad Completorium
Antiphonae
1. Ludovicus Dominum
de celis laudavit,
quando vite terminum
celo dedicavit.
P. Cum invocarem. [Ps. 4.2]

The crown of earthly justice
He traded for a crown on high,
Let him be given heaven's glories,
Who hears our grief in heaven's skies.

For God on high both Three and One,
May honor, praise, and virtue ring;
For He may crown us too with glory,
Assenting to our wondrous king.

Magnificat antiphon
Saint Louis' holy cult
And deeds of love
This college now exults.
To endless rest above,
His sacred soul has risen
Upon a throne sublime.
Among the holy saints of heaven,
God's kingdom beyond time.

Collect
Oh God, you who carried blessed Louis confessor from the earthly and temporal kingdom to the glory of the heavens and eternity, we beg that you make us, through his merit and intercession, the co-heirs of your son Christ Jesus, King of Kings, and allow us a share of that same kingdom.

Compline
Antiphons
1. Louis praised the Lord on high
When it was his time to die,
And gave his life to heaven.
P. When I called upon him ... [Ps. 4]

2. Coronatur gloria
sanctus et honore
quia mundi gaudia
duxit in timore.
P. Nunc dimittis. [Luke 2.29]

Ad Matutinum
Invitatorium
Ludovici leta solennia
leta colat mater ecclesia.
P. Venite. [Ps. 94]

Hymnus
Nova regis preconia
solenni digna cantico
devota promat Francia,
cantu plaudens angelico.

Regis huius religio
et aspectus gratissimus
monstrabant quid de premio
eius gustaret animus.

Monstrant quoque miracula
quantus sit in celestibus,
morbos, pestes, pericula
suis fugando precibus.

O quam dulce spectaculum
in Ludovico cerneret,
qui virtutis signaculum
eius vultum inspiceret.

Nam vultus eius claritas
nunquam in terra corruit,

2. Because the pleasures of the world
He held in mortal dread,
Honor and glory are the crown
Our saint bears on his head.
P. Now thou dost dismiss . . . [Luke 2.29]

Matins
Invitatory antiphon
Let the joyous church our mother,
The joyous rites of Louis honor.
P. Come let us praise . . . [Ps. 94]

Hymn for Matins
To praise the king
Let faithful France
New worthy plaudits bring,
In song the angels sing.

The King's demeanor
And his faith,
So full of grace,
Reveal the prize
His soul could taste.

His miracles as well display
His greatness in God's realm;
For with his prayers he drives away
All illness, plagues, and harms.

O, how sweet a vision
Our Louis is in heaven,
One sees upon his face
The mark of virtue's grace.

His face possessed a luminosity
On earth that never ceased to shine;

nec affectus benignitas
Deo presente caruit.

Trino Deo et simplici. *ut supra.*

In I Nocturno
Antiphonae
1. Beatus qui solium,
iter et consilium
malorum vitavit;
sanctus ab infantia
Ludovicus hec tria
semper declinavit.
P. Beatus vir. [Ps 1.1]

2. Regni sedem consequutus
humilem se prebuit
et in Syon constitutus
cultu Dei claruit.
P. Quare fremuerunt. [Ps. 2.1]

3. Susceptus ad meritum
gloria dotatur,
capud Deo subditum
celo coronatur.
P. Domine quid multiplicati. [Ps. 3.2]

Lectio prima
Beatus Ludovicus, quondam rex francorum illustris, patrem habuit
christianissimum regem nomine Ludovicum. Hic de Albigesio et comi-
tatu Tholosano hereticos debellavit et hereses extirpavit. Et dum

Nor did love's generosity
Fail our God who transcends time.

For God on high both Three and One ... (*as above*)[1]

First Nocturn
Antiphons
1. Blessed he who shunned the path,
The throne, or plans of evil men.
Saint Louis from his earliest days
Ever kept from these three ways.[2]
P. Blessed is the man ... [Ps. 1]

2. Even on the royal throne
He ever kept a humble look.
In worshipping his God he shone,
For Sion's was the rule he took.[3]
P. Why have the gentiles raged ... [Ps. 2]

3. Raised up to his merit
His glory is enthroned.
To his God a subject,
His head in heaven crowned.[4]
P. Why, O Lord, are they multiplied ... [Ps. 3]

First lection
Blessed Louis, the late illustrious king of the French, had as his father
the most Christian king, Louis [VIII], who fought the heretics from
Albi and the country of Toulouse, and rooted out heresy. As he was

---

1. An indication that one is to repeat the fifth stanza of the Hymn for First
Vespers.
2. Followed by Ps. 1.
3. Followed by Ps. 2.
4. Followed by Ps. 3.

reverteretur in Franciam, migravit ad Christum. Puer igitur sancte indolis, patre strenuissimo sic orbatus, sub tutela matris, videlicet Blanche regine, quondam regis Castelle filie, remansit. Quem ipsa te - nerrime diligens, sub cura specialis magistri et consilio religiosorum, maxime ordinis fratrum predicatorum et minorum,[1] in moribus et in scientia litterarum tradidit imbuendum. At ipse, velut alter Salomon, puer ingeniosus et bonam sortitus animam, supra coetaneos suos pro- fecit valde laudabiliter in utrisque.[2] Cujus sanctitati congaudens pia mater pluries dicebat eidem: "Plus vellem, fili karissime, te mortem incurrere temporalem quam per aliquod peccatum mortale te tuum offendere Creatorem." Quod verbum devotus filius in animo sic fir- mavit quod, divina se protegente gratia, nunquam sensisse letalis cri- minis contagium perhibetur.

Responsorium
Rex regum regis filio
regales parans nuptias,
post certamen in stadio
celi prebet delicias
glorioso commercio.

[v] Pro regno temporalium
regnum habet celestium
Ludovicus in premium.

Lectio secunda
Demum providentia matris ac procerum, ne tam nobile regnum re- gali successione careret, uxorem duxit, de qua susceptam sobolem generosam vir sanctus summopere studuit educari ad amorem Dei,

---

1. Note that the addition of "et minorum" to the sentence (in comparison to BL) is grammatically awkward.
2. "utriusque" in Epstein's edition

returning to France, he departed to Christ. This boy of saintly character, deprived in this way of his most resolute father, remained under the care of his mother, that is, of Queen Blanche, the late daughter of the king of Castile. Loving Louis most tenderly, she placed him under the care of a special master and the counsel of monks, especially from the order of the Preachers [and from the order] of the Minors,[5] for his education in good behavior and in knowledge of scripture. And he, just like another Solomon, a very clever boy having been allotted a good soul,[6] in many ways worthy of great praise, advanced beyond his peers in both things. His pious mother, rejoicing much in his sanctity, used to say to him: "I would rather, dear son, that you incur earthly death than that you offend your creator through some kind of mortal sin." This devout son so firmly held this saying in his heart that he never allowed himself, with divine grace protecting him, to feel the contagion of mortal sin.

Responsory 1
The King of kings
Prepares royal nuptial feasts
For the son of the king
Whose earthly battle's done
And by an exchange of glory
Provides delights of heaven won.

[v] Reward for a kingdom temporal,
Louis has gained rule celestial.

Second lection
After some time, owing to the solicitude of his mother and of the noblemen, in order that such a noble kingdom might not lack royal succession, he took a wife. This saintly man greatly desired that the noble

5. The reference to the Franciscans as participating in Louis' education is an addition to the text at this stage. See general introduction, n. 50.

6. Cf. Wisd. 8.19: "Puer autem eram ingeniosus et sortitus sum animam bonam." [And I was a witty child, and had received a good soul.] This sentence and the comparison to Solomon are additions to the text. Solomon was understood to be author of the Book of Wisdom.

contemptum mundi et cognitionem sui salutaribus monitis et exemplis. Et quando sibi secreto vacare poterat, eos personaliter visitans, et de eorum profectu requirens, velut alter Thobias dabat eisdem monita salutis, docens eos super omnia timere Deum et ab omni peccato iugiter abstinere. Serta quoque de rosis seu alios capellos eos portare sextis feriis prohibebat, propter coronam spineam tali die impositam capiti Salvatoris.

Responsorium
Felix terra cuius rex sapiens,
iustus, clemens, modestus, paciens,
cuius vultus est malos feriens,
bonos alliciens.

[v] Ludocivus sic terris prefuit,
quod regnando celos promeruit.

Lectio tertia
Et quia sciebat quod in deliciis, pietas, et in honoribus humilitas periclitari solent, ideo sobrietati, humilitati et misericordie animum dedit, ab insidiis mundi, carnis et diaboli sollicite custodians seme - tipsum. Et exemplo Apostoli corpus suum castigans, in servitutem redigens castigatione multiplici, suo spiritui servire cogebat. Multo enim tempore cilicio utebatur ad carnem. Et quando propter nimiam debilitatem corporis hoc dimittebat ad instanciam proprii confessoris, volebat quod idem confessor quasi in recompensationem pro qualibet die quadrigenta solidos parisientium secreto pauperibus erogaret.

offspring born of this [marriage] be educated in the love of God, contempt for the world, and self-knowledge through salutary admonitions and examples. And when he could spare the time for solitude, he himself visited [his children] and, as another Tobias,[7] inquired about their progress, offering warnings about their salvation and teaching them above all to fear God and abstain always from all sin. Further, he forbade them to wear either wreaths of roses or hats of any sort on Fridays on account of the crown of thorns which was placed on the head of the Savior on that very day.

Responsory 2
Happy the land who has a king
Both merciful and just,
Patient, wise, and modest,
A ruler they can trust;
A king whose face the evil fear
While good men will draw near.

[v] Louis ruled the earth in such a way
He well deserved his heavenly stay.

Third lection
And because [Louis] knew that piety was endangered in the delights of the flesh, and humility in striving for honors, he gave his heart over to sobriety, humility, and mercy, and with extreme care he protected himself from the snares of the world, the flesh, and the devil. And on the example of the apostle,[8] punishing his body and reducing it with frequent castigation to servitude, he would compel it to serve his spirit. For a long time he wore a hair shirt on his body. But when, because of excessive bodily harm, at his confessor's insistence, he renounced [this practice], he proposed that, in compensation, on those days this same

7. The reference to Tobias is an addition to the text. Cf. Tob. 4, in which Tobias offers salutary instructions to his son.
8. The reference to the apostle (Paul) is an addition to the text. Cf. 1 Cor. 9.27: "Sed castigo corpus meum et in servitutem redigo." [But I chastise my body and bring it into subjection.] Saint Paul was the author of 1 Corinthians. The reference to 1 Cor. 9.27 is in the original text.

Ieiunabat omni tempore sextis feriis, et maxime in Adventu et Quadragesima. Hiis diebus a piscibus et fructibus abstinebat, laboribus, vigiliis, orationibus, et aliis secretis abstinentiis et disciplinis iugiter se affligens.

Responsorium
Hunc natura genuit
regno fructuosum,
voluntas exercuit
mundo graciosum,
Deus ipsum prebuit
celo gloriosum.

[v] Normam vite posuit
hunc Deus et tribuit
signis virtuosum.

In II Nocturno
Antiphonae
4. Invocantem exaudivit
Deus regem humilem,
et preclaris insignivit
signis suum pugilem.
P. Cum invocarem. [Ps. 4.2]

5. Deductus in iusticia
clemens subiectis prefuit;
leges, penas et premia
sapienter instituit.
P. Verba mea. [Ps. 5.2]

6. Coronatur gloria
sanctus et honore

confessor secretly distribute forty Parisian *solidos* to the poor. He fasted throughout the year on Fridays, but with particular dedication during Advent and Lent. On these days he abstained from fish and fruit, continually subjecting himself to labors, vigils, prayers, and other secret abstinences and disciplines.

Responsory 3
This fruitfulness for the kingdom
Nature did unfurl.
Desire gave him power
To rule this earthly world;
But God placed him on high
Glorious in His sky.

[v] God made this man a model
For those who live on earth
And marked his many virtues,
With signals of his worth.

Second Nocturn
Antiphons
4. God heard the humble king
Who prayed to Him for aid
He marked him fighter in His ring,
Through the signs He made.[9]
P. When I have called upon him ... [Ps. 4]

5. Led by his sense of justice
His rule was merciful and good,
In wisdom giving laws and punishment,
Rewarding those he could.[10]
P. Give ear, O Lord, to my words ... [Ps. 5]

6. With glory and with honor
The saint is crowned on high;

9. Followed by Ps. 4.
10. Followed by Ps. 5.

quia mundi gaudia
duxit in timore.
P. Domine Dominus. [Ps. 8.2]

Lectio quarta
Omnium virtutum decor, humilitas, adeo refulgebat in eo ut quanto
magnus erat, velut alter David tanto humilius se gerebat et coram Deo
in oculis suis vilior apparebat. Quolibet namque Sabbato consueverat
in loco secretissimo quorumdam pauperum propriis manibus abluere
pedes, et deinde tergere ac humiliter osculari[3], similiter et manus, cuilibet certam summam pecunie tribuendo. Pluries etiam centum viginti
pauperibus, qui in curia sua omni die reficiebantur habunde et in vigiliis sollempnibus, ac quibusdam certis diebus per annum, ducentis pauperibus, antequam ipse comederet, manu propria fercula ministravit.
Semper enim in prandio et cena prope se tres senes pauperes recumbentes habebat, quibus de cybis sibi appositis karitative mittebat, et
quandoque scutellas et cybos quos Christi pauperes propriis manibus
contrectaverant [precipue offas quas libenter comedebat[4]], ut iterum
inde gustaret ante se reasportare precepit, Christum pauperem in suis
pauperibus venerando, de quorum reliquiis sic comedere non horrebat.

3. obstulari *in* MS (Paris BNF Lat 911)
4. *expunged in* MS

Because he held in terror
The joys that he denied.[11]
P. O Lord, our Lord . . . [Ps. 8]

Fourth lection
Humility, the glory of all virtues, shone forth in him in such a way that, as another David,[12] the greater that he was, with greater humility he bore himself, since he appeared more worthless in his own eyes before God. Thus, sometimes on Saturdays in a very secret place he would wash the feet of some poor men with his own hands, and then he dried them and humbly kissed them, and he did the same to their hands, while giving some of them a certain sum of money. Frequently he would, with his own hands, serve food to the 120 poor who were daily given meals at his court. On solemn vigils and on certain other days of the year he would, with his own hands, serve dishes to 200 poor guests before he himself would eat. At lunch and dinner he would always have three poor old men sitting near him, to whom he would charitably send over food placed before him, and sometimes he would order the dishes and food that the poor of Christ had touched with their own hands, bits of food that he was particularly willing to eat, to be brought before him again so that he might taste them a second time. He venerated Christ, the poor man, in his own poor, whose leftovers he did not

11. Followed by Ps. 8.
12. Cf. 2 Sam. 6.20–22: "Michol . . . ait quam gloriosus fuit hodie rex Israhel discoperiens se ante ancillas servorum suorum et nudatus est quasi si nudetur unus de scurris; dixitque David ad Michole ante Dominum qui elegit me potius quam patrem tuum et quam omnem domum eius et precepit mihi ut essem dux super populum Domini Israhel et ludam et vilior fiam plus quam factus sum et ero humilis in oculis meis et cum ancillis de quibus locuta es gloriosior apparebo." [Michol said {of David} how glorious was the king of Israel today, uncovering himself before the handmaids of his servants, and naked, as if one of the buffoons should be naked. And David said to Michol: Before the Lord who chose me rather than thy father, and than all his house, and commanded me to be ruler over the people of the Lord in Israel, I will both play and make myself meaner than I have done; and I will be little in my own eyes, and with the handmaids of whom thou speakest, I shall appear more glorious.] The comparison to David is an addition from BL. Here is a place where the lection is closely keyed to the responsory that follows it, in which Louis is described, like David, as "glorious in his appearance."

Scarleto etiam seu bruneto aut viridi vel alia veste pomposa uti nolebat, nec pellibus variis aut nimium sumptuosis, maxime postquam de partibus transmarinis rediit prima vice.

Responsorium
Gloriosus apparuit,
non cultu presidentis
sed cum incultus prefuit
more David ludentis;
nec ex hoc sibi defuit
auctoritas regentis.

[v] Virgam virtutis habuit,
in qua malos compescuit
sed sub norma clementis.

Lectio quinta
Dilatationem vero fidei ardenti desiderio cupiebat. Unde, tanquam verus amator fidei et zelator, dum ad huc esset iuvenis, apud Pontisaram de gravi infirmitate convalescens, de manu episcopi Parisiensis cum maxima devotione crucem accepit. Et fratres suos tres comites ac maiores regni barones et milites secum ducens, cum exercitu maximo applicuit in Aegyptum. Qui descendentes ad terram, illam famosam civitatem que Damiata dicitur et circumstantem regionem occuparunt vi armorum. Postmodum vero, iusto Dei iudicio sed occulto, exercitus christianus, infirmitate percussus multiplici, quam plurimis sublatis de medio, ut pie creditur, ad superna, de triginta duobus milibus bellatorum ad senarium est deductus. Volensque pater misericordiarum Dominus in sancto suo mirabilem se ostendere, pugilem fidei dominum regem tradidit impiorum manibus, ut mirabilior appareret. Et cum pius rex per navim propinquam evadere potuisset, spontanee tamen se reddidit, ut occasione sui[5] suum populum liberaret. Quis enim non recognoscat miraculum gentem ferocissimam tam faciliter parcere tanto regi et gentem cupidissimam regem ditissimum dimittere liberum pro

5. Should probably be "sua," but "sui" in all manuscripts

shrink from eating in this way. He refused to wear red or brown or green or any sumptuous garment, or mix-colored furs, or anything too extravagant, especially after he returned from his first overseas trip.

Responsory 4
His glorious appearance
Comes not from his attire;
He shines without adornment,
A David with his lyre;
His regal power is within
Authority that reigns in him.

[v] He held the scepter of virtue
Securely in his lands,
With it he chastised evil men
With mercy in his hands.

Fifth lection
With ardent desire, he sought to spread the faith. And thus, as a lover and zealot of the faith, while he was still young, although convalescing from a serious illness at Pontoise, he took up the cross from the hand of the bishop of Paris with the greatest devotion. He led his three brothers, the counts, with him and also the great barons and knights of the kingdom. He landed in Egypt with a very large army. And [the soldiers], disembarking, occupied that famous city (which is called Damietta) and all of the surrounding regions with the force of arms. And afterwards, by the just but hidden judgment of God, the Christian army, struck down by much illness, with as many as possible from the army having been taken from among them to heaven, as the pious believe, the [army] was reduced from thirty-two thousand fighters to just six thousand. The Lord Father of mercies, wishing to show Himself more wondrous in his saint, handed over this fighter for faith, the lord king, into the hands of the impious, so that He might appear even more wondrous. Although the pious king was able to escape to a nearby ship, he voluntarily surrendered in order to free his people. Who would not recognize as a miracle that this fierce people so easily spared so great a king, and that this most greedy people set free such a

multo minori redemptione quam habere potuissent. Pro cuius solutione complenda tenere carcerem preelegit pro aliis liberandis. Eductus itaque velud Ioseph de carcere Eegyptiaco, non ut effugiens vel timidus statim reversus ad propria, sed per quinque annos continue remansit in Syria, multos Sarracenos ad fidem convertens, et captivos redimens christianos, ac circumdans muris fortissimis plures civitates et castra. Tunc enim circa Sydonem multa invenit christianorum corpora occisorum, iam fetida et quamplura a bestiis lacerata; hec propriis manibus, cum aliquorum de suis adiutorio qui vix illorum fetorem sustinere poterant, recollegit et tradidit ecclesiastice sepulture humiliter et devote.[6] Post modum vero, audita morte regine matris sue, baronum suorum consilio, redire in Franciam acquievit. Et dum esset in mari, tercia nocte, prope diluculum, ad rupem seu terre lingulam navis deferens regem bina impulsione tam fortiter est collisa quod a nautis et aliis fracta et submergenda protinus credebatur. Tanta igitur concussione excitati et perterriti sacerdotes,[7] clerici et alii sanctum regem invenerunt devote orantem coram sacro corpore Ihesu Christi. Et fuit eorum omnium firma fides quod eius meritis et precibus eos omnipotens Deus a predicto mortis periculo liberasset.

Responsorium
Coram rege conspicitur
liber in preda perditus;
miraculose solvitur
rex sarracenis traditus,
et hostibus expositus.

[v] Ionas undis eripitur,
Ioseph detentus solvitur,
et David antro positus.

6. Note that this episode is not found in *Beatus Ludovicus.* It does appear in WSP *vie* 11 (pp. 99–102).
    7. et] *expunged in* MS

wealthy king for a much smaller ransom than they could have gotten. Instead of securing his own release, he chose to stay in prison so that others might be liberated. Having been, like Joseph, released from an Egyptian prison,[13] he did not behave like a fugitive or a fearful man who immediately turns around to go home, but stayed in Syria for five more years without interruption, converting many Saracens to the faith, redeeming Christian captives, and fortifying many cities and forts with very strong walls. At that time he also discovered the bodies of many slaughtered Christians near Sidon, by that time decomposing and torn up by wild animals. Humbly and devotedly he gathered up these bodies with his own hands (with the help of some of his men, who could hardly endure the stench) and handed them over for Christian burial. Later, hearing of his mother's death, and on the advice of his barons, he agreed to return to France. On his third night at sea, at daybreak, the king's ship collided twice against a rock (or a little slip of land) with such force that the sailors, along with the others [on board], believed that it had been torn open and was about to sink. Upset and completely terrified by such a great crash, priests, clerics, and others found the saint king in devout prayer before the sacred body of Jesus Christ [i.e., the consecrated host]. And it was everyone's firm conviction that almighty God liberated them from this mortal danger because of [Louis'] merits and prayers.

Responsory 5
The book lost in the looting
Appears before the king.
And he, to Saracens betrayed,
And to his enemy laid bare,
Miraculously is saved.

[v] A Jonah rescued from the waves,
A Joseph freed from prison.
A David from his cave.

---

13. This Old Testament reference is found initially in BL.

Lectio sexta

Reversus itaque in Franciam, cum ineffabili gaudio ab omnibus est receptus; et tunc ferventius proficiens de virtute in virtutem, ad omnimodam vite perfectionem pervenit. Et licet ab infantia secum creverit miseratio, ex tunc tamen evidentius super afflictos et pauperes pia gestabat viscera, necessitatibus omnium, prout commode poterat, succurrendo. Tunc enim coepit fundare hospitales domos pauperum, religiosorum edificare monasteria, et in diversis regni partibus plus aliis indigentibus multas annuatim pecunias erogare. Multos enim conventus ordinis fratrum predicatorum et minorum fundavit ex toto, et quamplurimis aliis pauperibus religiosis claustra, dormitoria, ecclesias, loca et edificia oportuna et largas elemosinas erogavit. Cecis, beguinis, filiabus Dei fere in omni civitate et castro regni, cum certis elemosinis de locis et domibus sibi competentibus providit; plura etiam monasteria diversorum ordinum, ab ipso fundata ex toto, magnis dotavit redditibus. In quibus mire humilitatis et caritatis officia pluries exercuit propriis manibus serviendo infirmis humiliter et devote. Unde quando veniebat Parisius aut ad alias civitates, hospitales domos in quibus magna copia infirmorum iacebat misericorditer visitans, nullius infirmi deformitatem vel immundiciam abhominans, omnibus infirmis pluries propriis manibus et flexis genibus cybaria ministrabat. In abbatia etiam Regalismontis, Cisterciensis ordinis, quam tam magnifice fundavit et dotavit, ut rei evidencia manifestat, pluries fecisse similia perhibetur. Unde, quod est mirabile dictu, cuidam monacho leproso abhominabili et horribili iam effecto, utpote naso et oculis dicti morbi corrosione privato, beatus Ludovicus, flexis genibus, in quodam ejus prandio cibum et potum immittendo in os ejus, absque aliqua abhominatione humiliter ministravit, abbate qui aderat et qui hoc vix videre poterat, in gemitus et lacrimas prorumpente. Et licet omni indigenti sinum misericordie aperiret, tamen divinis obsequiis et saluti anima - rum vacantibus maiores et frequentiores elemosinas faciebat. Unde de magna elemosina quam annuatim dabat conventibus Parisiensibus fratrum Predicatorum et Minorum sibi familiaribus dicebat quandoque: "O Deus, quam bene posita est hec elemosina tot et tantis fratribus de toto orbe terrarum[8] Parisius confluentibus, ut quod de

8. MS *reads* fratrum

Sixth lection

When he returned to France, he was greeted with ineffable joy by all. And then, advancing more fervently from virtue into virtue, he arrived at every kind of perfection of life. And although compassion had flourished in him since infancy [cf. Job 31.18], from this point onwards he bore himself even more visibly with a pious heart toward the afflicted and the poor, aiding everyone's needs as much as he was able. Then, he began to found hospitals for the poor, monasteries for religious, and in various parts of the kingdom, he gave out much money every year to other needy people. He founded *ex toto* many convents for the order of the Friars Preachers and [for the order] of the Friars Minor, and for as many other religious poor as possible he paid for cloisters, dormitories, churches, suitable places, and buildings and [gave] generous alms. And for the blind, for beguines, for the Filles Dieu, in almost every city and town of the kingdom, he provided a fixed sum for alms for housing and lodging to those who requested it of him. He endowed with great rents many monasteries of different orders that he had himself founded. In these matters he practiced the duties of wondrous humility and charity by often ministering to the infirm, humbly and devoutly, with his own hands. When he would come to Paris or arrive in other cities, mercifully visiting hospitals where a great number of infirm lay, hating the deformity or impurity of not a single one from among the ill, he would often on bended knee serve meals to all of them with his own hands. He is reported to have often done the same at the Cistercian Abbey of Royaumont, which he had founded and endowed so magnificently—as the evidence of the thing itself reveals. There, wondrous to say, blessed Louis, once at dinner, ministered on bended knee to a monk who was afflicted by an abominable and horrifying leprosy, deprived of his nose and mouth by the corrosion of this disease. With humility and without disgust, [Louis] placed food and drink directly into his mouth. When he did this, the abbot, who was present, and who could scarcely look at these things, broke out in groans and tears. Although he opened the bosom of his compassion to all those in need, he still also gave very great and frequent alms for divine worship and to those devoting themselves to the salvation of souls. Thus, with regard to the great alms that he gave yearly to the Parisian convents of the Dominicans and the Franciscans, he used to say from time to time to those close to him: "Oh God,

divinis Scripturis hic hauriunt, per totum mundum diffundant ad Dei honorem et animarum salutem." Ceteras autem elemosinas cotidianas et annuas quis sufficeret enarrare?

Responsorium
Cum esset in accubitu,
rex interne dulcedinis,
arcens potenti spiritu
pestes carnis et sanguinis
bonorum septus ambitu,
sceptro fulsit regiminis.

[v] David regis
sedit in solio,
Salomonis utens
iudicio.

In III Nocturno
Antiphonae
7. Habitabit confidenter
rex in monte Domini,
quia vixit innocenter
omni gratus homini.
P. Domine quis habitabit. [Ps. 14.1]

8. Rex virtutis in virtute
divina letatur,
quia sibi de salute
spes firma donatur.
P. Domine in virtute. [Ps. 20.2]

how well-spent are these alms given to so many great friars who have come together in Paris from around the world, as what they drink in from the divine scriptures here they may pour out throughout the whole world for the honor of God and the salvation of souls." Is there anyone who would be able to list all of his alms, daily or yearly?

Responsory 6
Even when he went to sleep
The king's sweet nature watch did keep.
Radiant with his ruler's scepter
He drove away all evil specters,
Lusts of the body or the blood,
Protected by a wall of good.

[v] A David on his royal throne,
A judge as wise as Solomon.

Third Nocturn
Antiphons
7. In confidence the king will live
On the mountain of the Lord;
Pleasing to all men below
Because his innocence they know.[14]
P. Lord, who shall dwell in thy tabernacle . . . [Ps. 14]

8. The king of virtue is joyful
In the virtue of our Lord,
Secure in hope that he was saved
Was the great gift to him He gave.[15]
P. In thy strength, O Lord . . . [Ps. 20]

14. Followed by Ps. 14.
15. Followed by Ps. 20.

9. Innocens manus prebuit
cordis quoque mundicia
Ludovico, quod meruit
regni celestis premia.
P. Domini est terra. [Ps. 23.1]

Lectio septima
Precipua vero devotione sanctas venerabatur reliquias; et Dei cultum
et honorem sanctorum iugiter augmentabat. Parisius siquidem, in regali palatio, capellam speciosissimam construxit, in qua sacrosanctam
coronam domini spineam, et maximam partem sancte crucis, ferrumque lancee quod latus aperuit salvatoris, cum pluribus aliis reliquiis dignissime collocavit, quas a Constantinopolitano imperatore
receperat cum immensis laboribus et expensis. Diem vero anniversarium quo in dicta capella huiusmodi reliquie sunt recepte solempnizari
instituit, magnis ad hec indulgentiis a sede apostolica impetratis. Et
tria festa in hujusmodi sollempnitate connectens, primum voluit fieri
per predicatores, secundum[9] per minores, tertium vero per alios religiosos communes. In ecclesia vero dum celebrarentur divina, nullius
colloquium admittebat, nisi urgeret necessitas aut evidens utilitas appareret; et tunc, ne sua impediretur devotio, breviter et succincte. Et
tanquam alter Ieremias, in sua devotione fontem lacrimarum siciens,
suo confessori quandoque familiariter recognovit quod aliquando in
oratione Deus lacrimas sibi dedit; quas cum sentiret per genas in os
defluere, non solum cordi sed et ori dulcissime sapiebant. Obprobria
vero fidei Christiane audire non poterat, sed zelando zelum Dei, tanquam Finees, graviter puniebat. Unde quemdam[10] civem Parisiensem,

9. secundum *in* MS
10. quamdam *in* MS

9. Louis' hand of innocence
To him a pure heart endowed,
For he had earned the recompense,
God's kingdom in the clouds.[16]
P. The earth is the Lord's … [Ps. 23]

Seventh lection
He revered sacred relics with particular devotion, and he continually sought to augment the veneration of God and the honor of the saints. At Paris in the royal palace he constructed an extremely beautiful chapel, in which he wonderfully gathered together the Lord's sacrosanct Crown of Thorns, the largest piece of the sacred cross, and iron from the lance that had pierced the Savior's side, along with many other relics, which he had obtained at great effort and expense from the emperor of Constantinople. With great indulgences from the apostolic see, he instituted the celebration of the anniversary of the reception of these relics at the chapel. Connecting three feasts in this type of celebration, he desired the first be celebrated by the Dominicans, the second by the Franciscans, and the third by other religious communities.[17] During the celebration of the divine services, he would allow no one to talk in church, unless the need were quite evident, and then only briefly and succinctly, lest his own devotion be impeded. And thus, like another Jeremiah,[18] drying the font of tears in his own devotion, Louis often revealed in confidence to his confessor that God sometimes gave tears to him when prayed, and when he felt them flow down over his cheeks and into his mouth they tasted very sweet to his heart and to his mouth. He could not bear to hear insults to the Christian faith, but in his fervent zeal for God, like another Phineas,[19] he punished these

16. Followed by Ps. 23.

17. In BL and GR, the author speaks only of two feasts, celebrated by the Dominicans and the Franciscans.

18. The comparison to Jeremiah is an addition to the text. Jeremiah famously wrote the laments of the people of Israel (Book of Lamentations).

19. The comparison to Phineas is an addition to the text. Cf. Num. 25.7–12 and Sir. 45.28–30. Eleazar punished violently those Israelites who defiled the community by frequenting prostitutes, and thereby expiated the cause of God's anger. Num. 25.10–11: "Dixitque Dominus ad Mosen. Finees filius Eleazari filii Aaron

qui turpiter iurando Christum blasphemaverat, iuxta regale statutum quod de consilio prelatorum et principum contra sic enormiter blasphemantes posuerat, in sui peccati penam et aliorum terrorem ferro candenti in labiis suis cauterizari[11] precipit. Cumque audiret propter hoc nonnullos in se maledicta congerere[12]: "Vellem, inquit, quoad vixero in labiis meis talem indecentiam sustinere, dummodo hoc pessimum iurationis vitium de regno meo penitus tolleretur." Similiter sarracenis petentibus in pactione facta de solvenda peccunia, pro sua et suorum liberatione habenda, addere quod fidem Christi negaret si pactum non teneret, velut alter Eleazarus, constans in fide constanter hoc facere denegavit, dicens quod si corpus occiderent, animam non haberent. Et persuadentibus qui sibi aderant quod hoc sine peccato poterat facere, clementer respondit: "Tantum," inquit, "horreo verbum de neganda fide etiam sub conditione audire, quod non possem illud exprimere sono vocis." Ibidem etiam quendam nobilem sarracenum, qui recenter soldanum occiderat, facere militem recusavit, dicens quod nec pro morte nec pro vita infidelem quemcunque insigniret baltheo militari.

11. *corr. in ms. from* caterizari

12. MS (BNF Lat 911): corrigere. BNF Lat 10872 (after RHF vol. 23, 163) has "congerere." BL used "corrigi" in a different construction at 8.2. GR uses "congerere" at 9.2.

words severely. Thus, he ordered that a certain citizen of Paris, who had blasphemed appallingly by swearing against Christ, be branded on his lips with a red hot iron in punishment for his crimes as an example to others, following a royal statute that he had instituted on the advice of prelates and nobles against those who blasphemed immoderately. When he heard that some men were heaping abuse on him on account of this, he said, "I would rather endure this shameful stigma on my own lips as long as I live so long as this terrible sin of swearing be entirely eradicated from our kingdom." In the same vein, the Saracens wanted to add to the pact being negotiated for his and his men's freedom the stipulation that Louis would deny his faith in Christ if he failed to keep to the agreement. Just like another Eleazar,[20] constantly constant in his faith, he refused to do so, saying that even if they killed his body, they would not have his soul. And to those present who were trying to persuade him that he could say this without incurring sin, he gently responded: "I have such horror at even hearing a word of negating the faith, even under these conditions, that I could never say this aloud." Further, he refused to bestow knighthood on a noble Saracen who had recently killed the sultan, saying that neither for death nor for life would he honor an infidel with the belt of knighthood.

---

sacerdotis avertit iram meam a filiis Israhel quia zelo meo commotus est contra eos ut non ipse delerem filios Israhel in zelo meo." [And the Lord said to Moses: Phineas the son of Eleazar the son of Aaron the priest, hath turned away my wrath from the children of Israel; because he moved with my zeal against them, that I might not destroy the children of Israel in my zeal.]

   20. Note that the comparison to Eleazar is an addition to the text. Eleazar refused to eat swine's flesh under pain of death. Cf. 2 Macc. 6.28–30: "Adulescenbibus autem exemplum forte relinquam si prompto animo ac fortiter pro gravissimis et sanctissimis legibus honest moret more perfungar. . . . sed cum plagis perimeretur ingemuit et dixit Domine qui habes sanctam scientiam manifeste scis tu quia cum a morte possim liberari duros corporis sustineo dolores secundum animam vero propter timorem tuum libenter haec patior." [And I shall leave an example of fortitude to young men, if with a ready mind and constancy I suffer an honourable death for the most venerable and most holy laws. . . . O Lord, who hast the holy knowledge, thou knowest manifestly that whereas I might be delivered from death, I suffer grievous pains in body; but in soul am well content to suffer these things, because I fear thee.]

Responsorium
Fulget signis rex insignis,
nam egrotis eius votis
prestantur remedia.

[v] Dati neci liberantur,
Claudi, ceci reparantur,
fugantur demonia.

Lectio octava
In tantam etiam veneratione habebat signaculum sancte crucis quod
desuper calcare cavebat, et a pluribus religiosis exegit ut in claustris
eorum in tumbis cruces non insculperentur, de cetero, et iam insculpte
penitus raderentur.[13] Quam reverenter et devote omni anno in Parasceve
ad adorandum lignum sancte crucis flexis genibus, resoluto crine ac
nudis pedibus procederet, testantur eorum oculi qui tunc ipsum sine
lacrimis non poterant intueri. In regimine vero regni ita potenter ac prudenter se gerebat, quod absque aliqua personarum acceptione cum diligenti causarum discussione reddebat iudicium et iusticiam unicuique.
Consiliarii quoque sui et potentes regni videntes sapientiam Dei esse in
illo, cum diletione sincera ipsum etiam plurimum formidabant. Timens
autem ne cause pauperum vix ingrederentur ad eos, ad minus bis in
ebdomada ad audiendum conquerentes in loco patenti se ponebat, et
mediante iusticia et plerumque misericordia faciebat celeriter expediri.
Et quando negotium fidei per prelatos seu inquisitores deferebatur ad
eum, omnibus aliis postpositis faciebat illud cicius expediri. Duella vero,
tanquam a iure prohibita, cuiusquam instancia, non admittebat; sed per
aliam viam iuri consonam etiam magnatum maleficia puniebat. Statuit
insuper ad abolendam voraginem usurarum ut obligatos iudeis aut aliis
publicis usurariis per litteras nullus iustitiarius compelleret ad solvendum. Et quia pacem operatur iusticia, dedit Deus illi[14] pacem et regno

---

13. *corr. from* rederentur
14. Written over in MS. In other versions of the text, this reads "sibi," suggesting that it is God who granted himself peace. This interpretation might be supported by BL 9.5, which is, in any event, vague.

Responsory 7
The king shines
With glorious signs
And to those ill,
Their prayers fulfilled,
Remedies they find.

[v] Freedom to those bound up tight
Healing for the lame or lacking sight,
And demons too were put to flight.

Eighth lection
He held the sign of the Holy Cross in such great reverence that he took care not to tread upon it, and in many monasteries he ordered that, from then on, crosses not be sculpted on the tombs of their cloisters, and that those that had already been sculpted be completely removed. The eyes of all those who could not look at him without tears bear witness to how devoutly and reverently he processed every year on Good Friday, on bended knee, hair loosened and feet bare, to adore the wood of the Holy Cross. In his rule of the kingdom he conducted himself with such force and prudence that, with favoritism to no one, he rendered justice to each individual after careful inquiry into the cases. His advisors as well as the leading men of the realm, perceiving that the wisdom of God was in him, with sincere affection held him in even greater awe. Fearing lest the cases of the poor be only rarely brought before (the counselors), he made himself available in a public place at least twice a week, in order to hear the plaintiffs, and he had these quickly expedited with impartial justice and great mercy. And if a matter of faith was brought to him by prelates or inquisitors, he had this expedited more quickly, postponing all other matters. He did not permit duels under any circumstance whatsoever, as if prohibited by law; rather, he punished crimes, even those of magnates, in other ways consonant with the law. In order to abolish the abyss of usury, he proclaimed that no judge could compel those bound through letters to Jews or to other public usurers to pay [their debt] back. And because justice serves peace, God granted peace to him and tranquility to his

tranquillitatem. De hoc etiam habebat gratiam specialem quod inter se
discordantes, ut communiter ad concordiam revocabat.

Responsorium
Pro se suisque subiectis
orans deum et cum rectis
rectum iter faciens
domum Dei rex intravit
et ad templum adoravit,[15]
ut predixit moriens.

[v] Felix cursus sic viventis,
felix finis sic currentis
Deo semper serviens.

Lectio nona
Tandem post multorum annorum curricula quibus se in omni genere
virtutum exercuit, audiens desolationes et pericula terre sancte, velut
alter Mathathias, cum filiis suis mala gentis christiane et sanctorum
ferre non sustinens, Deo inspirante, secundo transfretare curavit, cum
tribus filiis suis comitibus, et magnatibus ac nobilibus regni, et communis populi multitudine copiosa. Sed quando naves ascendere debu-
erunt, sanctus rex filios suos clementi vultu prospiciens, ad primogenitum specialius sermonem dirigens, sic ait: "Considera, fili, quod ego
grandevus alias transfretavi, et quod regina mater tua iam processit in
diebus suis, et quod regnum nostrum, favente Deo, possedimus pacifice
et quiete, diviciis, deliciis et honoribus quantum libuit et licuit, perfruentes. Vide igitur quod pro Christo et ecclesia nec mee parco senectuti,
nec matris tue desolate misereor; delicias et honores relinquo, et expono

15. Cf. Ps. 5.8.

kingdom. In this matter he had a special gift because he brought together in peace those who quarreled among themselves.

Responsory 8
To God, for self and subjects, he did pray,
His royal path with right men lay.
And in his Temple worshipped too,
Dying as he foretold true,
He entered God's house on his way.

[v] Happy the course of life he trod.
Happy, too, the end he met
Ever servant to his God.

Ninth lection
And finally, after the passage of many years in which he grew in every
kind of virtue, hearing of the hardships of and dangers to the Holy
Land, just like another Mattathias, with his sons,²¹ who was not willing that the evils to the Christian race and saints continue, [and] with
God inspiring him, [Louis] undertook to cross the sea a second time
with his three sons, the counts, and the magnates and nobles of the
kingdom, and a great multitude of common people. But as they were
about to board the ships, the saintly king, looking at his sons with a
gentle face, and directing his speech especially to his eldest son, said:
"Consider, son, that I, now aged, have crossed the sea before, that your
mother the queen is far advanced in years, and that we have possessed
our kingdom, through God's favor, peacefully and quietly, enjoying
riches, honors, and pleasures as was good and right. See thus that for
Christ and for the church I neither spare my old age, nor do I take pity
on your forsaken mother; I relinquish riches and honors, and I offer

21. The comparison of Mattathias is an addition to the text. Cf. 1 Macc. 2.
Mattathias was the father of Judas Maccabeus, who, with his sons, resisted Anti-
ochus. 1 Macc. 2.7: "And Mattathias said: 'Woe is me, wherefore was I born to see the
ruin of my people and the ruin of the holy city [of Jerusalem] and to dwell there,
when it is given into the hands of the enemies.'"

pro Christo et corpus et divicias. Te quoque ac fratres tuos et sororem primogenitam mecum duco, quartum etiam adduxissem filium si annos pubertatis plenius attigisset. Que idcirco te audire volui ut cum post obitum meum ad regnum perveneris, pro Christo et ecclesia et fide catholica sustinenda nulli rei parcas, nec uxori, nec liberis, nec etiam regno. Tibi enim et fratribus tuis do exemplum ut, si opus fuerit, similiter faciatis." Currente igitur navigio versus Tunicium et exercitu christiano libere capiente portum in Affrica, Carthaginis castrum et adiacentem regionem vi armorum ceperunt. Demum inter Cartaginem et Tunicium fixerunt tentoria, ibi aliquandiu moraturi. Illic enim beatus Ludovicus post tot laudabilia virtutum opera, post tot laboriosos agones, quos pro fide Christi indefesso animo toleraverat, disponente Deo, qui labores illius voluit feliciter consummare et sibi laborum bonorum fructum retribuere gloriosum, lecto decubuit, febre continua fatigatus. Et documenta sancta, que prius in gallico conscripserat, domino Philippo primogenito suo diligenter exposuit et imposuit efficaciter adimplenda. Invalescente igitur morbo, sana mente, integro aspectu et auditu, psalmos dicens, sanctos invocans, devote suscepit omnia ecclesiastica sacramenta. Demum vero ad extremam horam veniens, et supra stratum cinereum in modum crucis extensus, verba proferens ultima "Pater in manus tuas commendo spiritum meum" [Luke 23.46]. Anno Domini MCC septuagesimo migravit ad Christum, hora videlicet nona, qua Dei Filius pro mundi vita in cruce moriens exspiravit. Corpus vero beati Ludovici delatum fuit ad sepulchrum patrum suorum apud Sanctum Dyonisium in Francia, ubi et etiam alibi in diversis mundi partibus, crebris coruscat miraculis gloriosis.

Responsorium 9
Regnum mundi supergressus
et eius ornatum,
regnum celi iam ingressus

my body and wealth to Christ. I lead you along with your brothers and eldest sister with me, and I would have even brought my fourth son were he of age. And therefore I want you to listen so that when you attain the kingdom after my death, you spare nothing at all for Christ and the church and the preservation of the Catholic faith, not your wife, not your children, not even your kingdom. I give this example to you and your brothers so that, if need be, you will all do the same." The fleet sailed to Tunis and the Christian army boldly captured the harbor in Africa, and, with the force of arms, seized the city of Carthage and the surrounding region. They pitched their tents between Carthage and Tunis, where they would stay for some time. There, after many laudable works of virtue and many laborious struggles which for the faith of Christ he tolerated with a tireless soul, exhausted by continual fever, blessed Louis lay down on his bed. God wished that Louis' labors be happily brought to perfection and thus rendered to him the glorious fruit of his good labors. He carefully handed over to Lord Philip, his firstborn son, the saintly lessons that he had previously written in French, and he charged that they be carried out effectively.[22] And then, sick unto the point of death, but of sound mind and with sight and hearing intact, saying the psalms and invoking the saints, he devoutly received all the ecclesiastical sacraments. At last, approaching his final hour and stretched out upon a bed of ashes in the form of a cross, he offered up his final words: "Father, into your hands I commend my spirit" [Luke 23.46]. In the year of the Lord, 1270, he departed to Christ at the ninth hour, at which time the son of God, dying on the cross for the life of this world, breathed his last. The body of the blessed Louis was then borne to the burial place of his fathers at St.-Denis in France. Here, as elsewhere in many parts of the world, he shone forth with many glorious miracles.

Responsory 9
Louis left this earthly realm
And all its earthly splendor,
To reach the kingdom of the sky

---

22. A reference to the *Enseignements*, on which, see GR 4.6, n. 22 of the translation. This is an addition to the material found in BL.

sibi preparatum,
nostros ad se regat gressus
post hunc incolatum.

[v] Peregre Iacob egressus
patris ad mandatum,
Deum vidit sic professus
vite celibatum.

Ad Laudes
Antiphonae
1. Ludovicus hodie
decorem indutus
est celestis patrie
regnum consequtus.
P. Dominus regnavit. [Ps. 92.1]

2. Omnis terra iubilet
Deo leta serviens,
laudibus invigilet
novum festum faciens.
P. Iubilate Deo. [Ps. 99.2]

3. Ad te, Deus meus,
semper vigilavit,
sicque numquam reus
celos penetravit.
P. Deus Deus meus. [Ps. 62.2]

4. Benedixit creatorem
in suis operibus,
Ludovicus gerens morem
datum celi civibus
Benedicite. [Dan. 3.57–88, 56]

Prepared for him by God on high,
And may our steps to him he guide
Who follow to with him abide.

[v] Commanded by his father,
Jacob was a wanderer
Who chose to live in chastity
Because his God he came to see.

Lauds
Antiphons
1. Clothed in grace of heaven,
Louis on this day,
Joins God in His Kingdom,
Following the Father's way.[23]
P. The Lord hath reigned . . . [Ps. 92]

2. Let all the earth be joyful
Happy serving God;
For the new feast wakeful,
In the singing of the Lauds.[24]
P. Sing joyfully to the Lord . . . [Ps. 99]

3. For You, my Lord, did Louis
Keep an ever watchful eye;
Indeed no evildoer
Did penetrate Your sky.[25]
P. O God, my God . . . [Ps. 62]

4. Louis blessed our Maker so
In all his many deeds below
Behaving in his earthly days
A citizen of heaven's ways.[26]
All ye works of the Lord, bless the Lord . . . [Dan. 3.57–88, 56]

23. Followed by Ps. 92.
24. Followed by Ps. 99.
25. Followed by Pss. 62 and 64.
26. Followed by Dan. 3.57–88.

5. Ludovicus Dominum
de celis laudavit
quando vite terminum
celo dedicavit.
P. Laudate Dominum. [Ps. 148.1]

Capitulum
Dedit Dominus illi fortitudinem et usque ad senectutem permansit illi
virtus, ut ascenderet in excelsum terre locum, semen ipsius obtinebit
hereditatem. [Cf. Sir. 46.11]

Hymnus
Hymnum nove letitie
Regi canamus omnium,
qui sancto regi Francie
novi dat regni solium.

Ludovicus ex nomine
lucis dator exprimitur,
et custos in certamine
presentis vite ponitur.

Crucis hostes concuciens,
concussus egritudine,
vitam invenit moriens
tali felix certamine.

Nam sic in vita viguit
ut paciendo vinceret,
et hoc in morte meruit
ut moriendo viveret.

Vivit ergo feliciter
rex francorum in gloria,

5. Louis praised
The Lord on high,
And to Him
When about to die,
He offered up his life.[27]
P. Praise ye, the Lord . . . [Ps. 148]

Scriptural Reading
God gave fortitude to him and his strength lasted into his old age,
so that he would ascend to the highest place in the land; his seed will
obtain his inheritance. [Cf. Sir. 46.11]

Hymn for Lauds
Let us to the King of all that is,
Sing a hymn in fresh delight;
To France's saintly king God gives,
A throne in His new realm of light.

Louis' name defines him
As a giver of the light
And places him as guardian
In the battle of this life.

He, though struck by illness,
Fought enemies of the cross;
Happy in so great a strife,
And in his dying finding life.

For in this life he found the strength,
To conquer through his pain,
And thus in death he merited
Eternal life to gain.

And so the king of France did live
In glory and in joy,

27. Followed by Pss. 148–150.

quem Christus singulariter
sua replevit gratia.

Trino Deo et simplici. *ut supra.*

Ad Benedictus antiphona
Benedictus Dominus
qui nobis erexit
cornu, quod paulominus
a David dilexit;
hic virtute geminus
rex in pace rexit,
quem regendi terminus
ad celos direxit.
P. Benedictus. [Luke 1.68–79]

Ad Horas Minores
At Tertiam
In gentibus multis non erat rex similis ei et dilectus Deo suo erat et
posuit eum Deus regem super Israel. [Cf. 2 Ezek. 13.26]

Ad Sextam
In vinculis non dereliquit eum Dominus, donec afferret illi sceptrum
regni et potentiam adversus eos qui eum deprimebant. [Cf. Wisd. 10.14]

Ad Nonam
Magnificavit eum Dominus super omnem Israel et dedit illi gloriam
regni qualem nullus habuit ante eum rex. [Cf. 2 Chron. 29.25]

For to him Christ our Lord did give
His full grace to employ.

For God on high both Three and One . . . (*as above*)[28]

Benedictus antiphon
Blessed be the Lord and give him praise,
Who for all of us did raise
A horn he loved no less than David in his royal days,
A twin to him in virtue too,
Louis ruled in peace as kings should do.
Thus when his rule on earth was done
The goal of heaven Louis won.[29]
P. Blessed be the Lord God of Israel . . . [Luke 1.68–79]

The Little Hours
Terce
Among many nations there was not a king like him, and he was beloved
to his God, and God made him king over all Israel. [Cf. 2 Ezek. 13.26]

Sext
And in chains God left him not, till He brought him the scepter of the
kingdom, and power against those that oppressed him. [Cf. Wisd. 10.14]

None
And the Lord magnified him over all Israel: and gave him the glory of a
kingdom, such as no king of Israel had before him. [Cf. 2 Chron. 29.25]

28. An indication that one is to repeat the fifth stanza of the Hymn for First
Vespers.
29. Followed by Luke 1:68–79, the "Song of Zacharias." The "horn of salvation" (*cornu salutis*) at Luke 1.69, referenced in the third line of the antiphon, was
understood as the king who will bring salvation, and "the house of David" in the
same verse referred to the lineage of Christ. It may also have been intended as a reference to the royal house of France.

Ad II Vesperae
Ad Magnificat antiphona
Magnificat miraculis
Ludovicum divinitas,
in quo cunctorum oculis
David fulsit humilitas,
Salomonis serenitas
et Ezechie veritas,
quem gratiarum titulis
sollempnem fecit populis
Iosye par benignitas
Magnificat.
Capitulum et hymnus sicut in primis vesperis, supra.

Iste antiphone dicuntur per octavam[16]
Antiphonae
1. Ludovice rex francorum,
in felice beatorum
regno gaudes gloria
de hac valle miserorum
recto calle nos iustorum
duc ad celi gaudia.

2. Magnificat Dominum
et exultat spiritus
pauperum et divitum
in Deo salutari,
qui generi hominum
hunc regem divinitus
Ludovicum inclitum
dedit pro exemplari.

16. Note that the octave antiphons were not part of the original composition of LDR but were added a few years later, drawing mostly on prayers from other offices. They appear in Paris BNF Lat 911, but not Washington, DC, Library of Congress MS 15.

Second Vespers
Magnificat antiphon
Louis is made magnified
By miracles divine,
A David in humility,
With Solomon's serenity,
Ezechias's verity,
In the eyes of all mankind,
A Josiah in benignity,
For his people, a man of sanctity,
Honor's graces on him shine.
Magnificat.
Chapter and hymn as in first vespers, above.

These antiphons are sung for the Octave
Antiphons
1. O Louis, King of France's land,
In the happy kingdom of the blessed
Where you rejoice in glory's hand,
From the vale of men most wretched,
Lead us to the justs' right road,
To gain the joys in heaven's abode.

2. He magnified the Lord,
Exulting that the souls
Of rich and poor alike be saved
In God, who from heaven to men gave
This king renowned in fame
A paradigm for those who reign.

3. Iam sanctus post laborem
recepturus premium,
regnaturum maiorem
exhortatur filium
ad matris honorem,
de fide et moribus
testamentum condidit,
et bonis operibus
complementum addidit
divinum amorem.

4. O martyr desiderio,
quem pie mentis studio
crucifixo compateris,
cuius crucem in humeris
tuis bis affixisti;
passio tibi defecit
sed martyrem te effecit
fervor et zelus Christi.

5. Tu, cecorum oculus,
debilium baculus,
oppressorum clipeus,
perversorum malleus,
nutritor minorum,
miserere populi
te laudare seduli,
nobilis rex Francie,
Ludovice, glorie
consors beatorum.

6. O decus ecclesie,
pie rex francorum,
exemplar iusticie,
lex et norma morum,
post finem angustie,
mortis et laborum

3. Sanctified, his work now done,
Louis gains his final prize.
His reign he gave his elder son
And left for him instruction wise:
A testament of how to live
And honor to his mother give,
To faith and good works does he aspire,
Above all love of God desire.

4. O, you who wanted martyrdom
Were eager with your pious mind
To suffer crucifixion with Him.
Your shoulders twice did bear the cross
And by this act you suffered loss
But zeal for Christ and ardor too
A holy martyr made of you.

5. O Louis, noble king of France,
Who dwells in glory with the blessed,
Eyes for the blind are you
For the halt, a staff that's true,
A shield for the oppressed,
For the wicked a hammer too,
Nourisher of those with less,
Take pity on your people
Who praise you with largesse.

6. O, glory of the church,
For France the pious king,
Model of what is just,
In character and law,
Beyond the narrow sting
Of earthly tasks and death,

presta dono gratie
regnum beatorum.

7. Magnum magnatum speculum,
Ludovice rex Francie,
cunctis relinquens titulum
sanctitatis eximie,
prece iuvans in seculum,
commenda regi glorie
devotum tibi populum.

8. O patriarcha procerum,
piorum sator munerum,
curam gerendo pauperum,
Ludovice, rex beate,
efficaces sint oblate
tibi preces impetrate
pacis nobis indilate
fructum reportantes a te.

Magnificat, antiphona
Ora, pater Ludovice,
hac pro gente peccatrice
sui reatus conscia,
ut pax, Dei genitrice
tecum nobis adiutrice,
detur et indulgentia,
adiuva nos clementia,
que relicta cicatrice
carnis palma cum victrice
coronavit te gloria.
Magnificat.[17]

17. The manuscript, BNF Lat 911, here follows with readings for the octave, with the rubric, "Per octabas legitur de miraculis beati ludovici infra scriptis. Miraculum." These were adopted in the fifteenth century by the person who expanded *Gloriosissimi regis*, and can be found as GR 14.1–15.

Enhance the kingdom of the blessed,
With gifts of grace you bring.

7. Great mirror of great men,
O, Louis, King of France,
Who leave behind wondrous sign
Of saintliness for all mankind.
With prayer forever aiding
A people who adore you,
Praise them to glory's King.

8. O, father of nobility,
Fount of works of piety
Caring for our poverty
Louis, our blessed king,
May you succeed in all you will
Without delay our prayers fulfill,
For us the fruits of peace instill.

Magnificat Antiphon
Pray O father, Louis
For this race of sinners
Conscious of its crime,
So that the peace of Mary,
Helper with you for us,
May be given to us
Through your indulgency;
Aid us with your clemency,
For when you lost your scar of flesh,
You were made victorious,
Crowned with the palm of glory.
Magnificat.[30]

30. For octave readings that followed, see GR 14.1–15.

GAUDEAMUS OMNES:

MASS IN HONOR OF SAINT LOUIS

GAUDEAMUS OMNES:
MASS IN HONOR OF SAINT LOUIS

The text here is taken from BNF Lat 911, 29r–35r, as transcribed by P. Albanus Heysse, "Antiquissimum officium liturgicum S. Ludovici regis," *Archivum Franciscanum Historicum* 10 (1917): 559–75, but the items were fairly widespread. The two sequences, each labeled *hymnus* in BNF Lat 911 ("regem regum veneremur" . . . "and Letabunda psallat plebs"), are found in AH vol. 55, 255–56 (nos. 227–228) with an expansive list of manuscripts.

Note that italicized words in the Latin are read, not sung.

———

[1] *Ad missam [Introitus]*
Gaudeamus omnes in domino
Diem festum celebrantes
Sub honore beati ludovici
De cuius solennitate gaudent angeli
Et collaudant filium dei.
P. Domine in virtute tua letabitur rex & super salutare tuum exultabit vehementer. [Ps. 20.2]

[2] *Oratio*
Deus qui beatum ludovicum confessorem tuum de terreno ac temporali regno ad celestis et eterni regni gloriam transtulisti, eius quesumus meritis et intercessione regis regum ihesu christi filii tui nos coheredes efficias. Et eiusdem regni tribuas esse consortes.

[3] *Lectio libri sapientie [Epistola]*
Beatus vir [*sic,* for dives] qui inventus est sinemacula; et qui post aurum non abiit; nec speravit in thesauris pecunie. Quis est hic et laudabimus eum. Fecit enim mirabilia in vita sua. Qui[s] probatus est in illo et perfectus est et erit illi [in] gloria eterna. Qui potuit transgredi et non est transgressus, et facere mala et non fecit. Ideo stabilita sunt bona illius in domino, et elemosinas illius enarrabit. Omnis ecclesia sanctorum. [Wisd. 31.8–11]

Let Us Rejoice:
Mass in Honor of Saint Louis

———

[1] *Introit Antiphon*
Let us all rejoice in the Lord,
Celebrating this feast day,
For the honor of Blessed Louis,
In whose solemnity the angels rejoice
As they extol the son of God.
P. In thy strength, O Lord, the king shall joy; and in thy salvation he
shall rejoice exceedingly. [Ps. 20.2]

[2] *Collect*
God, who transported blessed Louis, your confessor, from the earthly and
temporal kingdom to the glory of the celestial and eternal kingdom, we
entreat by the merits and intercession of the King of kings, Jesus Christ,
your son, to make us coheirs; and that you might grant us inheritance.

[3] *Reading from the Book of Wisdom [Epistle]*
Blessed is the rich man that is found without blemish; and that hath
not gone after gold, nor put his trust in money nor in treasures. Who is
he, and how will we praise him? For he hath done wonderful things in
his life. Who hath been tried thereby, and made perfect, he shall have
glory everlasting. He could have transgressed, and hath not transgressed; and could do evil things, and hath not done them. Therefore
are his goods established in the Lord and all the church of the saints
shall declare his sins. [Wisd. 31.8–11]

[4] *[Graduale]*
Domine prevenisti
eum in benedictionibus
dulcedinis posuisti
in capite eius coronam
de lapide precioso.

[v] Vitam
petiit et tribuisti
ei longitudinem
dierum in seculum seculi.
Alleluya.

[v] Felix corona Francie
ludovici virtutibus
cuius corona glorie
refulget in celestibus.
Alleluya.

[v] Pater, sancte Ludovice
fusa deo precum vice
solve reos a sagena
peccatorum et a pena.
Alleluya.

[v] Ludovice lucens in gloria
cuius fuit mens meritoria
erga christum eiusque pauperes
piisimus gratus ad proceres
celesti heres martyr desiderio
pater in navigio bino transmarino
regni tui populum redde domino.
Alleluya.

[v] Qui dat salutem regibus
in benedictionibus dulcedinis prevenisti
eum eterne vite coronam
in capite ludovici posuisti.

[4] *Gradual*
Oh Lord, you surpass him
In sweet benedictions,
You placed
On his head
A crown of precious stones.

[v] He sought life
And you assigned to him
A great length of days
In the age of ages.
Alleluya.

[v] Happy is the crown of France
With Louis' virtues,
Whose crown of glory
Shines in the heavens.
Alleluya.

[v] O Father, O saint Louis,
By the broad repayment of prayers to God,
Release us sinners from the dragnet
Of sin and from its penalty.
Alleluya.

[v] Louis, shining in glory,
Whose mind was meritorious
Toward Christ and his poor,
Most pious, pleasing toward princes,
Heir of heaven, martyr by desire,
Father, twice on the ship across the seas,
Deliver the people of your kingdom to God.
Alleluya.

[v] He who gives salvation
To kings in sweet blessings,
You preceded him,
You placed the crown of eternal life
On Louis' head.

[5] *Hymnus*
Regem regum veneremur
et de regis gloriemur
ludovici gloria.

Ex francorum regni cura
beatorum regni iura
possidet in patria.

Christus Christo conformatum
magnum fecit et beatum
virtutum immensitas.

Longum fides, amor latum,
altum spes, sed non elatum,
profundum humilitas.

Vultum habens David regis
Ezechie zelum legis
et Josye studium.

Dictus vere lucis dator
vite custos et amator
in christo viventium.

Orbis signis illustratur
capto regi restauratur
liber preda perditus.

Vita datur morituris
claudis gressus lux obscuris
et captivis reditus.

[5] *Hymn of the mass*
Let us honor the King of kings
And let us glory in the glory
Of king Louis.

From the care of the kingdom of the French,
He [now] in the land [above]
Possesses the justice
Of the kingdom of the blessed.

Christ, in virtue boundless,
Has rendered the one conformed to Christ
Great and blessed.

Far reaching his faith made him,
And wide did his love,
High his hope raised him,
But he exulted not in pride,
His humility made him deep.

He held the countenance of king David,
Ezechias's zeal for law,
And the devotion of Josias.[1]

Said truly to be a giver of light,
A guardian and lover of the life
Of those living in Christ.

He is adorned by miracles in the world;
The book lost in battle
Is restored to the captured king.

Life is given to the dying,
Walk is given to the limping,
Light to those in darkness,
And return to the captured.

---

1. Note the echo here of the Magnificat for Second Vespers in the Office in
Honor of Saint Louis, *Ludovicus decus regnantium,* in this volume.

In extremis successorem
informavit et cultorem
esse dei docuit.

Certus demum de corona
maris undis dempto Iona
celi portum tenuit.

Vita vivens beatorum
felix regnat rex francorum
in beatis sedibus.

Supplicemus sancto regi
nos sanctorum iungi gregi
piis eius precibus.
Amen.

[6] *Hymnus*
Letabunda
psallat plebs cum mente munda
christiana.

Deum more
collaudet gens letiore[1]
gallicana.

Qui post regnum labile
ad inestimabile
sublimavit.

Ludovicum solium
turmisque letancium sociavit.

---

1. letiore] litiore *in* BNF 911. Cf. AH vol. 55, 256.

At the end of his life he instructed
His successor and taught him to be
A worshipper of God.[2]

Certain at last of his crown,
A Jonah released from the waves of the sea,
He beheld the harbor of heaven.

Living the life of the sainted,
The happy king of the French
Reigns in the home of the blessed.

Let us entreat the saint king
That we be joined with the flock of the saints
By his pious prayers.
Amen.

[6] *Hymn of the mass*
The joyful people are singing
With a pure, Christian mind.

Let the Gallic nation
Extol God
In a more joyful manner.

He who later raised up
The tottering kingdom
To one of priceless worth,

[His] throne joined Louis
To the crowds
Of those rejoicing.

2. A reference to the *Enseignements*. See GR 4.6, n. 22 of the translation.

Hic licet ex germine
prime natus femine
delinquentis

Fugato peccamine
mansit in dulcedine
pie mentis.

Celi rex delicias
filio familias
reservavit.

Invitavit filium
pater ad convivium
quem amavit.

Fulgentem in habitu
a celorum ambitu
cum ruboris exitu
non proiecit.

Quem sanctum miraculis
crebis in articulis
provectis & parvulis
patefecit.
In vite misere
lapsis itinere
ludovice rex compatere.

De nobis cogita
prece resuscita
quos facta premunt illicita
favente deo fiat ita.

Although this man was born
From the stalk of the
First fallen woman,

He remained in the sweetness
Of a pious mind,
His sin having been put to flight.[3]

Heaven's king has reserved delights
For the household's son.

The Father invited the son,
Whom He loved,
To the banquet.[4]

He did not cast down
From the embrace of heaven
That one, shining in appearance,
With the death of his shame.

He revealed this one to be a saint
With frequent miracles,
For the advanced in age and for the young.

O, Louis king, have compassion
For those who have lapsed
On the journey of wretched life.

Think of us;
Restore with prayer
Those whom evil deeds oppress;
Let it be thus, God willing.

---

3. Note the echo of the office's Responsory following the Scriptural Reading of First Vespers, repeated as the Sixth Responsory of Matins (Second Nocturn).

4. Note the echo of the office's First Responsory of Matins (during First Nocturn).

[7] *Evangelium*

Secundum Mattheum: In illo tempore dixit Ihesus discipulis suis. Dicit ihe discipulis suis. Considerate lilia agri quomodo crescunt. Non laborant neque vent? Dico autem nobis. Quoniam nec salomon in omni gloria sua. Coopertus est sicut unum existis. Si enim senum quod hodie est et cras inclibanum mittitur deus sic vestit. Quanto magis nos modice fidei. Nolite ergo soliciti esse dicentes quid manducabimus aut quid bibemus, aut quo operiemur. Hec enim omnia gentes inquirunt. Scit enim pater vester quia omnibus hiis indigentis. Querite autem primum regnum dei et iusteciam eius. Et hec. Omnia addicient nobis. [Matt. 6.28–33]

[8] *Offertorium*

Filie syon exultent in rege suo laudent nomen eius in choro in tympano et psalterio psallant ei alleluya. [Ps. 149.3–4]

[9] *Secreta*

Presta quesumus omnipotens deus ut sicut beatus Ludovicus confessor tuus per habundanciam gracie tue oblectamentis mundialibus spretis soli regi Christo placere studuit, ita eius oratio nos tibi reddat acceptos.

[10] *Communio*

Iustum deduxit dominus per vias rectas et ostendit illi regnum dei et dedit illi scientiam sanctorum honestavit illum in laboribus suis et complevit labores illius. [Wisd. 10.10]

[11] *Postcommunionem*

Deus qui almum confessorem tuum ludovicum mirificasti in terris, quesumus ut eundem in celis gloriosum ecclesie tue constituas defensorem eamque eius precibus et meritis ab omni adversitate liberare digneris. Per dominum nostrum ihesum christum filium tuum, qui tecum vivit et regnat.

[7] *Gospel Reading*

According to Matthew, In that time Jesus said to his disciples: Consider the lilies of the field, how they grow; they labor not, neither do they spin. But I say to you that not even Solomon in all his glory was arrayed as one of these. And if the grass of the field, which is today, and tomorrow is cast into the oven, God doth so clothe; how much more you, O ye of little faith? Be not solicitous therefore, saying, What shall we eat? or what shall we drink, or wherewith shall we be clothed? For after all these things do the heathens seek. For your Father knoweth that you have need of all these things. Seek ye therefore first the kingdom of God and his justice, and all these things shall be added unto you. [Matt. 6.28–33]

[8] *Offertory*

Let the children of Sion by joyful in their king; let them praise his name in the choir; let them sing to him with the timbrel and the psaltery. [Ps. 149.3–4]

[9] *Secret*

Fulfill these things, omnipotent God, just as blessed Louis, your confessor, has striven to please Christ, the one King, through the abundance of your grace, with worldly pleasures scorned, and thus may his prayer make us acceptable to you.

[10] *Communion*

The Lord conducted the just through the right ways, and showed him the kingdom of God, and gave him the knowledge of the holy things, made him honorable in his labors, and accomplished his labors.

[11] *Postcommunion*

God, you who exalted Louis, your dear confessor on earth, we beseech that you establish this same man, this glorious defender of your church, in the heavens, and that you deign to free her through his prayers and merits from all adversity. Through our Lord, Jesus Christ, your son, who lives and reigns with you.

4 ~

SERMONS OF
JACOB OF LAUSANNE

Paris BNF Lat 15962, 26r. *Videte regem* [siglum P3]. Courtesy
Bibliothèque nationale de France.

Jacob of Lausanne was a Dominican preacher who belonged to St.-Jacques, the Dominican convent in Paris, situated near the royal palace on the left bank of the Seine. Jacob, who was probably born in the last quarter of the fourteenth century, studied in Paris and was a member of the convent by 1303 (when he signed an oath of allegiance to the king). He received a license in theology in 1317, was elected Provincial of France (that is, of the area around Paris) in 1318, and died in 1322.[1] He was a prolific author, writing commentaries on both the Old and New Testaments, as well as a commentary on the *Sentences* of Peter Lombard and numerous other works. He was best known, however, for his preaching texts; more than fourteen hundred of his sermons survive.[2]

Jacob wrote sermons in every genre. Among these are five sermons in honor of Louis IX, meant to be preached on his feast day of August 25.[3] Many of Jacob's sermons, including those to Louis, survive in multiple copies and circulated widely. Clerics would often write "model sermons" in Latin, which were collected together into model sermon collections for others to consult or use in their own preaching. The great majority of sermons from this period survive in Latin, but they would have been preached in the vernacular to a lay audience. The fact that Jacob's sermons on Louis survive in multiple copies suggests that they had some measure of influence, although we should not assume that the surviving Latin texts matched the vernacular versions that reached the ears of the faithful.

Offered here are two of Jacob's sermons on Louis as examples both of how the (elite, Latin) hagiographic and liturgical tradition was translated into sermons that were designed to reach a broad audience, and also of how Louis' sanctity was presented as a model for preaching to the laity. Jacob, as a member of a religious house that had close ties to the palace and was devoted to the cult of Louis, probably had access to a range of hagiographical texts on Louis. Although he draws on numerous stories from different sources, he seems to have relied primarily on the liturgical vita BLQRF, which was itself a Dominican composition or

1. *Dictionnaire de spiritualité,* vol. 8, 46.

2. Schneyer, *Repertorium der lateinischen Sermones,* vol. 3, 54–157; HLF vol. 33, 459–79.

3. Gaposchkin, *Making of Saint Louis,* 286.

redaction. At numerous points he instructs the reader/preacher to "make a note of" or "consider" (*nota*) one story or another—indicating stories that were sufficiently well known not to need retelling or recording.

The two sermons presented here are *Rex sapiens* (The Wise King) and *Videte regem Salomonem* (Behold King Solomon!).[4] Their titles are simply their incipits, that is, the first two words of each sermon—themselves lines from scripture (Wisdom 6.26 and Canticles 3.11, respectively), which in turn influenced the themes of each sermon. These sermons follow a customary structure, in which the scriptural theme on which the sermon is based is broken down into its component parts and each word or phrase is glossed separately, one after the other. Traditionally, sermons, including these two, after an introductory section (or "protheme"), are divided into three main parts, each guided by words or phrases from the basic scriptural passage on which the sermon is based. The fact that the themes of both these sermons bear specifically on kingship is indicative of their predominant, overall message. This is especially the case with *Rex sapiens,* which engages ideas of political theology and the definition of the relationship between the king, God, and the community of those who are ruled. But the sermons are far more wide ranging than this suggests, taking up Louis' crusades, his good works, and his piety. *Videte regem,* which starts with an elaborate discussion of the winds that propel a ship toward salvation (an image that must have evoked, on some level, Louis' naval journey to the East on his first crusade and the saving of the ship on his return journey) engages Louis' crusades in a way that negotiates their historical failure, as well as taking up themes of piety and other anecdotes from his biography. It should be noted that the sermons are not really intended as narrative recapitulations. Rather, they work toward larger themes of Christian devotion and perfection, in which the figure of Louis is intended primarily as an exemplar and a source of inspiration.

The sermon transcriptions here are based, respectively, on two and four manuscripts. BNF Lat 14799 (93r/191r–94r/293r) has been used

4. For *Rex Sapiens,* see Schneyer, *Repertorium,* vol. 3, p. 105, no. 611. For *Videte regem,* see Schneyer, *Repertorium,* vol. 3, p. 104, no. 609. Schneyer offers a complete manuscript listing for each. For a brief discussion of *Rex sapiens,* see Gaposchkin, *Making of Saint Louis,* 119–23.

as the base manuscript for *Rex sapiens*. This text has been formally collated with Vatican Lat 1259; a version of the sermon found in BNF Lat 14966 (25r–26r) was also consulted. Because *Videte regem* survives in two forms (in which the second half of the sermon diverges), four manuscripts have been used, in order to have at least two witnesses of each version. The two versions follow the same essential outline and incorporate a number of the same scriptural materials, although they differ in some of their anecdotes and expand differently on various themes. *Videte regem₁* is found in BNF Lat 15962 (25v–26v) and Vatican Lat 1250 (102r–104r). *Videte regem₂* is found in Avignon 601 (460r–462r), Avignon 304 (68r–70r), Vatican Lat 1260 (62v–64v), Vatican Lat 1259 (164r–167r). BNF Lat 15962 has been used as the base manuscript for the first half of both versions of *Videte Regem* and for the entirety of *Videte Regem₁.* In the second part of *Videte Regem₂*, Vatican Lat 1259 has been used as the base manuscript. The relevant texts have been collated with Vatican Lat 1250 and Avignon 601. Avignon 304 and Vatican Lat 1260 have also been consulted, but variants have not been marked.

Scriptural references in interpolations and in the English translation follow the sequence 1–2 Samuel and 1–2 Kings, rather than 1–4 Kings.

Rex sapiens

REX SAPIENS

[1] *Rex sapiens stabilimentum populi est, etc.* Sapiencie vi [26]. A capite multum dependet regimen[1] et ordinacio corporis et membrorum, unde quando capud est infirmum membra incomposite et inordinate reguntur. Quando autem sanum est totum corpus et membra ordinacius[2] melius reguntur. Omnis congregatio sub uno rectore est sicut unum corpus sub uno capite. Cui concordat scriptura. Rom 12 [5] et 1[3] Cor 12 [12–19] *omnes sumus unum corpus in Christo.*

[2] Et in tota congregatione rector est caput et subditi sunt membra et merito rector vocatur caput, quia sicut in corpore humano, quamdiu vivit pulcherius membrum est caput, et maxime ratione faciei quando vero[4] mortuum est corpus turpius est et fcies abhominabilis[5] ad videndum est.[6] Sic in omni congregatione, tam seculari quam ecclesiastica, vel est ita pulchrum quam[7] rector bene vivens et bene regens, et vel est[8] ita turpe sicut rector[9] male vivens et male[10] regens. Rector ergo est capud quod[11] si sit infirmum cetera[12] membra dolent, id est,[13] omnes subditi inordinate se habent. Ysa i [5] *omne capud est languidum et*[14] *omne cor merens,* etc. Unde Bernardus ad Guillelmum, comitem pictavensis: "si quis de populo deviat, solus[15] perit.[16] Unde principis error

1. regimen] regnum V
2. ordinacius] et *add.* P₁
3. 1] ita V
4. vero] homo *in* V
5. abhominabilis] abhominabilior V
6. est] *om.* V
7. quam] sicut V
8. est] *om.* V
9. rector] *om.* V
10. reges *expunged* P₁
11. quod] quia V
12. infirmum] infirmus omnia V
13. dolent, id est] scilicet V
14. et] sequitur [seᶜ⁻] *add.* V
15. solus] salus P₁
16. perit] parit V

A Wise King

[1] *A wise king is the foundation of the people,* etc. [Wisd. 6.26]. Much of the rule and ordering of the body and its members depends upon the head, and thus when the head is infirm, the members are disordered and irregularly ruled. But if the entire body is healthy, the members are ruled better in a more orderly way. The entire congregation under one ruler is therefore one body under one head. Scripture is in agreement with this. Rom. 12 [5] and 1 Cor. 12 [12–19]: *We are all one body in Christ.*[1]

[2] And within a whole congregation, the ruler is the head and the subjects are the members. The ruler is deservedly called the head because, just as with the human body, so long as it lives, the head is the more beautiful member, especially in its appearance. But when [the head] is dead the body is more foul and its appearance is loathsome to behold. Thus, in each congregation, whether secular or ecclesiastical, [the body] is beautiful when the ruler lives and rules well and ugly when the ruler lives and rules badly. Thus the ruler is the head, because when it is sick the rest of the body suffers; that is, the subjects all find themselves in confusion. Isa. 1.5: *The entire head is ill and the whole heart mourns,* etc. And thus did [Saint] Bernard [write] to William, Count of Poitiers: "If any one person from among the populace errs, it is he alone who

1. The head-and-members metaphor for rulership was well established in medieval political thought and writing by 1300. It is generally believed that John of Salisbury (d. 1180), in the *Policraticus* (ca. 1159), first introduced and popularized the metaphor.

multos involvit et tantis[17] obest quantis[18] preest."[19] Si vero illud[20] capud
sic sanum sine corrumptione et difficultate[21] tunc omnia membra;
scilicet[22] subditi stant sub eo ordinate et secure. Id[23] est capud aureum.
Dan. 2: *et tunc est rex capud aureum.*[24] Et quia beatus Ludovicus fuit
tale capud ideo subditos suos utiliter rexit confirmando et stabiliendo
in[25] omni bonitate et hoc est quod dicunt verba proposita: *rex sapiens,*
etc. Et tanguntur tria: officium impositum *Rex*; adiutorium exhibitum.
Sapiens; sequtum beneficium. *Stabilimentum est populi.*[26]

I

[3] Quam[27] ad primum intelligendum[28] est quod sol non levat[29] nisi
purum et dulce, et dimitit[30] impurum et amarum ut patet in rore et
pluvia quamvis mare a quo potissime elevantur sit amarum et salsum.
Et ita[31] illa que sol elevat faciunt[32] inferiora fructificare sic Christus *sol
iusticie.* Malach 4.2.[33] Non elevat ad regnum[34] impios[35] et impuros.

17. ab] *expunged in* P₁
18. tantis obest quantis] tam obest quam V
19. praeest] potest V
20. illud] istud V
21. et difficultate] *om.* V. *Abbr. in* P₁ *as* diffcu
22. scilicet] id est V
23. Id] Istud V
24. Dan 2 . . . aureum] *om.* V
25. in] hoc *add.* V
26. officium . . . populi] Primo officum impositum rex adiutorium exhibitum. Secundo adiutorium exhibitum: sapiens. Tertio secutum beneficium stabilimentum. Talis le ofici a quoy dieux le orden, rex. Le ayde que deus li dona, sapiens.
li biens que [[163ra]] poples cuba. stabilitum, etc. V
27. Quam] quantum P₁
28. intelligendum] advertendum V
29. levat] elevat V
30. dimitit] dimittat V
31. ita] ideo V
32. faciunt] ista *add.* V
33. Malach 4] malum V; *corr. from* Malach 2 P₁
34. regnum] celorum *add.* V
35. impios] iniquos V

suffers. But the error of a prince involves many men and it is as harmful as he is powerful."[2] Thus indeed, if the head is healthy, without corruption and difficulty, so then are all the members, which is to say that the subjects remain ordered and untroubled under him. This is a golden head. Dan. 2: *and then the king is the golden head.*[3] And because blessed Louis was such a head, he ruled his subjects to their advantage by supporting and making [them] strong in all goodness. This is what the words put forth say: *the wise king* . . . . And these words touch on three things. The established office: *king.* The aid manifested: *wise.* The benefit that ensues: *the foundation of the people.*

I

[3] With regard to the first point, it must be understood that the sun only takes up [*levat*] what is pure and sweet, leaving behind the impure and bitter, as with the dew and rain which it takes up [*elevantur*] from the sea, although the latter is very bitter and salty. And thus those things which the sun takes up [*elevat*] make lesser things bear fruit, just as Christ, the *sun of justice* (Mal. 4.2), does not elevate [*elevat*] the

2. PL vol. 182, c. 281b. Bernard of Clairvaux, Epistola 127.
3. Cf. Dan. 2:32: "huius statue caput ex auro optimo erat"; and Dan. 2:38: "tu es ergo caput aureum."

Osee viii [8.4]. *Ipsi regnaverunt*[36] *et non in me*; sed puros et dulces per quos subditi[37] possint fructificare et foveri in bonis operibus;[38] talis fuit beatus Ludovicus. Unde potest dici de eo illud 3 Reg. x [1 Kings 10.9]: *Sit dominus deus tuus benedictus cui conplacuisti [. . .] et constituit te regem ut faceres iudicium et iusticiam.*[39]

[4] Nota quod curialitas que[40] non est recognita est perdita. Et ideo qui curialitatem recipit debet recognoscere[41] maior autem[42] curialitas quam Deus[43] faciat alicui communitati est quando dat ei bonum rectorem, hoc enim est signum quod diliget illam communitatem.[44] Et per contrarium[45] quando rector est malus signum est quod Deus[46] odit talem communitatem,[47] quia[48] rector[49] malus inimicus est Dei; et ideo quando Deus dimittit[50] aliquam communitatem[51] in manu[52] mali rectoris ponit eam in manu inimici extra manum suam.[53] Quod est signum magni odii. Osee 13: *Dabo vobis regem in furore meo.* Sed bonus rector est minister Dei et amicus et ideo communitas[54] commissa tali rectori commissa[55] est amico, quod est signum dilectionis, de qua dilectione

36. regnaverunt] regnabunt V
37. subditi] *corr. from* subdi P₁
38. fructificare . . . operibus] in rationis operibus foveri et fructificare operibus V
39. P₁ 191va
40. que] quam P₁
41. recognoscere] et regraciari *add.* V
42. autem] *om.* V
43. deus] dominus V
44. diligit illam communitatem] dominus diligit illam congregationem V
45. contrarium] oppositum V
46. Deus] Dominus V
47. talem communitatem] illam congregationem V
48. quia] quando *add.* V
49. rector] est *add.* V
50. manu] viam *add.* V
51. communitatem] congregacionem V
52. dei] *expunged in* P₁
53. eam in . . . manu suam] eum extra manu suam et in manu inimici [[192rb]] V
54. communitas] congregatio V
55. tali rectori comissa] *om.* V

impious and impure to royal power—Hos. 8.4: *They reigned but not by me.* Rather [He elevates] pure and sweet men through whom subjects can flourish and be nourished in good works. Such a man was blessed Louis. And thus can be said of him 1 Kings 10 [9]: *Blessed be the Lord God, whom you have pleased . . . and who has appointed you king to do judgment and justice.*

[4] Note that governance [*curialitas*] that is not appreciated is lost. Thus he who receives good governance ought to appreciate it. Governance which God provides for a given community is greater, however, when he provides a good ruler, for this is an indication that he loves that community. But on the other hand, when a ruler is a bad ruler, this is the sign that God hates that community, because a bad ruler is the foe of God. Therefore when God places any given community into the hands of a bad ruler, he places it into hostile hands and out of His own hands. This is the sign of great hatred. Hos. 13.11: *I will give to you a king in my fury.* But a good ruler is the minister and friend of God, and thus a community entrusted to such a ruler is entrusted as to a friend,

est Deo[56] valde regraciandum. Talis fuit beatus Ludovicus. Unde fertur dixisse quod prius vellet[57] quod omnes filii[58] essent mortui quam quod deum[59] offenderent[60] per peccatum[61] mortale.[62] Unde fuit[63] amicus Dei. In manu huius regis[64] amici sui[65] posuit Deus populum Francie.[66] Unde[67] signum est[68] specialis amoris Paralipomenon 2: *Quia enim diligit Deus Israhel et vult servare eum in eternum idcirco*[69] *posuit te regem super eum* [2 Chron. 9.8].

[5] Et ad quid ut faceret[70] iudicium et iusticiam?[71] Iudicium recte sentenciando, et iusticiam in ex[e]quendo.[72] Iudex enim debet esse sicut libra[73] in qua res ponderantur[74] que equaliter demonstrat pondus omnium rerum preciosarum et vilium,[75] auri et plumbi, argenti et stagni.[76]

56. dilectione est deo] est V
57. prius vellet] libericius [?] audiret rumores V
58. filii] sui *add.* V
59. deum] adeo V
60. offenderent] offenderet deum V
61. peccatum] per peccatum[?] V
62. Cf. GB 4 (p. 4): "Quod cum ille religiosus cum multa admiratione, quasi eam redarguendo, dominae reginae dixisset, illa super hac falsitate se et filium humiliter excusavit, verbum laudabile subinferens, videlicet, quod si dictus filius suus rex, quem super omnes creaturas mortales diligebat, infirmaretur ad mortem, et diceretur ei quod sanaretur, semel peccando cum muliere non sua; prius permitteret ipsum mori, quam semel peccando mortaliter suum offendere Creatorem. Hoc ego ab ore ipsius domini regis audivi."
63. fuit] verus *add.* V
64. regis] *om.* V
65. sui] *om.* V
66. francie] suum francorum V
67. Unde] *in* V
68. est] *om.* V
69. idcirco] iccirco P$_1$
70. faceres] faceret V
71. iusticiam] iudicium V
72. exequendo] exquendo V P$_1$; *spelled* exequendo P$_2$
73. libra] *om.* V
74. res ponderantur] respondeatur V
75. vilium] vililum P$_1$
76. et plumbi argenti et stagni (*corr. from* stangni)] plumbi etc. V

which is the sign of love, and for this love great thanks must be rendered to God. Blessed Louis was such a ruler. And thus, it is held that he had said that he would sooner wish that all [his] sons were dead than that they might offend God through mortal sin.[4] And thus he was a friend of God. Into the hand of this king, His friend, God placed the people of France. This is the special sign of love: 2 Chron. [9.8]: *Because God loves Israel, and will protect her for ever, therefore he placed you as king over her.*

[5] And how should one perform judgment and justice? By sentencing judgments rightly and by fulfilling justice. Truly, the judge ought to be like a pair of scales, in which things are weighed, [and] which, with equity, shows the weight of all things whether precious or vile,

---

4. Refers to a story that was originally about Blanche speaking about Louis (not Louis speaking about his own children) and that goes back to Geoffrey of Beaulieu (GB 4 [pp. 4–5]); the language here, however, draws from the tradition represented by WSP, GR, and BL. See GR 1, BL 1, BLQRF 1, YSD 1, and WSP *vie* 1 (p. 13).

Sic princeps in iudicando[77] debet[78] ponderare iura pauperum sine[79] acceptione personarum. Deutero 1[80] *ita parvum audietis*[81] *sicut magnum, et non*[82] *accipietis personam cuiusquam,*[83] *domini enim iudicium est* [1.17]. Sic fecit beatus Ludovicus. Unde semel vel pluries[84] in septimana sedebat in loco communi ut pauperes possent habere accessum ad eum. Item[85] puniebat magnos sicut parvos. Nota de[86] domino de Cociato. Sed nunc e contrario versum[87] est. Quia[88] dicitur Amos 5: *revelabitur iudicium in aqua et iusticia quasi torrens fortis.*[89] [5.24]. Nota quod baculum, quantumcumque rectus, si ponatur in aqua apparet tortuosus. Item in aqua non apparet proprium pondus rerum; videntur[90] enim maioris ponderis quanta sint.[91] Sic causa pauperum quantumcumque recta sit apparet tortuosa per falsos advocatos et falsos[92] consiliarios. Nec ius eorum ponderatur quantum deberet ponderari.[93] Illud[94] est iudicium in aqua. Iusticia[95] est quasi torrens fortis qui[96] si obviet turri forti non trahet eam secum. Sed res minutas trahit,[97] sic exequtio iusticie, nunc non trahit magnos dominos potentes, sed parvos et pauperes. Non sic

77. iudicando] iudicio V
78. debet] equaliter *add.* V
79. pauperum sine] per civem [?] sicut V
80. 1] quia V
81. audietis] audiens V
82. et non] nec V
83. cuiusquam] cuius V
84. pluries] bis V
85. Item] Ita P₁
86. V: 163vb
87. versum] impletum V
88. Quia] quod V
89. iudicum in aqua . . . torrens fortis] quasi aqua iudicium et iusciciam quasi torrens fortis V; torrens fortis] *corr. from* torretis P₁ to accord with Vulgate text
90. videntur] ibi V
91. sint] sit V
92. et falsos] propter usque V
93. ponderari] ponderare V
94. Illud] Istud V
95. Iusticia] enim *add.* V
96. qui] quod P₁
97. res minutas . . . potentis] minores sic execucio iusticie nunc non tangit magnos V

gold or lead, silver or tin. Thus the prince, in judging, ought to weigh equitably the rights of the poor without favoritism to anyone. Deut. 1 [17]: *You shall hear the little as well as the great; neither shall you show favor to any one in particular, because judgment is of God.*[5] And this is what blessed Louis did. Once or more each week he would make himself publicly available so that the poor could have access to him. And he punished the great just as the small. Consider the Lord of Coucy.[6] But now, things have changed to the opposite, as is said in Amos 5 [24]: *Judgment shall be revealed in water, and justice as a mighty torrent.* Note that a rod, however straight [*rectus*] it is, will appear twisted when placed in water. Similarly, the correct weight of things does not appear correct in water, but rather appears of greater weight, however much these things actually weigh. In this way any case of the poor, however just [*rectus*] it is, will appear twisted because of false advocates or false counselors. Nor is their right [*ius*] given as much weight as it ought to be. This is judgment in water. For justice is like a strong torrent which, if it meets a strong tower, will not drag it away, though it will drag away small things. So, too, in our times, the execution of justice does not drag away great men, lords, and potentates, but only the small and poor. This was not the case with blessed Louis, concerning

5. A variation from the Douay-Rheims translation.

6. Cf. WSP *vie* 18 (pp. 136–42). Jacob here instructs the preacher to tell the story of Enguerrand, Lord of Coucy, a high aristocrat whom Louis ruled against and punished harshly despite his high office. See BL, n. 61 of the translation.

fecit[98] beatus Ludovicus, de quo potest dici illud 2 Reg. 8 [2 Sam. 8.15]: *quod faciebat iudicium et iusticiam omni populo.*

II

[6] Secundo tangitur adiutorium exibitum: *Sapiens.*[99] Cuiuslibet viatori et maxime rectori vel directori necessarium est lumen,[100] non solum in[101] via pedum sed etiam[102] in via morum, rector aliorum est ductor[103] eorum. Et ideo indiget lumine sapientie.[104] Sapiens vi [23]: *Diligite lumen sapientie qui preestis populis.* Duplex est[105] lumen, scilicet ignis et stellarum.[106] Ita duplex est sapientia terrena et divina est. Lumen ignis consumit naturam in qua est, et omnem naturam quam tangit ut sepem,[107] altum lignum et huiusmodi. Et finaliter extinguitur cum exaltatione fumi et fetoris.[108] Sed lumen solis, lune, et[109] stellarum non fit. Fit terrena sapientia, consumit[110] in corde in quo est omnem humorem devotionis ad Deum, et compassionis ad proximum. Et quicquid tangit omnes[111] vicinos et subditos expoliat[112] et finaliter extinguitur in morte et non remanet nisi ferens memoria et infamia.[113] *Sapientes enim sunt ut faciant mala.* Jer. 4 [22]: Per istam sapientiam non regitur populus sed destruitur.

98. sed parvos . . . fecit] Et contrario V
99. et] Gal. lay'da a qui deus li dona *add.* V
100. rectori vel . . . lumen] ductori lumen est neccessarium V
101. in] *om.* V
102. etiam] magis V
103. 93vb/191vb P₁
104. lumine sapientie] lumen V
105. est] *om.* V
106. Duplex est lumen . . . lignum et huiusmodi] Istud lumen dedit deus beato ludovico. Rex inquit sapiens. Sed advertendum quod sicut est duplex lumen scilicet ignis [163vb] et stellarum, sic est duplex sapientia terrena et celestis et cum divina quia lumen ignis consumit materiam in quo est et omnem materiam quod tangit ceram, oleum, lignum, etc. V
107. sepem] *corr. from* sepum P₁ *and* P₂
108. fetoris] exaltatione, *expunged in* V
109. solis, lune, et] *om.* V
110. Fit terrena sapientia consumit] Sic sapientia terrena consumiter V
111. omnes] enim *add.* V
112. expoliat] spoliat V
113. et non remanet . . . infamia] cum fetore et fumo quia vel remanet declinibus [?] nisi ferens memoria sapientes nisi istud ut faciant mala V

whom we can say that of 2 Sam. 8 [15]: *And he did judgment and justice to all people.*

II

[6] Secondly, we consider the aid that is manifest: *Wise.* Light is necessary for any traveler and especially for a ruler or governor, not only for a journey by foot but also for a moral journey. A ruler of other people is their leader, and he thus requires the light of wisdom: *Love the light of wisdom, you who lead the people* [Wisd. 6.23]. And light is twofold: of fire and of the stars. And so, thus, wisdom is twofold: earthly and divine. Where the light of fire is, it burns up a natural object and every natural thing that it touches, such as a hedge, a tall tree, and the like. And finally it is extinguished with an exhalation of smoke and stench. But this does not happen with the light of the sun, moon, and stars. It does happen, however, with terrestrial wisdom; it consumes in the heart (where it is found) the entire desire [*humor*] of devotion to God and of compassion to neighbor. And it destroys whatever it touches—all neighbors and all subjects—and finally is extinguished in death and does not persist unless carried on by memory and infamy. *They are wise in doing evil*: Jer. 4.22. Through such wisdom people are not governed but instead brought to destruction.

[7] Sed sapientia divina nutrit humorem devotionis ad deum et com-passionis ad proximum.[114] Et dirigit populum spiritualiter et corpo-raliter.[115] Figura 2 Reg.[116] De Salomone qui petivit sapientiam a Deo ut sciret regere populum.[117] Et statim edificavit templum Domino et[118] pacifice rexit populum. Sed statim sapientia divina dimissa quoniam usus est sapientia humana oppressit populum.[119] Unde dixerunt[120] ad Roboam[121]: *Pater tuus durissimum iugum imposuit nobis* [1 Kings 12.4]. Ista sapientia non est[122] usus beatus Ludovicus, sed divina unde[123] potest ei dici illud secundo, Reg 14: *Tu domine mi rex* [cf. 1 Kings 1.13]. *Sapiens es sicut habet sapientiam angelus dei* [2 Sam. 14.20]. Hec est sapientia angelorum ministrancium nobis quod ex suo ministerio non querunt nisi honorem dei et nostram utilitatem. Sic beatus Ludovicus ex suo regimine nisi honorem dei et utilitatem proximi.[124]

III

[8] Ex quo[125] sequitur tercium: sequtum beneficium populi stabilimen-tum est.[126] Ubi sciendum[127] quod sicut Deus regit mundum corporeum

114. populum] *expunged and corr. with* proximum P₁
115. corporaliter] temporaliter V
116. Figura 2 Reg] Figuram habemus 2 Reg 2 V. Cf. 3 Kings 8.
117. populum] et dedit ei dominus *add.* V
118. et] optime et *add.* V
119. Sed statim . . . populum] Sed post a dimissa sapientia divina usus est sapientia mundana opprimens populum exactionibus.
120. dixerunt] dixsit [sic] V
121. Roboam] filium suum 2 Reg. 12 *add.* V
122. V: 164ra
123. unde] ideo added V
124. quod ex suo . . . utilitatem proximi] qui nonquam ex suo ministerio nisi Dei honorem et nostram utiltatem intendunt P₁
125. Ex quo] Propter quod V
126. secutum . . . stabilimentum est] beneficium secutum scilicet stabilimen-tum populi V
127. sciendum] notandum V

[7] But divine wisdom nourishes the desire [*humor*] of devotion to God and of compassion to neighbor. And it directs the people spiritually and bodily. [We have] the figure of Solomon from 2 Kings, who beseeched wisdom from God so that he might know how to rule his people. And he immediately built a temple to God and ruled his people peacefully. But immediately after having abandoned divine wisdom, since he used human wisdom, he oppressed his people. And thus they said to Rehoboam: *Your father laid a very heavy yoke on us* [1 Kings 12.4]. Blessed Louis did not use *this* sort of wisdom, but rather divine wisdom. Thus we can say of him, following 1 Kings 1: *You, my lord, the king* [1.13]. *You are wise, as the angel of God has wisdom* [2 Sam. 14.20]. This is the wisdom of the angels who minister to us because they do not ask for anything from their own ministry except the honor of God and usefulness for us. Thus did blessed Louis [ask] from his own rule nothing except the honor of God and what was useful for a neighbor.

III

[8] From this the third point follows: the ensuing benefit is the foundation of the people. Regarding this, it should be known that just as

per solem quantum ad effectus naturales sic regit regnum per[128] regem. Sol autem quantumcumque sit clarus, si[129] quiesceret et non moveretur, dissolveretur[130] in istis inferioribus, bonum regimen et bona[131] temperantia[132] calorum et frigorum[133] que omnia fiunt per motum celi. Sic quantumcumque rex et[134] rector sit nitidus lumine sapientie sicut sol, si tamen torpeat ocio[135] et non mutetur[136] per diversa loca ad sciendum qualiter sui officiales[137] regunt; subvertitur totum bonum regimen et bona ordinatio subditorum. Et[138] sicut in exemplo proposito; si sol staret tota[139] eius influencia esset ad unam partem[140] vicinam; et[141] alie privarentur lumine[142] et beneficio solis. Sic quando princeps est occiosus et negligens totum emolumentum venit ad collaterales et propinquos[143] consiliarios assistentes. Isti replent bursam suam[144] et[145] alii[146] remanent in frigore multiplicis desolationis. Non sic[147] beatus Ludovicus.[148] Sed circuibat[149] investigando per se et[150] per alios difficiliis[151] suorum officialium. Et bene[152]

128. per] secundum *add.* V
129. si] tamen *add.* V
130. dissolveretur] solveretur V
131. temporalia] *expunged* P₁
132. bona temperantia] bonum temperanientum V
133. calorum et frigorum] caloris et frigoris alternacio estatis et hyemis die et noctis V
134. rex et] *om.* V
135. ocio] occio P₁
136. mutetur] permutetur V
137. officiales] *absent* V
138. Et] *om.* V
139. tota] totam V
140. partem] scilicet ad partem V
141. et] *om.* V
142. lumine] calore V
143. et propinquos] *om.* V
144. bursam suam] bursas suas V
145. et] *om.* V
146. V: 164rb
147. sic] fecit *add.* V
148. P₁: 192ra. vero *add.* V
149. circuibat] crescebant V
150. et] vel P₁
151. difficiliis] defactus V
152. bene] *om.* V

God rules the corporeal world through the sun for the production of the things of nature, so does He rule the kingdom through the king. The sun, however bright it may be, if it were to stand still and not move, would be dissipated[7] in those things beneath it—good direction, good moderation of heat and cold, which all come to pass because of heavenly motion. Thus, however much the king and ruler might shine with the light of wisdom like the sun, if he becomes le - thargic in idleness and does not move from place to place in order to know how his officers are ruling, then the entire good rule and good order of his subjects would be overturned. And thus, just as in the example advanced here, if the sun were to stand still, its entire effect would be focused only on the area to which it was closest, and other places would be deprived of its light and its benefits. And thus when the prince is idle and negligent, every benefit goes to his right-hand men and the advisors who closely attend upon him. These men fill up their purses, and other people are kept outside in the cold of manifold ruin. This was not blessed Louis, for he circulated around investigating the failures of his officials, both on his own and through his men.

7. Note here the pun: the sun (*sol*) dissolves (dis*sol*veretur), literally "un-suns-itself."

puniebat et[153] propter hoc regnum eius firmum fuit[154] et populus ei[155] adhesit. Unde de eo potest exponi quod[156] dici de Ioseph. Eccli. 49:[157] *Natus est homo princeps fratrum suorum firmamentum gentis et stabil-imentum populi.* Sequitur.[158] *ossa eius visitata sunt* [Sir 49.18], quando scilicet[159] crescentibus miraculis canonizatus est et ossa eius revelata sunt[160] ut honoraretur corpus in terris cuius spiritus fruitur in celis[161] cum angelis.

153. et] *om.* V
154. fuit] stetit V
155. ei] firmiter *add.* V
156. quod] illud V
157. 49] 19 V
158. Sequitur] quod *add.* V
159. scilicet] *absent* V
160. sunt] *om.* V
161. celis] celo V

And he punished them appropriately, and, on account of this, his kingdom remained strong and his people were loyal to him.[8] And thus of
him we can say that which was said of Joseph; Sir. 49 [17]: *He was born
a man, prince of his brothers, mainstay of the nation and the foundation
of his people.* And then follows: *And his bones were visited* [Sir. 49.18];
which is to say that, miracles having grown in number, he was canonized, and his bones were made available to the public, so that the body
could be honored on earth whose spirit rejoices in the heavens with
the angels.

8. Jacob here refers to Louis' establishment of the *enquêteurs,* a group of
men—largely drawn from the Franciscans and Dominicans—who went into the
kingdom to hear and redress complaints against royal officials.

VIDETE REGEM SALOMONEM

VIDETE REGEM SALOMONEM

[1] *Videte regem Salomonem in dyademate.*[1] Can. 3 [11]. Nova[2] et mirabilia libenter videntur.[3] Figura iii[4] Reg. vi.[5] Salomon in principio regni sui fuit novus et[6] mirabilis in duobus[7] precellens[8] diviciis et sapientia omnes[9] reges.[10] Ideo dicitur de ipso[11]: *magnificatus est rex Salomon*[12] *super omnes reges in*[13] *universa terra, et*[14] *omnis populus*[15] *desiderabat videre vultum Salomonis* [cf. 1 Kings 10.23–24] Licet[16] magnum sit in[17] omni persona,[18] pertingere ad[19] honorem et gloriam paradysi tantum maius est et[20] mirabilius[21] sita in honoribus[22] huius mundi.[23] Eccli. 31[24]: *Beatus est*[25] *dives qui inventus est sine macula, et qui post non aurum*

1. dyademate] etc. *add.* V₁
2. Nova] Magna V₁
3. videntur] audiuntur V₁
4. iii] quidem V₁; *om.* W
5. vi] x V₁
6. novus et] *om.* V₂
7. in duobus] *om.* V₁; scilicet *add.* W
8. precellens] in *add.* V₁
9. omnes] *om.* W
10. Cf. 3[1] Kings 10.23: "magnificatus est ergo rex Salomon super omnes reges terre diviciis et sapientia."
11. ipso] eo V₁
12. Solomon] vehementer W
13. in] et W
14. et] in V₂
15. et omnis populus] *om.* V₁; omnis populus *om.* W
16. Licet] hoc *add.* V₁
17. in] dici W
18. magnum sit in omni personam] ei sit magnum in dei persona V₂
19. persona pertingere ad] persona non habente V₁
20. est et] *om.* V₁
21. mirabilius] de persona *add.* V₁ W
22. honoribus] et diviciis *add.* V₁ W
23. Licet magnum . . . huius mundi] Licet hoc sit magnum in persona non habente gloriam et honorem paradysi maius tantum et mirabilius de persona sita in honoribus et diviciis huius mundi V₁
24. 31] 3 V₁; 1 P₃
25. est] *om.* V₂ W

BEHOLD KING SOLOMON

[1] *Behold King Solomon in his crown* [Song 3.11]. People willingly see new and wondrous things. For example, in 3 Kings 6: Solomon, from the beginning of his reign, was new and wondrous, surpassing all kings in two things: his wealth and his wisdom. And thus is said of him: *King Solomon exceeded all kings on the entire earth, and all the people desired to see Solomon's face* [cf. 1 Kings 10.23–24]. Although in every person it is a great thing to attain the honor and glory of paradise, it is all the greater and more marvelous if that person has been placed amidst the honors of this world. Sir. 31: *Blessed is the rich man who is found without stain, and who hath not gone after gold*; and then it follows: *he has*

abiit.[26] Sequitur: *fecit*[27] *mirabilia in vita sua* [cf. Sir. 31.8−9]. [2] Ratio est: non est magnum si navis habens ventum post se, recte[28] venit ad portum quia ventus eam inpellit;[29] unde talis[30] ventus quanto maior est[31] navis cicius venit ad[32] portum[33] dum tamen bene[34] regitur ne inpugnat[35] in[36] aliquid[37] et[38] frangatur. Sed quando navis habet ventum ex transverso mirum est si veniat[39] ad portum. Ventus[40] navem quandoque ita agitat quod evertit[41] eam et precipitat, quandoque tamen [ita] proicit[42] de aqua quod submergit. Tribulationes[43] huius mundi sunt ventus directe sequens[44] navem[45] nature humane infliguntur[46] a Deo[47] propter peccatum. Unde iuvant nos et impellunt[48] ad Deum. Unde[49] Gregorius. *Mala que nos hic*[50] *premunt ad Deum*[51] *ire*[52]

26. abiit] nec speravit in peccunie et thesauris *add.* V₁
27. fecit] enim *add.* V₁ W, V₁: 164va
28. post se recte] rectum poste se V₂
29. inpellit] et vivat *add.* W
30. unde talis] eam et vivat bonus autem V₂; talis] *om.* W
31. est] tanto *add.* W
32. P₃: 26ra. P₃ includes second ad.
33. portum] quia ventus eam impellit *add.* V₂
34. bene] *om.* V₂, inpug *expunged*
35. regitur ne inpugnat] regitur ne inpugnet V₂; regatur nec inpingat V₁; regatur ne inpinguat W
36. in] *om.* V₂
37. in aliquid] *om.* W
38. et] nec V₁
39. veniat] venit V₁
40. Ventus] enim *add.* V₁
41. evertit] vertit V₁
42. proicit] pricit V₂; *add.* per P₃
43. Tribulationes] Tribulatio V₂; et miserie *add.* V₁; miserie huius seculi *add.* W
44. sequens] insequentes V₁
45. navem] *corr. from* ventum P₃; quia *add.* W
46. infliguntur] inflicte V₁
47. deo] pro *add.* V₁; a deo] propter W
48. impellunt] impellit V₁; compellunt ire W
49. Unde] sicut ad bonum portum V₁; *om.* W
50. hic] habet V₁
51. deum] nos *add.* V₁
52. V₂: 102rb

done wondrous things in his life [cf. Sir. 31.8–9]. [2] This is the reason:
it is no wonder that a ship that has the wind at its back arrives directly
into the harbor, because the wind pushes it forward; the greater the
wind, the more quickly the ship comes to harbor, provided that it is
steered well so that it does not crash into something and break. But
when a ship has the wind coming at its side, it is wondrous that it ever
arrives at port at all. The wind sometimes blows a ship in such a way
that it overturns it and casts it down, and even sometimes casts it
forth from the water in such a way as to submerge it. The winds are
tribulations of this world that directly pursue the ship of human nature; [these tribulations] are inflicted by God on account of sin. And
thus they aid us and drive us toward God. So said Pope Gregory the
Great: *Evil things that overwhelm us here drive us to go toward God.*

compellunt.[53] Unde quanto[54] ventus persecucionis et[55] tribulationis maior est tanto cicius duxit[56] ad portum salutis[57] dum tamen navis ducatur[58] recte nec[59] frangatur per inpacientiam.[60] Sicut patet in martyribus qui[61] mediante vento passionis[62] statim pervenerunt[63] ad portum salutis de isto vento dicitur, Numeri xi [31]. *Ventus egressus*[64] *a domino*[65] *trans mare cocurnices*[66] *transtulit.* [3] Honor,[67] dominacio[68] mundi, non[69] venit[70] directe ex conditione[71] nature;[72] ventus est[73] veniens ex adverso; venit quandoque idcirco[74] ut[75] personam[76] agitat, et

53. ad deum ire compellunt] etc. W. Aquinas (ST Ia., qu. 21, art. 4) attributed this phrase to Gregory the Great in the Middle Ages. I am unable to locate the phrase in Gregory's work, but (as the editors of the Blackfriars edition of Aquinas note), see *Moralia in Job,* 26:13 (PL vol. 76, col. 360; CCSL vol. 143B, p. 1280). See also Guido of Pisa, *Expositiones et glose super Compediam Dantis,* vv. 82–84.

54. quanto V₁] quando P₃; tamen *add.* V₂

55. et] *om.* W

56. duxit] ducit V₂ V₁ W

57. salutis] ducente ad deum sequere salutem V₂

58. ducatur] regatur bene et W

59. nec] propterea V₁; ne frangatur ut scilicet patientia sustineat amore dei *add.* W

60. inpacientiam] in pacienciam V₂, sed sustineat amore dei *add.* V₁; W: 460v

61. qui] que V₁

62. passionis] huius mundi compassionis V₁

63. pervenerunt] perveniunt V₂ V₁

64. egressus] transmissus W

65. domino] areptas *add.* V₁

66. V₁: 164vb

67. Honor] et *add.* V₁

68. dominacio] huius *add.* V₁

69. non] que V₂

70. dir] *expunged* P₃

71. conditione] consideracione P₃

72. directe ex consideracione nec] directione excisione nature V₂; nec] nature sed V₁

73. est] *om.* W

74. idcirco] itaque V₂

75. venit quandoque idcirco ut] multa veniunt ad statum honoris non recte nec secundum rationem sed ex adverso per coactiones dolos et malitias. Et quia iste ventus ex adverso verso venit quandoque W

76. personam] ut *add.* W

Thus, the greater the winds of persecution and tribulation, the more quickly they lead to the port of salvation, provided that the ship is steered straight [*recte*] and is not shattered by a want of endurance. This is clear with the martyrs who arrive immediately at the port of salvation by means of the winds of suffering; of this wind it is said, in Num. 11 [31]: *And a wind coming out from the Lord transported the quails across the sea.* [3] Honor[1]—lordship in the world—does not come directly out of our natural condition, but is a wind blowing against us. And therefore, when it comes, it disturbs a person and casts

1. The word *honor* in Latin denotes not only honor in the English sense of the word, but also public office, power, and the dignity associated with it, hence, here, rulership.

quandoque[77] evertit[78] eam[79] et precipitat;[80] quandoque ventus honoris tantum dat et proicit persone de aquis diviciarum et deliciarum quod navis submergitur, ut[81] Mt. viii.[82] *Venerunt flumina et*[83] *flaverunt venti et*[84] *irruerunt*[85] *in*[86] *domum illam et*[87] *cecidit.* [4] Et[88] sic habemus duo.[89] Unum[90] est quod difficilius et mirabilius est personam[91] existentem in dominio et honore venire ad gloriam et coronam glorie[92] paradysi quam personam simplicis status. [5] Secundum[93] est[94] quod[95] mira - bilia libenter videntur.[96] Et quia ecclesia recolit quando beatus Lu- dovicus de honore regni mundani venit ad honorem[97] paradysi, ideo quasi proponens rem mirabilem[98] et spectabilem[99] dicit *Videte regem,*[100] *etc.* ubi[101] proponit tria videnda[102] de ipso. [6] Primum est fortitudo sue potentie. *Videte regem.* Licet vigor potentie requiratur in omni

---

77. et quandoque] quod W

78. venit quandoque idcirco . . . quandoque evertit] multi veniunt ad sta- tum honoris nec recte nec secundum rationi, sed ex adverso quod tractus, scilicet, dolos et malicia; et quia iste venit ventus ex adverso venit quandoque personam ita agitat quod vertit V₁

79. eam] ea V₂

80. precipitat] quia *add.* V₁

81. ut] *om.* V₂ W

82. viii] ci V₁; v W

83. et] *om.* W

84. flaverunt venti et] *om.* V₂

85. irruerunt] *corr. from* irruunt P₃

86. in] *om.* V₁

87. et] *om.* V₁

88. Et] *om.* V₂ V₁ W

89. sic habemus duo] Habemus igitur duo V₁ W

90. Unum] Primum V₁ W

91. personam] persona V₁

92. et coronam glorie] *om.* V₂ V₁; glorie] *om.* W

93. Secundum] Sic secundum V₂

94. est] *om.* W

95. quod] nova et *add.* W

96. videntur] audiuntur V₁

97. honorem] honores V₁; regni *add.* W

98. mirabilem] mirabile V₁

99. spectabilem] expectabilem V₁

100. regem] *om.* P₃ V₁; Solomonem *add.* W

101. ubi] et W

102. ubi proponit tria videnda] et tangit 3 mirablia V₁; indicia W

him down and knocks him over. And when the wind of honor gives so much to a person that it blows [him] out of the waters of riches and delights, the ship founders, as in Matt. 7 [27]: *And the floods came, and the winds blew, and they beat upon that house and it fell.* [4] And so we have two points. One is that it is more difficult and more wondrous for a person living in lordship and honor to achieve glory and the crown of glory in paradise than it is for a person of simple status to do so. [5] The second point is that, people look upon wondrous things willingly. And because the church recalls the moment when the blessed Louis went from the honor of an earthly kingdom to the honor of paradise, it says, as if it were setting forth some wondrous thing worth seeing, *Behold the King,* etc., where it sets forth three things about him that should be considered. [6] The first point is about the strength of his power. *Behold the king.* Although the force of power is a requirement

bellatore magis tamen in duce vel[103] rege; quia ad ipsum[104] omnes
alii aspiciunt,[105] eo stante, alii[106] pugnant, et[107] eo[108] cadente, ceteri[109]
fugiunt. Id est[110] [1] Mach ix [18]. *Iudas cecidit*[111] *et reliqui*[112] *fugerunt.*
Judas erat dux aliorum. Ideo[113] cervi[114] ducem faciunt forciorem[115] in
transfretando, cuius adiutorio ceteri innitentes[116] transfretant,[117] sic[118]
ecclesia romana, volens[119] transfretare pro terra sancta[120] recuperanda,
Ludovicum,[121] sicut forciorem et potenciorem filium quem haberet,[122]
fecit[123] ducem. [7] Qui assumpta[124] cruce de manu episcopi Parisiensi
duxit[125] secum tres comites fratres suos[126] barones alios et milites Francie
et[127] cum maximo[128] exercicu applicuit[129] in Egyptum et[130] vi armo -
rum[131] expugnavit Damiatam[132] civitatem famosam et totam regionem

103. vel] et in V₁
104. V₂: 102va
105. aspiciunt] respicunt et V₁
106. alii] omnes W
107. et] *om.* W
108. eo] *om.* V₂
109. cadente, ceteri] cessante alii V₁; ceteri] omnes W
110. id est] ptuno [?] V₂; *om.* W V₁
111. V₁: 165ra
112. reliqui] ceteri in Vulgate
113. Ideo] Unde V₁
114. cervi] servi V₂; tamen W
115. forciorem] etiam *add.* V₁
116. invitentes] intrantes V₂
117. transfretant] transeunt V₁
118. sic] est in *add.* V₁
119. volens] *om.* V₁
120. ru] *expunged* P₃
121. pro terra sancta recuperanda Ludovicum] peccatum romanum recuperanda et terra sancta V₁; Ludovicum] *om.* W
122. haberet] habeat V₂; habebat V₁
123. fecit] ipsum *add.* W
124. Qui assumpta] Unum beatum Ludovicum qui assumens V₁
125. duxit] ducit V₂; ducens V₁ W
126. suos] scilicet V₂; fratres suos] *om.* V₁ W
127. et] *om.* V₂ W; Francie et] faciens V₁
128. maximo] magno W
129. applicuit] applicavit V₁
130. et] *om.* V₁
131. vi armorum] sarracenorum V₂
132. Damiatam] Damascum W

for every soldier, it is even more so in a leader or a king, because all others look to him. When he stands firm, others fight, and when he falls, others flee. Thus it is said in 1 Macc. 9 [18]: *And Judas fell, and the rest fled away.* Judas represents the leader of other men. Just as deer choose a stronger leader whose help allows the whole herd to make a crossing, so, in this way, the Roman church, wishing to cross the sea in order to take back the Holy Land, made Louis, its stronger and more powerful son, the leader.[2] [7] After taking the cross from the hand of the bishop of Paris, and taking with him his three brothers, the counts, other barons, and knights of France, he landed in Egypt with a very great army and by force of arms conquered Damietta, that famous city, and the whole of the surrounding region. And thus it was right to

---

2. Cf. Blangez, ed., *Ci nous dit: Recueil d'exemples moraux,* vol. 2, 530, nos. 1–6, where the rich should help the poor through alms, as the strong deer help the weaker ones so that all can cross the river.

circumstantem.[133] Unde bene fuit actum[134] sumere[135] tam[136] potentem[137] et tam fortem regem ductorem.[138] Judic[ium] 9.16.[139] *Recte*[140] *constituistis super vos*[141] *regem Abymelech bene egistis cum Ieroboam. et domo*[142] *eius […] qui*[143] *pugnavit pro vobis*[144] *et animam suam dedit periculis ut erueret vos de manu Madian.*[145] [8] Et[146] tangit[147] auctoritas[148] tria puncta fortitudinis que habuit Ludovicus propter que laudandus est. [9] Primus est pugnare fortiter contra hostem: *Pugnavit.*[149] Secundum est[150] expo - nere se periculo: *dedit animam*[151] *periculis.* Tertium[152] est iustam causam eligere: *ut erueret vos de manu*[153] *Madian.*[154]

I

[10] Primus[155] punctus fortitudinis beati Ludovici fuit pugnare[156] contra hostem: *pugnavit.*[157] Volens pugnare contra hostem ita[158] quod[159]

133. Cf. BLQRF 5.
134. actum] *om.* W with space left for word
135. sumere] acuum *add. [illeg]* V$_1$
136. tam] *om.* V$_1$
137. potentem] potem V$_2$
138. ductorem] facere *add.* W
139. Judic 9.16–17] *corr.* Judic 3.
140. Recte] *om.* V$_1$ W
141. vos] nos W
142. domo] domus V$_1$
143. qui] *om.* V$_1$
144. vobis] nobis W
145. Madian] Madiar V$_2$
146. Et] Ubi V$_2$; Hec V$_1$
147. tangit] tanguntur W
148. auctoritas] *om.* W
149. Pugnavit] Qui pugnavit W
150. est] *om.* W
151. animam] scilicet *add.* W
152. Tertium] Tertio W
153. W: 461r
154. 15692: 26rb
155. Primus] Primum V$_1$
156. pugnare] pungnare P$_3$
157. Secundum est exponere … hostem: pugnavit: *om.* V$_2$; Primus punctus fortitudinis … hostem: pugnavit] De primo notandum quod W
158. ita] *om.* W
159. Pugnavit. Secundum est exponere … hostem ita quod] *om.* V$_1$

make such a powerful and strong king the leader. Judg. 9 [16]: *Rightly you have appointed Abimelech as king over you, and have dealt well with Jerobaal, and with his house . . . who fought for you and gave his life to dangers so as to deliver you from the hands of Midian.* [8] This [scriptural] authority touches on the three points of fortitude that Louis had and for which he ought to be praised. [9] The first is that he fought with strength against the enemy: *He fought.* The second is that he exposed himself to danger. *He exposed his life to dangers.* The third is that he chose a just cause: *to deliver you from the hands of Midian.*

I

[10] The first point of blessed Louis' strength was that he fought against the enemy: *he fought.* Desiring to fight against the enemy in such a

non[160] ledatur debet esse armatus, et secundum[161] quod[162] hostes diver-
simode invadunt[163] oportet habere diversa[164] arma. Tres[165] hostes habuit
beatus[166] Ludovicus[167] sicut nos habemus mundum, carnem, et demo-
nem.[168] Mundus:[169] Pugnat[170] sicut luctator[171] qui maxime conatur[172] so-
cium[173] levare de[174] terra quia quando[175] potest ipsum elevare[176] a terra
faciliter[177] ipsum deicit.[178] Sic mundus[179] dat divicias[180] genus honores
ad[181] elevandum[182] cor per superbiam et statim ipsum deicit per peccatum. Ps [72.18]: *deiecisti eos*[183] *dum*[184] *allevarentur.* [11] Bene[185] pugnans[186] contra mundum debet esse[187] armatus[188] virtute humilitatis; de apro legitur quod[189] non pungnat[190] nec percutit nisi sursum

160. non] ne V₁
161. secundum] hoc *add.* V₂
162. secundum quod] ut W
163. V₂: 102vb
164. diversa] diversemode V₂
165. Tres] *om.* V₁
166. beatus] *om.* V₂
167. Tres hostes habuit beatus Ludovicus] Dicens hostes habuit W
168. demonem] dyabolem V₁; carnem et demonem] carnem, dyabolum et mundum W
169. V₁: 165rb
170. pugnat] pugnaret V₂
171. luctator] vita morum [?] V₁
172. conatur] habet V₁
173. socium] suum *add.* V₂ V₁
174. de] a V₂ V₁ W
175. quando] quod W
176. elevare] levare W
177. faciliter] facile V₂; *om.* W
178. ipsum deicit] eum devincit V₁
179. mundus] maxime *add.* V₁
180. divicias] et *add.* W
181. ad] *om.* V₂; *add.* etc. W
182. elevandum] levandum W
183. eos] illos V₂
184. dum] ut V₁
185. Bene] Unde V₂ W; Et ideo V₁
186. pugnans] pungnans P₃
187. esse] *added in right margin* P₃
188. armatus] amatus V₂
189. De apro legitur quod] Aper W
190. non pungnat] ned pugnat V₂

way that he would not be wounded, he had to be armed, and because different kinds of enemies were attacking, he needed to have different kinds of weapons. Blessed Louis had three enemies, just as we do: the world, the flesh, and the devil. The world: He fights like a wrestler who tries most of all to lift his opponent off the ground since, if he can raise the other, he can easily throw him down. So, the world gives riches, nobility, [and] honors to elevate the heart through pride and then, at once, it knocks it down through sin: Ps. [72.18]. *When they were lifted up thou has cast them down.* [11] He who fights well against the world must be armed with the virtue of humility. It is said about the boar that he does not fight or strike a blow except by lifting upwards.

elevando.[191] Si deicit se deorsum est in tuto.[192] Sic pugnavit .N. contra genus,[193] divicias, etc., quia[194] non elatus.[195] Sed[196] fuit tante humilitatis[197] quod vestes preciosas forraturas[198] de vario[199] abhorrebat.[200] Pauperibus serviebat[201] propriis manibus lavando pedes,[202] etc.,[203] etiam[204] quantumcumque informes essent[205] infirmi. [12] Nota de monacho[206] leproso horribili[207] cuius oculos lepra excecaverat et[208] faciem corroserat; quem propria manu[209] pavit[210] et osculatus est. Unde[211] pungnavit[212] contra mundi superbiam per humilitatem. Secundum illud 1[213]

191. elevando] Unde pugnans contra eum si elevatum sursum est in periculo *add.* W

192. Si deicit se deorsum est in tuto] Unde pugnans contra eum si elevetur sursum propter quod aliud mundatum est in periculo quod deiciatur si tenet se deorsum stat in tuto V_1; Sic pugnans cum mundum si elevat sursum propter aliud mundanum est in periculo. Si tenet se deorsum propter nichil mundanum superbiens est in tuto *add.* W

193. genus] Ludovicus *add.* V_2

194. quia] *om.* W

195. Sic pugnavit. N . . . non elatus] Sic persona pugnans contra mundum si elevetur sursum propter aliquid mundanum est in periculo; si tenet se deorsum per humilitatem propter vel mundanum superbiens est in tuto. Sic pugnavit Beatus Ludovicus non fuit elatus propter genus nec propter divicias, etc. V_1.

196. Sed] *om.* V_2 W; Ymmo V_1

197. humilitatis] et est *add.* V_1

198. forraturas] fulraturus V_1, *om.* W

199. vario] colore *add.* V_2; variis V_1 W

200. abhorrebat] *add.* et. V_2

201. serviebat] *add.* et pauperibus serviebat V_2

202. pedes] *om.* V_2

203. Cf. BLQRF 4.

204. etc., etiam] *om.* V_1 W

205. informes essent] deformes vel V_1; deformes et W

206. monacho] *add.* religioso V_1

207. horribili] *add.* fetido V_2 V_1; et horri et fetido W

208. et] *om.* V_1 W

209. V_1: 165ra

210. pavit] paraverat V_2

211. Unde] *add.* bene W

212. pungnavit] bene pugnavit V_2

213. 1.] *om.* W

If one throws oneself down, one is safe. Thus [Louis] fought against no-bility, riches, and so forth, because he did not raise himself up high.³ In truth, he was of such great humility that he hated costly garments, [and] mixed-coloured furs. He ministered to the poor with his own hands, washing their feet, and so forth, no matter how deformed were the in-firm.⁴ [12] Consider the horribly leprous monk whose leprosy had eaten away his eyes and gnawed away at his face, whom [Louis] fed with his own hands and then kissed.⁵ In this way he fought against the pride of the world through humility. According to 1 Kings [1 Sam.] 17.32:

3. *elatus* = proud; we have rendered it as "up high" to carry on the boar metaphor, but have put it in the reflexive to indicate this meaning.

4. BLQRF 4.

5. The story of Louis kissing the leprous monk at Royaumont was among the most popular. See GB and WC. Jacob probably took the episode from BLQRF Lection 6.

Reg. vii[214] [1 Sam. 17.32]. *Servus*[215] *tuus*[216] *vadam et*[217] *pugnabo con-tra*[218] *philisteum,* id est mundum superbum.[219] [13] Secundus hostis[220] est[221] caro. Caro enim[222] pungnat[223] mordendo, sicut castor[224] de quo dicit Solinus,[225] quia[226] ita fortiter mordet quod[227] vulnerata carne non laxat dentes, nisi etiam[228] ossa frangat,[229] sic voluptas[230] ita fortiter mordet quod non sufficit ei[231] ledere[232] carnem exterius;[233] sed pene-trat usque ad ossa,[234] usque ad consensum cordis interius.[235]

[From this point forward there are two different traditions for the ser-mon. Each line is represented by two manuscripts. Because both ver-sions follow a similar outline, and their comparison is instructive, we include both versions side by side.]

214. vii] v W
215. Servus] Ego servus W
216. tuus] *add.* sum P$_3$
217. et] *om.* V$_1$
218. contra] adversus in Vulgate
219. id est mundum superbum] *om.* V$_1$; mundum superbum] superbum et vacandum W
220. V$_2$: 103ra
221. est] *om.* W
222. Caro enim] *om.* V$_2$ W
223. Caro enim pungnat] que propugnat V$_1$
224. castor] pastor V$_2$
225. Solinus] Libanus V$_1$
226. quia] quod V$_2$ W; quid V$_1$
227. quod] quid V$_1$
228. etiam] omnia W
229. nisi etiam ossa frangat] quosque perveniat ad ossa et tamen hostibus surgat V$_1$
230. voluptas] *add.* carnalis V$_1$
231. ei] *om.* V$_2$
232. ledere] mordere V$_1$
233. exterius] *add.* nec ledere V$_1$
234. ossa] *add.* scilicet V$_1$
235. cordis interius] *om.* P$_3$ V$_2$

I thy servant will go, and will fight against the Philistine, that is, the prideful world. [13] The second enemy is the flesh. Indeed, the flesh fights by biting, just like the beaver, of whom Solinus[6] said that he bites so forcefully that once the flesh is wounded he will not loosen his teeth until he has broken bones. Carnal desire bites in this way, with such force that it is not content with just a flesh wound, but it penetrates all the way to the bones, that is, as all the way to the consenting of the inside of the heart.

[From this point forward there are two different traditions for the sermon. Each line is represented by two manuscripts. Because both versions follow a similar outline, and their comparison is instructive, we include both versions side by side.]

6. Gaius Julius Solinus, third-century author of the *De mirabilibus mundi,* ch. 14: "Per universum Pontum fiber plurimus, quem alio vocabulo dicunt castorem. Lytris similis est, animal morsu potentissimum, adeo ut quum hominem invadit, conventum dentium non prius laxet, quam concrepuisse persenserit fracta ossa." Solinus, *Collectanea rerum memorabilium,* ed. Theodor Mommsen (Berlin: Weidmannos, 1985).

Version A
P_3*/ V_2

Version B
V_1*/W

[14A] Et ideo contra istum inimicum[236] armavit se sobrietate et
penitencia; quia portabat cilicium
ad carnem, in qua erat[237] crux fer-
rea, cum quatuor dentibus acu-
tissimis pungentibus.[238] Etc. Sic
vicit carnem. *sic pungnavit quasi
in incertum*[239] *etc*[240] enim ad Cor
[cf. 1 Cor. 9.26].

[14B] Arma contra istum hostem[241] sunt asperitas penitentie.
Legitur quod lucius qui anguil-
lam et alios pisces teneram pellem habentes et[242] mordet et de-
vorat. Sed perticam[243] habentem
scalinas duras et plenam[244] aculeis
non audet tangere. Sic peccatum
carnis, licet mordeat delicatos
tamen non audet tangere ar-
matos[245] dura[246] penitencia, sed[247]
dimitat eos[248] in pace. Sic fuit
beatus Ludovicus[249] armatus[250]
portans cilicium et crucem[251] fer-
ream ad carnem nudam, verberans se cathenis ieiunans in pane et
aqua;[252] unde poterat dicere illud
1 Cor [9.26–27]. *Sic pugno non
quasi*[253] *aerem verberans*[254] *sed castigo corpus meum.*

236. inimicum] *corr. from* immicum V_2, innicum P_3
237. portabat ... erat] oportebat in qua erat V_2
238. BLQRF 3 refers to Louis' hairshirt.
239. incertum] *corr. from* incircuitu, P_3
240. etc.] *om.* V_2
241. hostem] *om.* W
242. teneram pellem habentes et] habentes pellem teneram et mollem W
243. perticam] *om.* W
244. scalinas duras et plenam] pellem duram plenam scamis [?] duris et
245. tamen non audet tangere armatos] et armatus W
246. dura] *add.* pelle W
247. sed] *om.* W
248. eos] *om.* W
249. beatus Ludovicus] *om.* W
250. armatus] iste *add.* W
251. crucem] cathenam W
252. ad carnem ... pane et aqua] etc. W; V_1: 165vb
253. non quasi] ut V_1
254. verberans] *corr. from* similans; cf. Vulgate text.

Version A

[14A] And thus he armed himself against this enemy with sobriety and penance, for he wore a hair shirt on his body, in which there was an iron cross with four very sharp teeth that bit into him, etc.[7] Thus he conquered the flesh; *Thus he fought as if aimlessly, etc.* as in Corinthians [cf. 1 Cor. 9.26].

Version B

[14B] The weapons against this enemy are the hardships of penance. We read that the pike bites and devours eel and other fish with tender skins, but does not dare to touch the perch, which has hard scales and is full of spikes. Thus a sin of the flesh, although it bites the weak, does not dare touch those who are armed with harsh penance, but leaves them in peace. Blessed Louis was so armed, as he wore a hair-shirt and an iron cross on his naked body, beat himself with chains, [and] fasted on bread and water.[8] Thus he could say as in 1 Cor. [9.26–27]: *I fight not as if beating the air, but I chastise my body.*

7. BLQRF 3 treats Louis' bodily asperities, but not in as much detail; for which, see GB 17; GR 5; WSP *vie* 14; BL 3. The sermon takes liberties.
8. See note 7.

[15A] Item tertio. Pugnavit[255] contra dyabolum qui temptaciones apponit[256] contra fidem. Item[257] se armavit scuto fidei. Scutum enim ponitur a parte sinistra ad protegendum cor et latitudo eius maior[258] est superior. Ita[259] spiritualiter in sinistra adversitatis, debet apparere virtus fidei, ne cor, id est, conscientia ledatur per impacienciam. Item[260] latum fidei debet esse supra appetendo celestia.

[15B] Tertio. Hostis scilicet dya - bolus[261] pugnat spiritualiter contra fidem temptando contra sacramenta;[262] arma[263] contra istum hostem sunt scutum[264] fidei. Eph.[265] 6: *In omnibus sumentes scutum fidei ut possitis omnia tela nequissimi ignea extinguere.*[266] [Eph. 6.16] Scutum[267] deffendit corpus[268] ne vulneretur a lancea et portatur ad sinistrum[269] partem nec ad dexteram. Item elatum[270] superius et[271] strictum inferius, sic[272] deffendit cor ne sagitta infidelitatis ad ipsum veniat per consensum et debet deportari[273] ad sinistrum[274] adversitatis contra quosdam confidentes in

255. tertio pugnavit] *om.* V_2

256. apponit] ponit V_2

257. Item] ideo V_2

258. maior] *om.* V_2

259. Ita] Item V_2

260. Item] Ita V_2

261. scilicet dyabolus] est demon quasi W

262. contra fidem temptando contra sacramenta] pro temptando contra fidem W; 461v

263. arma] armata V_1

264. scutum]scutu V_1

265. Eph] *corr. from* Phi V_1

266. fidei ut possitis omnia tela nequissimi ignea extinguere] etc. W

267. Scutum] Nota scutum W

268. corpus] carnem W

269. sinistrum] sinistra W

270. partem nec ad dexteram. Item elatus] latum W, *corr. from* elatum V_1

271. et] *om.* W

272. sic] fides *add.* W

273. et debet deportari] portatur W

274. sinistrum] sinistra W

[15A] Point three. He fought against the devil who sets up temptations against faith. So, he armed himself with the shield of faith. The shield is held up at the left side to protect the heart, with its greater width higher up. Spiritually, the virtue of faith should be found on the left side against adversity, lest the heart—that is, conscience—be wounded through a lack of constancy. And so, the breadth of faith ought to be held on high in the quest for the heavenly.

[15B] Point three. The enemy, i.e., the devil, fights spiritually against the faith by tempting against the sacraments. The weapon against this enemy is the shield of faith. Eph. 6 [16]: *In all things taking the shield of faith, wherewith you may be able to extinguish all the fiery darts of the most wicked one.* This shield defends the body so it not be wounded by a lance, and it is carried on the left side and not on the right. Likewise, a shield raised high and held closely below defends the heart so that the arrow of faithlessness does not come to it by consent, and it ought to be held up to the left of adversity against anyone who trusts in prosperity but despairs in adversity.

prosperitate[275] sed in adversitate desperantes. Item debet esse maior et lacior sursum in bonis spiritualibus quam deorsum in temporalibus contra[276] confidentes in mundanis.[277] Sic fuit armatus beatus Ludovicus.[278]

II

[16A] Ita[279] legitur de ipso quod si videret Christum in specie humana ex una parte et sacramentum altaris[280] ex alia,[281] ita firmiter

[16B] Nota quando navem sua oratione collisa fractione servavit.

275. prosperitate] et mundani *add.* W
276. contra] *om.* V₁
277. Item debet esse . . . confidentes in mundanis] *om.* W
278. Beatus Ludovicus] N. W
279. Ita] add ledabatur V₂
280. altaris] *om.* V₂
281. alia] *add.* parte V₂

And thus the upper part [of the shield of faith] ought to be greater and wider in spiritual goods than is the lower part in temporal goods, [guarding] against those who trust in the world. Blessed Louis was so armed.

II

[16A] And thus it is said of him that if he were to see Christ in human form, on the one hand, and the sacrament of the altar, on the other, so firmly did he believe

[16B] Note the time that [Louis] saved the ship from a crushing

credebat Christum esse in sacramento quod non dimitteret videre sacramentum propter Christum in specie humana. Exemplum de eo: cum pertransiret[282] semel ante ecclesiam fiebat elevacio nec tamen amovit[283] capellum[284] suum. Quid[285] cum quesisset quidam miles: Quare esset hoc quia consueverat, respondit[286] quod[287] Deus revelaverat sibi quod hostia nec[288] erat consecreta. Bene igitur fuit armatus scuto[289] fidei contra insultus dyaboli. Iosue 1:[290] *Salus vel*[291] *salvaturus*[292] *pungnavit multo tempore contra tres reges et devicit eos* [cf. Josh. 11:18].

Item quando voluit videre[293] hostiam media[294] parte rubeam, etc. Unde optime fuit armatus scuto fidei.[295] Ps. [90.5] *Scuto circumdabit te veritas tua.* Sic igitur pugnavit[296] bene contra hostes quod nunquam ab aliquo lesus esset per peccatum mortale. Josue xi. *Multo tempore pugnavit Josue contra reges istos* [Josh. 11.18] et occidit istos.[297]

282. pertransiret] transiret V₂
283. amovit] ammovit V₂. V₂: 103rb
284. capellum] capussium V₂
285. quid] quod V₂
286. Respondit] sibi V₂
287. quod] hostia sibi quod hostia rex quod V₁
288. ned] non V₁
289. scuto] sacramento V₂
290. 1] primo V₂
291. vel] et V₂
292. salvaturus] salvatus V₂
293. Item quando voluit videre] *repeated in* V₁ (assumed accidental)
294. media] mediam
295. Nota quando nave . . . Unde optime fuit armatus scuto fidei] Sic fuit armatus N. et ideo impletum est in eo illud W; *add.* quando dixit quod non avertet oculos ab altari dum levatur [levat Avignon 304] hostia si Christus a tergo [argo? Vatican Lat 1260] corporaliter transieri under impletum es in eo illud Avignon 304, Vatican Lat 1260
296. V₁: 166ra
297. Sic igitur pugnavit . . . et occidit istos] *om.* W

that Christ was present in the sacrament that he would not stop
gazing upon the sacrament to
look upon Christ in human form.
Hence, the exemplum about him:
Once, when he passed before a
church at the moment of the elevation [of the host], he did not
remove his hat. When a certain
knight asked him why not, because he usually did so, he answered that God had revealed to
him that the host had not been
consecrated.[9] Indeed he was well
armed with the shield of faith
against the assault of the devil:
Josh. 1 [11.18]: *Safe and about
to save, he fought for a long time
against the three kings and de-
feated them.*

collision through his prayer.[10]
And also, when he desired to see
the host, red in its middle part,
etc.; thus he was best armed by
the shield of faith. Ps. [90.5] *Your
truth will encompass you with
a shield.* And so he fought well
against these enemies, because
he was never wounded by anything through mortal sin. Josh. 11
[18]: *Joshua made war a long time
against these kings,* and killed
them.

9. This exemplum is related to the one recorded in Blangez, ed., *Ci nous dit:
Recueil d'exemples moraux,* vol. 1, 145, no. 40.
    10. For this story, see GB 30 (p. 18).

[17A] Secundo fuit audax in periculis quia posuit[298] animam suam. Multi bene pugnant[299] quamdiu habent advantagium[300] sed imminente periculo statim fugiunt.[301] Sic spiritualiter quamdiu temptacio est levis, satis bene pugnant. Sed quando aggravatur statim cadunt per peccatum.

[17B] Secundum punctum fortitudinis est exponere se audacia in periculo.[302] *Audacter*[303] *dedit animam suam periculis*[304] [Judg. 9.17]. In hoc patet audacia in periculo quando homo[305] non fugit nec abscondit se. Quidam licet bene pungent[306] in prelio[307] temp-tacionis tamen[308] in periculo consensus cadunt et succumbunt.[309] Sed verus audax dicitur exponere vitam suam periculo mortis antequam succumbat suggestioni demonis. Iudic. 5. *Qui*[310] *sponte obtulistis de israhel etc animas vestras ad periculum benedicite Deum* [Judg. 5.2]. Sic fecit beatus Ludovicus vitam suam exponens periculis multis propter Christum. Fuit sicut elephas qui inebriatus vino rubeo deponit timorem assumens tantam audaciam quod viso tali vivo non timet

298. posuit] dedit V$_2$

299. pugnant] *emended from* pugnans P$_3$

300. bene pugnant quamdiu habent advantagium] quamdiu habent advantagium pugnant

301. statim fugiunt] *om.* V$_2$

302. audacia in periculo] se exponere V$_1$ [phrase repeated in MS]

303. Audacter] *om.* W

304. periculis] etc. W

305. homo] *om.* W

306. Quidam licet bene pungent] Quidem bene pugnant V$_1$

307. prelio] preli W

308. Tamen] sed V$_1$

309. succumbunt] etc. Non sic iste *add.* W

310. Qui] *corr. from* Que

[17A] Second, he was bold in that he placed his own soul in danger. Many men fight well while they have the advantage, but when imminent danger is at hand, they flee at once. And in the same way, spiritually, when temptation is light, [many men will] fight well enough, but [once temptation] becomes weightier, they immediately fall through sin.

[17B] The second point of fortitude is to expose oneself boldly in times of danger. *Boldly, he gave his soul over to danger* [Judg. 9.17]. In this, boldness in danger is evident when a man does not flee or hide. Indeed, some men might fight well in the battles of temptation, but they fall and succumb to the danger of consent. A truly bold man is said to expose his life to the danger of death before surrendering to the suggestion of the devil. Judg. 5 [2]: *Bless God, you of Israel who have willingly offered your lives to danger.* Thus did blessed Louis expose his life to many dangers for Christ. He was like an elephant, which, when drunk on red wine, sets aside his fear, assuming such boldness that he fears

hostes nec gladium. set omni periculo se exponens.[311] Sic[312] Ludovicus[313] considerans passionem Christi et sanguinem[314] per devotionem inebriatus.[315]

311. Sed verus audax . . . set omni periculo se exponens] *om.* W
312. sic] N [Nomen] expunged V₁
313. Sic Ludovicus] Nomen sic iste, sed W
314. passionem Christi et sanguinem] sanguinem passionis Christi W
315. inebriatus] ad. est, etc. W

neither enemies nor the sword, but indeed exposes himself to every danger—and I have seen such an animal alive. Thus Louis, when contemplating the passion and blood of Christ, was intoxicated by devotion.

III

[18A] Non sic beatus Ludovicus quia sicut legitur de eo[316] quando quidam miles[317] qui bene novit modum paganorum dixit Ludovico[318] quod oporteret eos[319] illa die mori vel capi a sarracenis et ideo rogavit regem quod ipse recederet,[320] ne per captionem suam[321] corona Francie perderetur.[322] Respondit autem rex militi: "O[323] bone Guillelme, nunquam audisti quod[324] heredes Francie verterent[325] inimicis[326] fidei," et sic intravit bellum et fuit captus;[327] sed confidens in domino tandem miraculose[328] liberatus est quia pro modica[329] pecunia.[330] Ideo po - test dici de eo: *Macchabeus hor - tatus est eos* [2 Macc. 13.12] qui secum erant subire periculum. Machabeus interpretatur protegens vel percuciens.

[18B] ii. Mach [11.7]. *Machabeus sumptis*[331] *armis ceteris*[332] *est hortatus similis*[333] *secum periculum subire.* Nota quando solus militi dicenti quod fugeret respondit etc.

---

316. de eo] *om.* V₂

317. P₃: 26va

318. Ludovico] *om.* V₂

319. eos] *om.* V₂

320. rogavit . . . recederet] rogo nos quod recedatis per V₂

321. suam] nostram V₂

322. perderetur] perdatur V₂

323. autem rex militi O] *om.* V₂

324. audisti quod] vidisti V₂

325. vereterent] vertere V₂

326. inimicis] in negociis initis V₂

327. et fuit captus] *om.* V₂

328. miraculose] *om.* V₂

329. pro modica] prmodicat V₂

330. The quotation is not known elsewhere, but the sentiment of Louis' trust in the Lord and the idea that his ransom was miraculous for being so small was part of the tradition. Cf. GB 25 (p. 16); BLQRF 5.

331. V₁: 166ra

332. ceteris est] socios W

333. similis] *om.* W

III

[18A] Not so, blessed Louis, because, as can be read about him, when a certain knight who knew well how the pagans operated said to Louis that [the French] would either die or be captured by the Saracens on that day, and for that reason he asked the king to retreat so that the crown of France would not be lost if he were captured, the king responded to the knight: "O good William, never have you heard that the heirs of France would flee from the enemies of the faith." Therefore, he engaged in battle and was captured, [and] trusting in the Lord he was, at last, miraculously freed for a very small sum of money. And thus it can be said of him: *Maccabeus exhorted those* [2 Macc. 13.12], who were going to undergo danger with him. Machabeus here represents a protector or fighter.

[18B] 2 Macc. [11.7] *Machabeus, having taken up arms, exhorted the rest likewise to subject themselves to danger with him.* Consider what [Louis] replied to the knight who said that he should flee alone, etc.

[19A] Tertio pugnavit pro iusta causa, quia pro populo³³⁴ suo: *ut erueret eos de manu Madian*³³⁵ [Judg. 9.17]. Madian interpretur iniquitas. Multi pugnant et habent multa sustinere pro mundo, sed³³⁶ tales sunt martyres dyaboli. Sed Ludovicus pugnavit pro populo suo et fide Christi quem zelabat, similis cete pungnanti³³⁷ pro fetibus³³⁸ suis quos³³⁹ diligit. Beatus autem Ludovicus reprehendebat omnes domini blasphemantes, in cuius³⁴⁰ exemplum fecit signari quemdam civem Parisiensis propter blasphemiam; qui cum super hoc redargueretur, respondit quod vellet ita signari et talis blasphemia de regno suo penitus tolleretur.³⁴¹ Unde de eo³⁴² dicitur: *Dimicabo pro vobis et eruam vos de periculo.* [Cf. Deut. 20.4.]

[19B] Tertium punctum fortitudinis est pugnare propter iusticiam³⁴³ causam *ut erueret nos de manu Madian* [Judg. 9.17]. Non enim decet princeps pugnare propter vindictam et odium³⁴⁴ inimicorum, sed per liberationem subditorum a periculo.³⁴⁵ Sicut cete quod³⁴⁶ fetus suos multo tempore circumcidit³⁴⁷ per mare in periculo pugnat propriorum liberatione, sic beatus Ludovicus fetus suos, id est, subditos, fratres et alios filios, duxit per mare pugnans³⁴⁸ non solum pro defensione mortis corporalis³⁴⁹ sed etiam spiritualis. Nota quando contra peccatum blasfemie erexit scalas,³⁵⁰

334. populo] tempore V₂
335. eos de manu Madian] etc. V₂
336. sed] et V₂
337. cete pungnanti] repugnani V₂
338. fetibus] fecibus V₂
339. quos] quosque V₂
340. Beatus autem ... blasphemantes in cuius] meus V₂
341. penitus tolleretur] amoveretur V₂. Cf. BLQRF 7.
342. eo] ipso V₂
343. iusticiam] bonam W
344. propter vindictam et odium] pro vindicta vel odio W
345. periculo] *add.* etc. W
346. quod] fecit *expunged* V₁
347. circumcidit] circumducit 304
348. *om.* Per mare V₁; scribe copied twice, and not found in Avignon 304 or Vatican Lat 1260.
349. corporalis] corporis V₁; "corporalis" supplied by Vatican Lat 1260.
350. Cf. WSP *vie* 3 (p. 27): "Et fesoit aucune foiz ceus qui encontre fesoient, cuire ou seignier es levres d'une fer chaut et ardant, roont qui avoit une vergete par mi et estoit especiaument fet a ce. Et a la foiz, il fesoit estre en l'eschiele devant le pueple, boiaux de beste pleins d'ordure penduz a leur cous, et comonda que l'en

[19A] Third, [Louis] fought for a just cause, because [he fought] for his people, *so that he might deliver them from the hands of Midian* [Judg. 9.17]. Midian here represents iniquity. Many men fight and have to endure many things for this world, and these men are martyrs of the devil. But Louis fought for his people and for the faith of Christ whom he loved, just like a whale fights for its young whom [she] loves. Blessed Louis condemned all blasphemers of the Lord; he had a certain citizen of Paris branded on account of blasphemy as an example.[11] When he was criticized about it, he replied that he would rather himself be branded in this way [if it meant] that all blasphemies of this kind would be expunged entirely from his kingdom. Whence of him it is said: *I will fight for you and pluck you out from danger.* [Cf. Deut. 20.4.]

[19B] The third point of fortitude was that [Louis] fought for a just cause; *so that he might deliver us from the hands of Midian* [cf. Judg. 9.17]. It is not fitting that a prince should fight out of vengeance [or out of] hatred of his enemies, but [rather he should fight] to free his subjects from danger. Just as the whale, which often circles its offspring in the sea, will fight for their deliverance when in danger, so blessed Louis led his offspring, that is, his subjects, his brothers, and his other sons overseas, fighting overseas not only for protection against bodily death but also from spiritual death. Note that when he erected ladders against the sin of blasphemy, he ordered branding with a hot

11. The story of Louis cauterizing the Parisian blasphemer is a commonplace; cf. GB 33 (p. 19); BL 8.2; GR 9.2; BLQRF 7. For the ladders, see n. 350 of the Latin. WSP *vie* 3 (p. 27) explains that Louis erected ladders in several cities on which to display the punished blasphemers (who had animal guts hung around their necks) before the people.

fecit cauteria[351] cum ferro cadenti. Et quando unum parisius cauterizari fecit propter turpe iuramentum, propter quod cum argueretur respondit. "Vellem quod hec durissima pestis de regno meo tolleretur penitus."[352] Unde implevit illud Deut. 20[353][4]: *Contra adversarios dimicavit ut eruat eos a periculo* [Deut. 20.4].[354]

---

meist eschieles es bonnes viles en lieu commun, seur les queles tex blaphemeurs de Dieu fussent mis et liez en despit de cel pechié. Et fist metre espies contre tex qui les acusassent, et estoient les eschieles a ce especiaument ordenées es citez et es lieux sollempnez par le commandement du benoiet roi."

351. cauteria] *corr. from* caucacia V₁

352. Cf. BLQRF 7. The original quote is "Vellem quoad vixero in labiis meis talem indecentiam sustinere, dummodo hoc pessimum juracionis vitium de regno meo penitus tolleretur."

353. 20] *corr. from* 2, V₁

354. Sicut cete quod fetus . . . Contra adversarios dimicavit ut eruat eos a periculo] *om.* W

iron. And once he had branded a certain Parisian on account of his evil oaths, and being criticized for this, he responded: "I would prefer that this most horrible plague be completely removed from my kingdom." Thus he fulfilled Deut. 20 [4]: *he fought against your enemies to deliver them from danger.*

[20A] Circa secundum nota. In principe[355] sapientia plus est necessaria quam fortitudo. Unde Sapiens[356] dicit sapientiam esse[357] meliorem fortitudine [cf. Eccles. 9.16]. Sapiens pugnator non dimictit inimicum suum nimis approprinquare. Ita spiritualiter qui sapienter vult pugnare contra temptaciones carnis, etc. non debet appropinquare ad verba dissoluta vel ad[358] tactus[359] dissolutos, qui alliciunt ad consensum. Nota torpedo[360] est quidam[361] piscis qui[362] statim quod percutitur amictit fortitudinem suam. Sic multi quando percuciuntur verbo vel tactu inpudico. Ideo beatus Ludovicus sicut prudens pungnator[363] elongavit se a talibus.

[20B] Secondo tangitur magnitudo sue[364] sapientie. Salomonem. Non sufficit solum in rege potentia, sed oportet etiam sapientia, quia sapientia melior est.[365] Eccl. 9 [16] *Ego dicebam esse[366] meliorem sapientiam fortitudine.* Ratio est; confidencia fortis cuilibet[367] permittit hostem nimis appropinquare. Ita quod vulneratur et tollitur fortitudo sua,[368] ita quod homo non potest se deffendere, vel si deffendit se,[369] non sit quin turpiter vulneretur. Sed sapiens non permittit hostem[370] appropinquare sed[371] a longe vincit eum[372] cum minori dampno.[373] Sic in bello spirituali quidam sinunt[374] hostem[375] appropinquare confidentes de sua virtute

---

355. principe] principio V$_2$
356. Sapiens] sapientia V$_2$
357. esse] *om.* V$_2$
358. vel ad] et V$_2$
359. tactus] tractus illicitos et V$_2$
360. torpedo] *corr. from* crepedo P$_3$; crepetudo V$_2$
361. est quidam] quedam
362. qui] *om.* V$_2$
363. pugnator] pugil V$_2$
364. sue] *om.* W
365. Non sufficit ... melior est] Non enim sufficit in rege potentia sive sapientia quia [166va] sapientia melior est V$_1$
366. esse] *om.* W
367. fortis cuilibet] fortitudine quandoque W
368. Vulneratur et tollitur fortitude sua] vulneart tolli fortitudine V$_1$
369. se] *om.* W
370. Sed sapiens non permittit hostem] Sapientia non sinit hostis W
371. sed] portat eum W
372. eum] ideo W
373. dampno] *add.* et periculo W
374. sinunt] sumunt V$_2$
375. hostem] hostes W

[20A] With respect to the second point it should be noted that in a prince, wisdom is more necessary than fortitude. Whence the wise one [Solomon] said that wisdom is better than bravery [cf. Eccles. 9.16]. A fighter who is wise does not permit his enemy to get too close. Thus spiritually, he who wishes to fight wisely against the temptations of the flesh, etc., should not go near degenerate words or degenerate touching, which entice one to consent. Note that the ray is a fish which, after being struck, immediately loses its strength.[12] It is the same with many men when they are struck by a shameless word or a touch. Thus blessed Louis, a prudent fighter, distanced himself from such things.

[20B] Second, we treat the magnitude of his wisdom. Solomon: Power alone is not sufficient in a king, but wisdom is also necessary, as wisdom is the better. Eccles. 9.16: *I said that wisdom is better than fortitude.* Here is the reason. Over-confidence in strength permits the enemy to come too close, so that he is wounded and his strength is taken away and the man is unable to defend himself, or if he does defend himself, he is still badly wounded. But a wise man does not permit the enemy to come close but conquers him from a distance with little damage. Thus in a spiritual war certain men allow the enemy to approach, confident in their virtue

12. Cf. Isidore of Seville, *Etymologies,* Book 12, 6.45, citing Pliny (*Naturalis Historia* 32.7).

et fortitudine. Nota periculum est eis torpendo.[376] Piscis est[377] in mari luto se[378] infingens et occultans qui[379] si tangatur virga vel lancea brachia, tangentis quantumcumque fortis obstupescunt.[380] Sic peccatum carnis lutosum, quando tangatur[381] per moram[382] delectacionis, corda fortissima facit torpere. Ideo contra tale peccatum melior est sapientia docens ipsum fugere. I Cor. 6[383][18]. *Fugite fornicationem,* quam confidencia[384] quandoque permittit[385] ipsam nimis appropinquare.[386]

---

376. Nota periculum est eis torpendo] Sed est quidam W; corpedo *expunged* W

377. est] *om.* W

378. luto se] in luto in W

379. qui] quid V_1

380. obstupescunt] obtupescunt V_1. We are puzzled by the author's shift to the plural here. One manuscript (Avignon BM 304) put this in the singular.

381. tangatur] tangitur W

382. moram] modum V_1

383. 6] *corr. from* 5 V_1

384. *add.* que, all MSS

385. permittit] *om.* V_1, supplied by Vatican Lat 1260; permittunt Avignon 304. Passage *om.* W.

386. quam confidencia que ... approprinquare] *om.* W; *add.* sunt V_1

and fortitude. Note that there is danger to these men of being made numb. There is a fish in the sea, hiding and sticking itself in the mud such that, if it be touched with a stick or spear, the arms of the person touching, no matter how strong, will be debilitated. Likewise, the muddy sin of the flesh, touched by the obstacle of pleasure, numbs [even] the strongest hearts. Thus, against such a sin, wisdom is better, teaching a man to flee. 1 Cor. 6.18: *Flee fornication,* which confidence sometimes allows to come too close.

[21A] *Dedit Dominus sapientiam*[387] *Salomoni* [cf. 1 Kings 5.12], quam[388] ad spiritualia et prudenciam quoad temporalia gubernanda. Unde quam[389] bene se habuit beatus Ludovicus in talibus quam[390] ad spiritualia et temporalia, patet in legenda sua.[391] Sed nota aves bene peditantes male[392] volant. Et bene volantes male peditant. Sic certe multi bene peditant de foro ad forum ad sua negocia et peccata et tales non possunt volare in celum per contemplationem ad bona spiritualia. Non sic beatus Ludovicus.

[21B] Istam sapienciam dedit Dominus beato Ludovico[393] 3 Reg. 4 [1 Kings 4.29]. *Dedit deus sapienciam salomoni et prudenciam.*[394] Hoc fuit mirabile sic[395] habere sapientiam[396] divinorum et prudenciam terrenorum, quod[397] dicitur impossibile.[398] Aves, bene[399] peditantes super terram sicut perdix naturaliter male volant, et econtra bene volantes sicut yrundo male peditant.[400] Sed[401] N. habuit utrumque speciali dono dei. In hoc fuit[402] similis cani custodi domus qui unum occulum semper habuit[403] ad mensam domini[404] ut inde aliud recipiat;[405] alium ad ostium[406] domus quam custodit ne latro subintret.

387. V₂: 103vb
388. quam] quantum V₂
389. quam] quantum V₂
390. in talibus quam] quantum V₂
391. sua] *om.* V₂
392. male] male *add.* V₂
393. beato Ludovico] Nomen W
395. sic] similis W
396. sapientiam] *add.* eternorum W
397. quod] *add.* est W
398. impossibile.] Quia *add.* W
399. bene] enim V₁
400. W: 462r
401. Sed] beatus *add.* W
402. in hoc fuit] nihil V₁
403. habuit] habet W
404. domini] deo W
405. recipiat] accipiat W
406. ostium] hostium V₁

[21A] *The Lord gave wisdom to Solomon,* as much in governing spiritual things as foresight in temporal things. And so did blessed Louis conduct himself in spiritual and temporal matters, as he reveals in his writings. But note that birds that walk well fly badly, and [birds] that fly well walk badly. Thus, of course, the many men who walk well from market to market to conduct business, sinful activities, and other similar things, cannot fly into the sky toward spiritual wealth through contemplation. This was not blessed Louis.

[21B] The Lord gave this very wisdom to blessed Louis. 1 Kings 4 [29]: *The Lord gave wisdom and prudence to Solomon.* It is wondrous thus to have [both] wisdom in divine things and prudence in earthly things, because it is said to be impossible. Birds that walk well on the earth, like the partridge, naturally fly badly. And, on the other hand, those that fly well, like the swallow, walk badly. But N. [Louis] had both [kinds of wisdom] by a special gift of God. In this he was similar to the house's watchdog that always keeps one eye on the master's table in order to get something from it, and keeps the other on the door of the house that he is guarding lest a thief break in.

Sic enim oculum dextrum semper habebat ad[407] mensam domini ad ecclesiam et eius sacramenta.[408] Nota quam devote communicabat et[409] visitabat ecclesias in parasceve,[410] quando sapiebant ei[411] lacrime.[412] Alium oculum habebat ad custodiam domus.[413]

---

407. ad] deo *add.* W
408. eius sacramenta] ad sacramentum W
409. et] *om.* W
410. in parasceve] et W
411. ei] sibi W
412. lacrime] *om.* W
413. domus] *om.* V₁

Likewise, [Louis] always had his right eye on the table of the Lord, on the church and her sacraments. Note how devoutly he took communion and visited churches on Good Friday when he was tasting his tears. With the other eye he guarded the house.

[22A] Sed[414] nota quod ipse[415] sedebat in communi loco ad audiendas causas pauperum. Ergo[416] dicit *Sapientie soror mea es et prudenciam,*[417] etc. [Prov. 7.4[418]] Secundum iura, soror dimittit fratri partem hereditatis. Sed amicus amico mobilia.[419] Spiritualiter per sapientiam, id est, per sorororsam[420] scientiam et devotionem de divinis habetur hereditas. Sed per prudenciam de inferioribus habentur mobilia fortuita.

[22B] Nota quando sedebat in palacio[421] semel in septimana pro causis pauperum[422] quando faciebat iusticiam implens consilium Sapientis.[423] Prov. [7.4][424] *Sapientia soror mea est et prudenciam*[425] *vocavit amicam*[426] *meam.* Nota quod[427] quandoque frater succedit sorori in hereditate qua soror ipsum privare non potest. Set persona amica si aliqua[428] dimittat[429] alteri,[430] hec sunt mobilia[431] in magno dubio. Quia si mutetur[432] eius voluntas non dimittet[433] ei unum obolum. Sic sapientia dicitur soror dei quia reliquit vobis[434] hereditatem paradisi

414. Sed] *om.* V$_2$
415. quod ipse] quando V$_2$
416. Ergo] Can v V$_2$
417. We have translated "prudentia" in this passage as "good sense," as in "foresight," "prepared concern," and so forth.
418. Prov 7.4: "Dic sapientiae soror mea es et prudentiam voca amicam tuam."
419. Sed amicus amico mobilia] *om.* V$_2$
420. sororosam] saporosam P$_3$
421. palacio] *add. saltem* W
422. pauperum] *add. et* W
423. Sapientis] Salomonis W
424. Prov. [7.4] 7 et a. & 4, et 24 *add.* V$_1$; *om.* W
425. prudenciam] prudencia V$_1$
426. amicam] animam V$_1$
427. Nota quod] *om.* W
428. aliqua] aliud W
429. V$_1$: 167ra
430. alteri] *om.* W
431. mobilia] et *add.* W
432. mutetur] imitetur V$_2$
433. dimittet] dimittit W
434. vobis] nobis W

[22A] Note also how he sat in a public place in order to hear the cases of the poor. Therefore, he says *Wisdom, you are my sister and call prudence [your friend]* [cf. Prov. 7.4]. According to law, the sister gives up her part of her inheritance [of property] to her brother. But a friend to a friend [gives up only] movable goods. Spiritual [property] inheritance is acquired through wisdom, that is, through sisterly knowledge about and devotion to divine things. But through prudence concerning lesser things, merely moveable goods of little import are acquired.

[22B] Make note of how he sat in his palace once a week to hear the cases of the poor, at which time he did justice, fulfilling the counsel of the wise one [Solomon].[13] Prov. 7.4: *Wisdom is my sister and called prudence my friend.* Make note that whenever a brother follows a sister in inheriting [property], the sister cannot deprive him of [that inheritance]. But if someone who is only a friend bequeaths something to someone else, these movable good are in great doubt. Because if he changes his mind, he will leave not even a single coin to that person. Thus wisdom is called the sister of God because she indisputably leaves to you the inheritance of paradise, unless we are

13. Cf. BL 9.2; BLQRF 8; Joinville, *Vie de Saint Louis,* §5.9.

indubitanter[435] nisi proprium peccatum prepediat.[436] Sed[437] prudentia de natura[438] terrenorum
est animata,[439] quia quandoque
dat bona temporalia, quandoque
subtrahit secundum quod fortuna
mutatur. Ergo magis est diligenda
sapientia[440] quam prudencia.

435. indubitanter] indeficienter W
436. prepediat] inpediat W
437. Sed] Et W
438. de natura] *om.* W
439. est animata] dicitur amica W
440. sapientia] *om.* W

blocked by our own sins. In contrast, prudence is animated by the nature of earthly things, because it might give temporal goods, but it might also take them away according to the whim of fortune. Therefore, wisdom is to be preferred over prudence.

[23A] Circa tertium, nota quod dyadema dicitur quod⁴⁴¹ duo demens scilicet miserias corporis et tristicias anime. Sed qui⁴⁴² non possunt a deo demi, qui non habet eas, qui sustinebat in hac vita istas angustias corporis et anime. Sicut fecit beatus Ludovicus cum eo habebat dyadema in paradyso. Unde de eo⁴⁴³ dicitur: *Insuspicabilis portabat dyadema⁴⁴⁴ regni in capite eius cum Christo in gloria ad quam nos perducat,* etc. [cf. Sir. 11.4 and Esth. 2.17]

[23B] Tertio tangitur honor sue⁴⁴⁵ excellencie. *In dyademate.* Dyadema dicitur quasi duo demens quia dyadema⁴⁴⁶ paradisi demit duos defectus⁴⁴⁷ corporis famem et⁴⁴⁸ sitim,⁴⁴⁹ etc. Item defectus⁴⁵⁰ anime⁴⁵¹ dolorem tristiam et ignorantiam, etc.⁴⁵² Sed non potest demere quod non est ipsa.⁴⁵³ Ergo qui⁴⁵⁴ propter Deum nullum vult pati defectum nec miserias cordis volens dimittere ludos solacia etc. Dyadema paradisi non habet locum ibi nec⁴⁵⁵ invenit quod demat. Sed N. propter

441. quod] quasi P₃
442. qui] quia V₂
443. de eo] *om.* V₂
444. V₂: 104va
445. sue] eius W
446. dyadema] corpora V₁; "corona" found in Vatican Lat 1260 and Avignon 304.
447. defectus] scilicet *add.* W
448. et] *om.* W
449. sitim] frigus *add.* W
450. Item defectus] *om.* W
451. anime] scilicet *add.* W
452. et ignorantiam etc.] ignorandum V₁
453. sed non potest demere quod non est ipsa] Sed peccatori non potest demere quia non est ibi in parus [?, paradisus?] W
454. qui] *om.* V₁
455. nec] quia vel W

[23A] Concerning the third point, note what is said of the *crown*: that it takes away two things—the miseries of the body and the sadnesses of the soul. But these things cannot be taken away from God, who does not have them [and] who sustains in this life the tribulations of body and soul. Just so with blessed Louis, [who] had the diadem in paradise with Him. And therefore, it is said of [Louis], *Unexpectedly, he wore the diadem of the kingdom on his head with Christ, in glory, to which may he lead us.* [Cf. Sir. 11.4 and Esth. 2.17.]

[23B] Thirdly, the honor of his excellence is treated: *In the crown.* It is called "diadem," as if "duo demens," because the diadem of paradise removes two weaknesses of the body, namely, hunger and thirst, etc., likewise, weaknesses of the soul, namely, sorrow, sadness, and ignorance. But it cannot remove what is not there. Therefore, whoever wishes to suffer no weakness for God's sake, nor, wishing to set aside the sorrows of the heart, [pursues] games, comforts, etc., the diadem of paradise has no place there nor does it find what it may remove. But N. [Louis] endured many

Deum,[456] sustinuit multas miserias cordis et corporis. Ideo dyadema bene invenit in eo quid de-
mendum.[457] Ecc. xi. *Insupicabilis
portabit dyadema.* Hest 2[17]: *posuit dyadema regni*[458] *capite eius.*
Rogabimus Deum etc. Amen.[459]

456. N. propter deum] si W
457. demendum] demandum V$_1$
458. regni] in *add.* W
459. Roga … Amen] quod nobis concedat, etc., W

miseries of the heart and body for the sake of God. Therefore the diadem has indeed found in him something to remove. Sir. 11.4: *He, who no one suspects of it, will wear the crown.* Esther 2.17: *He placed the crown of the kingdom on his head.* We will entreat God etc. Amen.

BIBLIOGRAPHY

Allirot, Anne-Hélène. *Filles de roy de France: Princesses royale, mémoire de saint Louis et conscience dynastique (de 1270 à la fin du XIVe siècle)*. Culture & Société Médiévales 20. Turnhout: Brepols, 2010.

Armstrong, Regis J., J. A. Wayne Hellmann, and William J. Short, eds. *Francis of Assisi: Early Documents*. 3 vols. New York, London, and Manila: New City Press, 1999–2001.

Aubert, Édouard. *Trésor de l'abbaye de Saint-Maurice d'Aguane*. 2 vols. Paris: A. Morel et cie, 1872.

Baltzer, Rebecca A. "A Royal French Breviary from the Reign of Saint Louis." In *The Varieties of Musicology: Essays in Honor of Murray Lefkowitz*, edited by John Daverior and John Ogasapian, 3–25. Warren, MI: Harmonie Park Press, 2000.

Beaumont-Maillet, Laure. *Le Grand couvent des Cordeliers de Paris: Étude historique et archéologique du XIIIe siècle à nos jours*. Paris: Champion, 1975.

Beaune, Colette. *The Birth of an Ideology: Myths and Symbols of Nation in Late-Medieval France*. Translated by Susan Ross Huston. Berkeley: University of California Press, 1991.

Bériou, Nicole. *L'avènement des maîtres de la Parole: La prédication à Paris au XIIIe siècle*. 2 vols. Série Moyen Âge et Temps Modernes 31. Paris: Institut d'Études Augustiniennes, 1998.

Berlioz, Jacques, and Marie Anne Polo de Beaulieu. *Les Exempla médiévaux: Nouvelles perspectives*. Nouvelle bibliothèque du Moyen Âge 47. Paris: Champion, 1998.

Bibliotheca hagiographica latina antiquæ et mediæ ætatis. Brussels: s.n., 1898.

Blangez, Gérard, ed. *Ci nous dit: Recueil d'exemples moraux*. 2 vols. Paris: Société des anciens textes français, 1979–1986.

Boureau, Alain. "Les Enseignements absolutistes de Saint Louis, 1610–1630." In *La monarchie absolutiste et l'histoire en France: Théories du pouvoir, propagandes monarchiques et mythologies nationales*, 79–97. Paris: Presses de l'Université de Paris-Sorbonne, 1987.

Bournazel, Eric. "Suger and the Capetian." In *Abbot Suger and Saint-Denis: A Symposium*, edited by Paula Lieber Gerson, 55–72. New York: Metropolitan Museum of Art, 1986.

Boutet, Dominique. "La méthode historique de Joinville et la réécriture des *Grandes chroniques de France.*" In *Jean de Joinville: De la Champagne aux Royaumes d'outre-mer,* 93–108. Langres: Dominique Guénior, 1998.

Branner, Robert. *Manuscript Painting in Paris during the Reign of Saint Louis: A Study of Styles.* California Studies in the History of Art 18. Berkeley: University of California Press, 1977.

Brown, Elizabeth A. R. "Burying and Unburying the Kings of France." In *Persons in Groups: Social Behavior as Identity Formation in Medieval and Renaissance Europe: Papers of the Sixteenth Annual Conference of the Center for Medieval and Early Renaissance Studies,* edited by Richard Trexler, 241–66. Binghamton, NY: Medieval and Renaissance Texts & Studies, 1985.

———. "The Chapels and Cult of Saint Louis at Saint-Denis." *Mediaevalia* 10 (1984): 279–331.

———. "Philippe le Bel and the Remains of Saint Louis." *Gazette des Beaux-Arts* 97 (1980): 175–82.

Carolus-Barré, Louis. "Consultation du cardinal Pietro Colonna sur le IIe miracle de saint Louis (Arch. du Vatican, A. A. Arm. C, 493)." *Bibliothèque de l'École des Chartes* 117 (1959): 57–72.

———. "Les enquêtes pour la canonisation de Saint Louis de Grégoire X à Boniface VIII et la bulle *Gloria Laus,* du 11 Août 1297." *Revue d'Histoire de l'Église de France* 57 (1971): 19–31.

———. "Guillaume de Chartres clerc du roi, frère prêcheur, ami et historien de saint Louis." *Collection de l'Ecole Française de Rome* 204 (1995): 51–57.

———. *Le procès de canonisation de Saint Louis (1272–1297): Essai de reconstitution.* Edited by Henri Platelle. Collection de l'École Française de Rome 195. Rome: L'École Française de Rome, 1994.

Catalogus Codicum Hagiographicorum Bibliothecae Regiae Bruxellensis. Analecta Bollandiana, vols. 2–5. 1886.

"Catalogus codicum hagiographicorum qui vindobonae asservantur in bibliotheca privata serenissimi caesaris austriaci." *Analecta Bollandiana* (1895): 231–83.

Chapotin, Marie-Dominique. *Histoire de Dominicains de la Province de France: Le siècle des fondations.* Rouen: Cagniard, 1898.

Chennaf, Sharah, and Odile Redon. "Les Miracles de Saint Louis." In *Les Miracles Miroirs des Corps,* 53–85. Paris: Université de Paris VIII, 1983.

Cherubini, Paolo. "Un manoscritto occitanio della *Legenda aurea* con note di Bottega in volgare (Reg. Lat. 534)." *Miscellanea Bibliothecae apostolicae Vaticanae* 13 (2006): 119–66.

Cohen, Meredith. "An Indulgence for the Visitor: The Public at the Sainte-Chapelle of Paris." *Speculum* 83 (2008): 840–83.

Constable, Giles. *Crusaders and Crusading in the Twelfth Century.* Burlington, VT: Ashgate, 2008.

Corpus Catalogorum Belgii: The Medieval Booklists of the Southern Low Countries. Edited by Albert Derolez. Vol. 4, *Provinces of Brabant and Hainault.* Brussels: Paleis der Academiën, 2001.

D'Avray, David L. *Death and the Prince: Memorial Preaching before 1350.* Oxford and New York: Clarendon Press, 1994.

———. *The Preaching of the Friars: Sermons Diffused from Paris before 1300.* Oxford: Clarendon Press, 1985.

"De codicibus hagiographicis Iohannis Gielemans canonici regularis in rubea valle prope Bruxellas." *Analecta Bollandiana* 14 (1895): 5–88.

Delaborde, Henri-François. *Jean de Joinville et les seigneurs de Joinville, suivi d'un catalogue de leurs actes.* Paris: Imprimerie nationale, Picard et fils, 1894.

———. "Une oeuvre nouvelle de Guillaume de Saint-Pathus." *Bibliothèque de l'École des Chartes* 63 (1902): 261–88.

Deshusses, Jean. *Le Sacramentaire Grégorien: Ses principales formes d'après les plus anciens manuscrits.* Spicilegium Friburgense. 2nd ed. Fribourg Suisse: Éditions Universitaires, 1979.

Dictionnaire de spiritualité: Ascétique et mystique, doctrine et historie. 17 vols. Paris: Beauchesne et ses fils, 1932–1995.

Dreves, Guido Maria, and Clemens Blume, eds. *Analecta hymnica medii aevi.* 55 vols. Leipzig: Fue's Verlag (R. Reisland), 1886–1922. Reprint, New York: Johnson Reprint Corp., 1961.

Dubreil-Arcin, Agnès. *Vies de saints, légendes de soi: L'écriture hagiographique dominicaine jusqu'au Speculum Sanctorale de Bernard Gui (†1331).* Turnhout: Brepols, 2011.

Duchesne, André. *Historiae Francorum scriptores coaetanei . . . Quorum plurimi nunc primum ex variis codicibus mss. in lucem prodeunt: alij vero auctiores & emendatiores. Cvm epistolis regvm, reginarvm, pontificvm . . . et aliis veteribus rerum francicarum monumentis.* 5 vols. Paris: Sumptibus S. Cramoisy, 1636–1649.

Dumas, Antoine. *Liber Sacramentorum Gellonensis.* CCSL, 159–159A. 2 vols. Turnhout: Brepols, 1981.

Elliott, Alison Goddard. *Roads to Paradise: Reading the Lives of the Early Saints.* Hanover, NH: Published for Brown University Press by University Press of New England, 1987.

Epstein, Marcy. "*Ludovicus Decus Regnantium*: Perspectives on the Rhymed Office." *Speculum* 53 (1978): 283–334.

Erlande-Brandenburg, Alain. "Art et politique sous Philippe le Bel: La priorale Saint-Louis de Poissy." *Comptes rendus de l'Académie des Inscriptions et Belles Lettres* (1987): 507–18.

———. "La Priorale Saint-Louis de Poissy." *Bulletin Monumental* 129 (1971): 85–112.

Farmer, Sharon. "Down and Out and Female in Thirteenth-Century Paris." *American Historical Review* 103 (1998): 345–72.

————. *Surviving Poverty in Medieval Paris: Gender, Ideology, and the Daily Lives of the Poor.* Ithaca: Cornell University Press, 2002.

Fay, Percival B., ed. *Guillaume de Saint-Pathus: Les miracles de saint Louis.* Paris: Champion, 1932.

Folz, Robert. *Les saints rois du Moyen Âge en occident (VIe–XIIIe siècles).* Subsidia hagiographica 68. Brussels: Société des Bollandiste, 1984.

Fros, Henri, ed. *Bibliotheca hagiographica Latina antiquae et mediae aetatis. Novum Supplementum.* Brussels: Imprimerie Cultura, 1986.

Gaposchkin, M. Cecilia. "*Ludovicus Decus Regnantium*: The Liturgical Office for Saint Louis and the Ideological Program of Philip the Fair." *Majestas* 10 (2002): 27–90.

————. *The Making of Saint Louis: Kingship, Sanctity, and Crusade in the Later Middle Ages.* Ithaca: Cornell University Press, 2008.

————. "The Monastic Office for Louis IX of France: *Lauda Celestis Regio.*" *Revue Mabillon* (2009): 143–74.

————. "Philip the Fair, the Dominicans, and the Liturgical Office for Louis IX: New Perspectives on *Ludovicus Decus Regnantium.*" *Plainsong and Medieval Music* 13, no. 1 (2004): 33–61.

————. "Place, Status, and Experience in the Miracles of Saint Louis." *Cahiers de Recherches Médiévales et Humanistes/Journal of Medieval and Humanistic Studies* 19 (2010): 235–48.

————. "The Role of the Crusades in the Sanctification of Louis IX of France." In *Crusades: Medieval Worlds in Conflict,* 195–209. Burlington, VT: Ashgate, 2010.

Guillaume of Saint-Pathus. *Vie de Saint Louis.* Edited by H. François Delaborde. Collection de textes pour servir à l'étude et à l'enseignement de l'histoire 27. Paris: A. Picard, 1899.

Hallam, Elizabeth M. "Aspects of the Monastic Patronage of the English and French Royal Houses, c. 1130–1270." Ph.D. diss., University of London, 1976.

————. *Capetian France, 987–1328.* London and New York: Longman, 1980. 2nd ed., 2001.

Hazebrouck-Souche, Veronique. *Spiritualité, sainteté et patriotisme: Glorification du Brabant dans l'oeuvre hagiographique de Jean Gielemans (1427–1487).* Hagiologia 6. Turnhout: Brepols, 2007.

Heffernan, Thomas J. *Sacred Biography: Saints and Their Biographers in the Middle Ages.* New York: Oxford University Press, 1988.

Heysse, P. Albanus. "Antiquissimum officium liturgicum S. Ludovici regis." *Archivum Franciscanum Historicum* 10 (1917): 559–75.

Histoire littéraire de la France. 41 vols. Paris: Imprimerie Nationale, 1832–1974.

The Hours of Jeanne d'Evreux, Queen of France. New York: Metropolitan Museum of Art, 1957.

Jacob of Voragine. *The Golden Legend, or, Lives of the Saints.* Edited by Wil-
    liam Caxton. London: J. M. Dent, 1900.
———. *Legenda Aurea vulgo historia lombardica dicta.* Edited by Th. Graesse.
    1850.
Joinville, Jean de. *Vie de Saint Louis.* Edited by Jacques Monfrin. Paris: Gar-
    nier, 1995.
Joinville, [Jean de,] and [Geoffroi de] Villehardouin. *Chronicles of the Cru-
    sades.* Translated by Caroline Smith. London: Penguin, 2008.
Jordan, Alyce. *Visualizing Kingship in the Windows of the Sainte-Chapelle.* In-
    ternational Center of Medieval Art Monograph Series. Turnhout: Bre-
    pols, 2002.
Jordan, William Chester. *The French Monarchy and the Jews: From Philip Augus-
    tus to the Last Capetians.* Philadelphia: University of Pennsylvania Press,
    1989.
———. *Louis IX and the Challenge of the Crusade: A Study in Rulership.* Prince-
    ton: Princeton University Press, 1979.
Kaeppeli, Thomas, and Emilio Panella. *Scriptores Ordinis Praedicatorum Medii
    Aevi.* 4 vols. Rome: Ad S. Sabinae, 1970–1993.
Kemp, Eric Waldram. *Canonization and Authority in the Western Church.* Lon-
    don: Oxford University Press, 1948. Reprint, New York: AMS Press, 1980.
Kienzle, Beverly Mayne, ed. *The Sermon.* Typologie des sources du Moyen
    Âge occidental 81–83. Turnhout: Brepols, 2000.
Klaniczay, Gábor. *Holy Rulers and Blessed Princesses: Dynastic Cults in Me-
    dieval Central Europe.* Edited by Lyndal Roper and Chris Wickham. Past
    and Present Publications. Cambridge: Cambridge University Press, 2002.
Lamarrigue, Anne-Marie. *Bernard Gui (1261–1331): Un historien et sa méth-
    ode.* Paris: Champion, 2000.
LeGoff, Jacques. "Saint de l'Eglise et saint du peuple: Les miracles officiels
    de saint Louis entre sa mort et sa canonisation (1270–1297)." In *Histoire
    sociale, sensibilités collectives et mentalités: Mélanges Robert Mandrou,*
    169–80. Paris: Presses Universitaires de France, 1985.
———. "La sainteté de Saint Louis: Sa place dans la typologie et l'évolution
    choronlogique des roi saints." In *Les Fonctions de saints dans le monde oc-
    cidental (IIIe–XIIIe siècle): Actes du colloques,* 285–93. Rome: École fran-
    çaise de Rome, 1991.
———. *Saint Louis.* Paris: Fayard, 1996.
———. *Saint Louis.* Translated by Gareth Evan Gollrad. Notre Dame, IN:
    University of Notre Dame Press, 2009.
Leroquais, Victor. *Les bréviaires manuscrits de bibliothèques publiques de
    France.* 5 vols. Paris: Macon Protat frères imprimeurs, 1934.
Levillain, Léon. "La Vie de Saint Louis par Guillaume de Saint-Pathus." *Le
    Moyen Âge* 16 (1903): 110–24.

Maes, A. *Sur les traces des chanoines reguliers de Rouge-Cloître, 1368–1796.* Brussels: Créadif, 1983.

Maier, Christoph T. *Crusade Propaganda and Ideology: Model Sermons for the Preaching of the Cross.* Cambridge and New York: Cambridge University Press, 2000.

Menestò, Enrico, and Stefano Brufani, eds. *Fontes Franciscani.* Assisi: Porziuncola, 1995.

Moeller, Dom Edmond Eugène, ed. *Corpus benedictionum pontificalium.* Édité avec une étude, un index scripturaire et liturgique et un index verborum. Turnhout: Brepols, 1971–.

Molinier, Auguste, and Louis M. Polain. *Les sources de l'histoire de France des origines aux guerres d'Italie (1494).* Vol. 3, *Les Capétiens, 1180–1328, Les sources de l'histoire de France depuis les origines jusqu'en 1815.* Paris: A. Picard, 1903.

Monfrin, Jacques. "Introduction." In Jean de Joinville, *Vie de Saint Louis,* 11–142. Paris: Garnier, 1995.

Mostert, Marco. *The Library of Fleury: A Provisional List of Manuscripts.* Hilversum: Verloren Publishers, 1989.

O'Connell, David. *The Teachings of Saint Louis: A Critical Text.* North Carolina Studies in the Romance Languages and Literatures 116. Chapel Hill: University of North Carolina Press, 1972.

Paris, Gaston. "La composition du livre de Joinville sur saint Louis." *Romania* 23 (1894): 508–24.

Paris, Paulin. "Le Confesseur de la Reine Marguerite, auteur de la Vie et des Miracles de saint Louis." In *Histoire littéraire de la France,* vol. 25, 154–77. Paris: Firmin Didot, 1869.

Potthast, Augustus, ed. *Regesta Pontificum Romanorum inde ab a. Post Christum natum MCXCVIII ad A. MCCCIV.* 2 vols. London and Paris: Berolini, 1875.

Rathmann-Lutz, Anja. *"Images" Ludwigs des Heiligen im Kontext dynastischer Konflikte des 14. und 15. Jahrhunderts.* Berlin: Akademie Verlag, 2010.

Reames, Sherry. *The Legenda Aurea: A Reexamination of Its Paradoxical History.* Madison: University of Wisconsin Press, 1985.

Reitzel, J. M. "The Medieval Houses of 'Bons-Enfants.'" *Viator* 11 (1980): 179–207.

Riant, Paul Edouard Didier. "Déposition de Charles d'Anjou pour la canonisation de saint Louis." In *Notices et documents publiés pour la Société de l'histoire de France à l'occasion du cinquantième anniversaire de sa foundation,* 155–76. Paris, 1884.

Richard, Jean. *Saint Louis: Crusader King of France.* Translated by Jean Birrell. Edited by Simon Llyod. Cambridge: Cambridge University Press, 1992.

Ripoll, Thomás, and Antonin Brémond. *Bullarium Ordinis FF. [i.e. Fratrum] Prædicatorum: Sub auspiciis SS. D.N.D. Benedicti XIII, pontificis maximi, ejusdem Ordinis.* Rome: Ex Typographia Hieronymi Mainardi, 1729.

Saint Andrew Daily Missal: With Vespers for Sundays and Feasts. Bruges, 1962.

Samaran, Charles, and Robert Marichal. *Catalogue des manuscrits en écriture latine portant des indications de dates, de lieu ou de copiest.* 7 vols. Paris: Centre National de la Recherche Scientifique, 1959–1984.

Schmid, Karl, and Joachim Wollasch, eds. *Memoria: Der geschichtlice Zeugniswert des liturgischen Gedenkens im Mittelalter.* Münstersche Mittelalter-Schriften 48. Munich: W. Fink, 1984.

Schneyer, Jean-Baptist. *Repertorium der lateinischen Sermones des Mittelalters für die Zeit von 1150–1350.* 11 vols. Beiträge zur Geschichte der Philosophie und Theologie des Mittelalters 43. Münster: Aschendorff, 1969–1973.

Skoda, Hannah. "Representations of Disability in the Thirteenth-Century *Miracles de Saint Louis.*" In *Disability in the Middle Ages: Reconsiderations and Reverberations,* edited by Joshua Eyler, 53–66. Burlington, VT: Ashgate, 2010.

Slattery, Maureen. *Myth, Man and Sovereign Saint: King Louis IX in Jean de Joinville's Sources.* New York: Peter Lang, 1985.

Smith, Caroline. *Crusading in the Age of Joinville.* Burlington, VT: Ashgate, 2006.

Spiegel, Gabrielle. *The Chronicle Tradition of Saint-Denis: A Survey.* Brookline, MA, and Leiden: Classical Folia Editions, 1978.

Stahl, Harvey. *Picturing Kingship: History and Painting in the Psalter of Saint Louis.* University Park: Pennsylvania State University Press, 2008.

Strayer, Joseph R. "The Crusades of Louis IX." In *A History of the Crusades.* Vol. 2, *The Later Crusades, 1189–1311,* edited by Kenneth M. Setton, 343–76. Madison: University of Wisconsin Press, 1969.

Tillemont, Sébastien Le Nain de. *Vie de Saint Louis, Roi de France.* 6 vols. Paris: J. Renouard et cie, 1847–1851.

Vauchez, André. *Sainthood in the Later Middle Ages.* Cambridge: Cambridge University Press, 1997.

Viard, Jules Marie Édouard. *Les Grandes chroniques de France.* 10 vols. Paris: Société de l'histoire de France, 1920.

Viollet, Paul. "Les Enseignements de saint Louis à son fils." *Bibliothéque de l'École des Chartes* 35 (1874): 1–56.

Wailly, Natalis de. *Histoire de Saint Louis, par Jean sire de Joinville, suivie du Credo et de la lettre à Louis X.* Paris: Jules Renouard, 1868.

Weinstein, Donald, and Rudolph Bell. *Saints and Society: The Two Worlds of Western Christendom, 1100–1700.* Chicago: University of Chicago Press, 1982.

Weiss, Daniel. *Art and Crusade in the Age of Saint Louis.* Cambridge and New York: Cambridge University Press, 1998.

Wright, Georgia Sommers. "The Royal Tomb Program in the Reign of St. Louis." *Art Bulletin* 56 (1974): 224–43.

———. "The Tomb of Saint Louis." *Journal of the Warburg and Courtauld Institutes* 34 (1971): 65–82.